PROCESS
OF
DISCOVERY

A Writer's Workshop

PROCESS OF DISCOVERY

A Writer's Workshop

R. J. WILLEY
JENNIFER BERNE
Oakland Community College

The McGraw-Hill Companies, Inc.

New York St. Louis San Francisco Auckland Bogotá Caracas
Lisbon London Madrid Mexico City Milan Montreal New Delhi
San Juan Singapore Sydney Tokyo Toronto

McGraw-Hill

A Division of The McGraw-Hill Companies

PROCESS OF DISCOVERY
A Writer's Workshop

This book is printed on acid-free paper.

1 2 3 4 5 6 7 8 9 0 DOC DOC 9 0 9 8 7 6

ISBN 0-07-070316-7

This book was set in Melior by Graphic World, Inc.
The editor was Tim Julet;
the designer was Karen K. Quigley;
the production supervisor was Denise L. Puryear;
project supervision was done by Graphic World Publishing Services.
R. R. Donnelley & Sons Company was printer and binder.

Credits for Part-Opening Photographs
Part One   Cristina Thomson/Woodfin Camp & Assoc.
Part Two   Michael Krasowitz/FPG
Part Three Ron Chappel/FPG
Part Four   Hugh Rogers/Monkmeyer
Part Five   Ursula Markus/Photo Researchers
Part Six   Mike Kagan/Monkmeyer

Library of Congress Cataloging-in-Publication Data

Willey, R. J.
    Process of discovery: a writer's workshop / R. J. Willey, Jennifer Berne.
        p.   cm.
    ISBN 0-07-070316-7
    1. English language--Rhetoric.   2. English language--Grammar.
3. College readers.   I. Berne, Jennifer.   II. Title.
PE1408.W5855   1997
808'.042--dc20   96-23361

http://www.mhcollege.com

To Our Students

About the Authors

Jennifer Berne holds degrees from the University of Michigan and Northeastern University. She teaches writing at Oakland Community College and lives in suburban Detroit with her husband, a one-year-old daughter, and two cats. She tries out all her writing assignments on her family: the cats take turns facilitating writing groups.

R. J. Willey, who teaches writing and literature courses at Oakland Community College in Farmington Hills, Michigan, graduated as a creative writing major from California State University, Long Beach, sometime after the invention of the typewriter, and went on to take his Master of Fine Arts degree in creative writing and Ph.D. in rhetoric and composition from the University of Arizona around the time personal computers were first introduced. His oldest daughter and her husband live in California, and he lives in suburban Detroit with his wife, son, younger daughter, a dog, two birds, miscellaneous fish, a collection of ants (some in an ant farm, others in the kitchen cupboards), and a hermit crab.

Table of Contents

Preface

To Instructors:

This book grew from a sense of frustration, the same sense of frustration many of you, our friends and colleagues, had expressed for years. As teachers, we do our best to keep informed about the theories, research, and pedagogy current in our field. We read journals, attend conferences, symposia, and workshops. We share information formally and informally via phone conversations, letters, e-mail, discussion groups, and the like. We attempt to constantly challenge and evaluate our assumptions and our methods. The frustrating part comes in when the tools available to us don't really reflect our philosophies, don't help us out much with what we want to do in the classroom.

Often in both basic writing and first year composition, we've found that textbooks are lagging well behind the paradigm shift our field has undergone. Too many rhetorics still put too much emphasis on grammar, mechanics, and basic skills instruction, on the modes of discourse; whereas we wish to teach skills and modes of thinking within the very real contexts of our students' writing. Drills, workbooks, and traditional rhetorics of all sorts have been of little value to our students and thus to us. The writing process, we've come to believe, especially concentration on good invention and revision strategies, can help writers improve dramatically in ways that grammar drills or sentence-level workbooks or careful instruction in the modes of discourse cannot. And too often, treatment of the writing process, particularly thorough, specific advice about invention and revision, is sketchy in the books currently available to us.

As have many of you, we often found ourselves using our required texts only tangentially, sometimes not at all, and we often found them more of a hindrance than a help. We ended up putting so much work into photocopied writing assignments, invention strategies, revision strategies and the like, that we were finally convinced by Tim Julet, the English editor at McGraw-Hill, to write a book of our own. That is why we say that our book was born of frustration, ours and others'.

What we have attempted, then, is a holistic, process-based approach to the instruction of student writers. In the first section, we talk with students about what good writing is and isn't, and try to address many of the misconceptions so many of our students come into our courses with.

In section two, we attempt to teach students that writing is first and most importantly an act of discovery. Student writers often don't think they have anything worthwhile to say or write about. Good invention strategies are absolutely essential. We also give students lists of ideas to brainstorm and freewrite about, as well as a series of more detailed writing assignments, both academic and personal/expressive, giving us instructors a good deal of flexibility. We have included assignments that students of many different levels can work well with.

In sections three and four, we try to show students that good writing is a result of good composing and revising strategies. Yes, we chant the litany: Writing *is* revising. Much of this book is dedicated to discussions of composing and revising. We talk with students about numerous revision strategies, provide heuristics for meaningful group work, discuss working effectively with tutors and instructors while revising, and proselytize about the computer's particularly important role in helping students make successful, global revisions. We believe that student writers can learn to do meaningful revisions. We have seen ours do it, and some of their work is also shared here.

Because our students' work ultimately becomes the course's primary text, we use only their work as models in part five. Here we give students examples of multiple drafts our own students have written in response to many of the writing assignments in the book. (You, of course, can choose to publish as many of your students' essays as you wish during the course of a semester.) These are not perfect essays in their final forms; they *are* the sorts of essays all of our students write, they demonstrate different levels of revising from draft to draft, and they end up working pretty well.

And because we firmly believe that matters of grammar and mechanics are best treated as an editing operation, and are best addressed on an individual basis, in section six we treat only the most common errors, again farmed from our students' work. Our explanations are simple and direct and are only meant to stimulate students' questions about the contexts and reasons for their own errors.

To students:

We wrote this book because we wanted to give our own students every opportunity to write well. We felt that a lot of the books we had used in the past stifled student writers because they didn't teach them the tools that real writers use every day. We didn't want our students to merely learn the correct placement of a semicolon, or to distinguish between a subject and an object, or to write essays that fit the descriptions of various "modes of discourse." These things may be important, but they aren't the essence of meaningful writing. Good writing affects its readers, making them think, feel, respond. Though this idea may have been lurking in the corners of many books, we wanted to bring it to the forefront.

We hope some of our experiences working with student writers will help you. We have spent a lot of time in our classes listening to what students say, for we believe that our students know much of what they need to learn. They tell us they want to learn how to come up with ideas; they tell us they want to know how to begin revising; they tell us they want assignments that they can relate to; they tell us they want to know how to find their own mistakes; they tell us they want to know how to use feedback; they tell us they want to learn to appreciate their own writing. So these are some of the things we spend time talking about in this book.

Here we focus on the writing process. Writing is a series of steps. Once you have studied the writing process, you will understand these steps and have the tools necessary to go forth as a writer practicing the craft. Writers are not made in a day or a month or a semester, and much of the work you need to write with skill you will only begin to develop in this course, but that's okay. With practice and patience, time and energy, you will develop into a writer.

The course you are taking will help you understand what it takes to write with power, but this book and this course are only as instructive as you allow them to be. We know that students who truly are writers write lots and lots beyond the confines of their class and their institution.

Your instructor will be your primary resource as you go through this class. He or she will possess a lot of information and strategies that will help you as you begin writing more and more. And we imagine that your instructor will assign you parts of this book to read, parts of it to analyze, parts of it to discuss. We wish to be a resource for you both. There are assignments, strategies, papers from our own students, and model questions that will help you to respond to your peers' writing more comfortably (this is an important part of a writer's workshop). There are also clues on how to use feedback that your instructor gives you, ways to help identify your own persistent writing problems, advice on when to see a tutor.

This book may be the most help to you outside the classroom setting. When you are home, working on your writing, we would like you to turn to this text for advice, strategies, problem-solving.

We felt it was important to write you a text that would support your work in your writing class. So here it is. When you are rifling through this late at night, it may be helpful for you to know what comprises each section.

Part 1   WHO WRITES? WHY WRITE?—A discussion of what makes good writing good. You may particularly want to note the misconceptions about good writing.

Part 2   INVENTION—Strategies for generating ideas on what to write about. Lots of suggestions for topics in case you are given free reign to pick your own subjects. Some detailed writing assignments that your instructor may assign. Turn here when you have a case of writer's block.

Part 3   COMPOSING—Beginning with a discussion of taking ideas and making a first draft, this moves through discussions of introductions, organization and conclusions.

Part 4   REVISION—How to give feedback, how to get and use feedback from all sorts of places, how to learn to identify your own writing problems.

Part 5   STUDENT WRITERS AT WORK—Multiple drafts, complete with comments by the instructor, of real students tackling the assignments found in Part 2. Browse through these to look at strategies for handling writing tasks.

Part 6   RECOGNIZING AND CORRECTING COMMON ERRORS—A discussion of ten of our students' most common writing problems.

Acknowledgments:

Writing, teaching, and learning are perhaps the three most collaborative endeavors. In this, we would like to thank those who, sometimes even without their knowledge, truly were our collaborators:

Our colleagues at Oakland Community College: Carolyn Carty, Ben Reilly, Dick Trombley, Aaron Stander, Mary K. Monteith, Christine Francis.

Our tutors, who have shown us the grace of running a truly fine writing group: Tom Edwards, Courtenay Hendricks, Jennifer Biggs, Carolyn Thomas, and others.

Our administrators, past and present: Carol Brown, Mary Ann McGee, George Keith, Paul Batty, Patsy Calkins, Mike Crow, Dave Doidge, Jim Warner.

Our teachers and colleagues: Sherry Abrahms, Lillian Back, Charles Davis, Theresa Enos, Kathleen Kelly, Bob Mittan, Clyde Moneyhun, Duane Roen, C. Jan Swearingen, Susan Wall.

Our supporters at McGraw-Hill: Tim Julet, David Damstra, Christopher Fitzpatrick, Lesley Denton.

Our reviewers from around the country:

Joseph G. Anthony, Lexington Community College
Alan Brown, University of West Alabama
Pam Dusenberry, Shoreline Community College
Steffeny Fazzio, Salt Lake Community College
Dolores Johnson, Marshall University
Robert K. Mittan, Casper College
Stephen Straight, Manchester Community-Technical College
Bartholomew Trescott, Piedmont Technical College

And most especially, our students, from the University of Arizona, Barry University, Northeastern University, and Oakland Community College.

Part

WHO WRITES?
WHY WRITE?

1

HOW GOOD WRITING IS A LOT LIKE GOOD MUSIC

■ ■

As we were thinking about how to begin a discussion on good writing, we remembered a paper that a student once wrote, a nice piece on the characteristics of rock music. This student was passionate about his subject, so he spent a good deal of time presenting his theory of what rock music is and is not. His paper was lively and fast-moving, a pleasure to read.

As we continued to think about and enjoy this paper, it became clear that it had many of the qualities that he was arguing good rock music had. He had spent enough time working with his paper to get it to begin to flow the way a piece of music does. It made us draw connections in our minds between the music he was so passionate about and the writing he was doing.

A Writing Exercise

Before we talk any more about this student's paper, we'd like you to do some writing. On a sheet of paper, by yourself or with a group, ask yourself questions about what makes you enjoy certain kinds of music. Don't be concerned about being "right" or "wrong"; just generate ideas. Once you have a whole lot of ideas, discuss them with others and try to come up with several of the most meaningful characteristics. You'll be surprised how listing your ideas and putting your head together with others—which we later label with fancy titles like *brainstorming* and *peer editing*—can really spur your thinking.

Next, in a small group or perhaps as a whole class, share what your brainstorming sessions came up with; then begin to consider the ways that the traits of good music might also be true of good writing. You may be surprised by how many similarities you can come up with.

When our students freewrite and brainstorm about what they think good writing and good music have in common, they come up with many of the same things you probably have: good writing and good music have a sound, a rhythm, and a purpose that they drive home by means of that sound and rhythm. In each, the "feeling" is unique—you wouldn't mistake one musical group for another or your paper for someone else's.

Think of the Beatles, Arrested Development, Nirvana, Pearl Jam, Elvis Presley, Bruce Springsteen. When you hear these artists, you know who they are, and you don't have to think long about it. You don't mistake one band's sound for another's, and you couldn't re-create their music in a studio with synthesizers, computers, drum machines, and the like. Each of these artists has a sound of their own.

Writing is like that, too; good writing is, anyway. It has a sound that the writer creates with phrases, clauses, and sentences of various lengths and types; it has a purpose that readers perceive a certain way because of that sound; and it has voice—once we get to know their work, we'd never mistake one writer's work for another's

And while few of us will achieve the unique mixture of talent, discipline, and luck that made stars of Pearl Jam and The Who, each of us can become a pretty good writer. Each of us can learn to write clearly, with our own unique voices.

So that was what we made out of this idea. By comparing writing to rock music, we were able to articulate some important aspects of writing in very concrete terms. Simile making, comparing one thing to another, often serves to help us understand things in just this way. By comparing something that we had a good handle on—rock music (at least after reading that student's paper)—to something we were still trying to articulate—good writing—we learned something about both.

Another Writing Exercise

Next, alone or in a group, compare good writing to something besides music. What else is good writing like? Stretch your mind to create your own simile. Once you've collected your thoughts and written them down in some form, share them with your classmates. Talk about the different ways that different people think about writing. Then, after reading the remainder of this chapter, maybe you will add your voice to our conversation.

You and your class can probably come up with any number of similes for what good writing is like: a good meal, a good ballet, a good ball game, a good date. Play with your similes and support them with the sorts of details we did for music.

Notice that, in addition to reading about our ideas, we have asked you, in this beginning chapter, to try out some of your own. This is a way for you to start to think carefully about writing and to do some of the preliminary steps to actual writing. Listing, jotting things down, and discussing are all important ways to begin to write. If you've done both exercises so far, you probably have done a lot of listing, doodling, and talking already. You may be surprised at how much information you have about what you think about writing. By the time you have concluded this chapter, you may have done a whole lot of writing about writing. Your instructor may ask you to gather all this material together to use as the basis for a first paper. So it is important to keep all the responses you make handy. Even if you have no formal assignment on your ideas about writing, you may find it useful to go back to your notes as you struggle with future writing tasks.

WHAT MAKES GOOD WRITING GOOD?

Some of what we've learned about good writing follows. Much of it we have learned from our students, so our examples throughout this book are taken from their writing. Writing students can write well much of the time. Concentration, devotion to the task, understanding of the basics, and just plain desire propel a lot of beginning writers toward good, solid writing.

Another Writing Exercise

So what is good writing? Perhaps we should throw this question at you first. Sure, we have ideas of what *we* think, but other people's ideas are more meaningful and more thought-provoking when you have first organized your own thoughts. Before you listen to our ideas, try to come up with some of your own. By yourself, in small groups, or as a class, come up with as many elements of good writing as you can. List these elements, without evaluating them, on a computer, the chalkboard, or a piece of paper. This technique of listing without bothering to edit is called *brainstorming,* and it is something we'll discuss and practice a lot. Once you have a whole mess of ideas, discuss them and compare them to what we've come up with. No doubt, you're going to think of some ideas about writing that we don't cover here. Some of them may even fall into the category of "misconceptions" about good writing, which we cover in the next chapter.

Here are some elements of good writing from our students' brainstorming sessions:

Purpose

Many people make up a society. And within the society there are many rules both written and understood. I find myself torn between two societies. Being born of Chaldean decent, I have learned to accept the traditions and social do's and don'ts. But being born and raised in American society, I've also had to learn to adapt to their expectations. I find myself torn between these different expectations.

This is a paragraph from "Torn in Two" by Sandra. Just a paragraph is about all you need to get a pretty good indication of what Sandra's essay is about. Good writing is always *about* something. Sometimes you may have heard this reason, this central point, referred to as a *topic sentence,* a *thesis statement,* or a *main point.* What you call it doesn't really matter. We like to use the term *purpose* because, if you have one, all those other terms take care of themselves.

Any of us can articulate Sandra's purpose from her opening paragraph. We expect that she will go on to describe her conflicts in growing up with a foot in each of two different societies. This idea is important to Sandra, and she successfully communicates it in her work.

Although at many points in this book we'll ask you to just sit down and write, to use writing to explore your thoughts and experience, and to treat writing as an act of discovery, ultimately, by the time you prepare drafts for other people to read, you'll subject your writing to a few key questions: What is my paper really about? How do I want to affect my readers? What's my point, my purpose? Will anyone care?

There are any number of purposes for writing, for a writer giving something to the reader, saying, "Here, this is what I want to share with you." You may be trying to share painful or memorable experiences, searching for the sort of common ground of experience that draws all of us together as people. You may be trying to inform or educate us about something you know well and we may not, such as a student who shares with us her personal experiences of living with an alcoholic or Sandra's paper on living in two cultures at once. You may be trying to persuade us to do something—to see or not bother seeing a movie, to buy an American car, to recycle, to try a new pizza place. A main purpose in a given piece of writing could even be to entertain us as humorists do—those people we laugh at in the newspaper every Sunday morning, for example. But note that we said *a* main purpose; while these writers usually are very entertaining, even downright funny, the best often explore some serious underlying themes.

A piece of writing gets its energy from its purpose. Writing can't be very successful if it is created only to fulfill an assignment. Unfortunately, writing classes sometimes make purpose hard for students. In many writing classes, you are given an assignment or topic that you did not choose. Because you did not choose it yourself, you may have trouble finding a purpose for writing on it. This doesn't mean that you are doomed to fail; it merely means that you need to spend time creating a purpose as you plan your writing. Even the most structured writing assignments have room for students' personalities and interests to come through. As a writer, it is your job to take an assignment and make it worthwhile for you. This is the only way it can be meaningful for your readers.

Sound

Consider this passage from another student paper:

```
I sat in the dining room, drinking coffee, thinking about my
unfinished housework. Dishes, dusting, laundry. The list was
endless, yet I couldn't get started. Moving seemed impossi-
ble. Just like my life.
```

or this one:

```
"Go back to the country you came from! YOU ARAB!" How would
you like hearing that? First of all, I was born in the
United States, and second of all, I am Chaldean, not Arab.
```

Even in these very short passages, you can see that these lines are written to capture the sound of the writers' moods. Jane is angry at being attacked for her ethnicity. Her choice of short, concise sentences and her word emphasis leave little doubt in our minds how she feels about this encounter. Similarly, Josie's flat monotone reveals how dull her life has become. These writers gain much from paying close attention to the way their language sounds to their reader. Good writers care about the sound of their prose. They use shorter and longer sentences in deliberate ways and learn from experience that sounds help create meaning.

Some of this happened naturally for these writers, no doubt, but not all of it. In fact, one of the greatest falsehoods about writers is that their writing is some sort of gift that flows forth effortlessly. No doubt there are some "gifted" writers, but of the gifted writers we know, we can assure you that all of them work very hard on their writing. Sometime during the composing and revising of their work, these writers cast a critical eye on it and craft the language to work the way it does in their final products. Skilled writers think long and hard about words—what they do, how they function, the feelings they convey. The effects of the writing do not happen merely by accident, merely because of a gift. Josie and Jane wanted to place their readers in their shoes, so they selected a form that would do that most effectively.

Voice

The final ingredient we'll discuss here is voice, and a unique voice is generally very difficult for writers to achieve. So much of the writing that we teachers read in college sounds the same. We can't tell you how many times we've read in student papers "In today's modern society" or "There are many disturbing aspects of human nature." Pretty strange that such a diverse group of people from Los Angeles city streets, Missouri farms, and Texas suburbs suddenly all sound the same when they begin to write papers for college. "In today's modern society"—where is the voice, the accent, the rhythms peculiar to this student in this place at this time?

Sure, part of the reason students do this is that they've been taught that there's standard, edited English, a way that writing should sound. They've been taught that they can't write exactly the way they talk: The tone is different, not to mention the vocabulary. Sure, some of that is true. We don't often punctuate our writing quite the same way we punctuate our speech, and most of us write more complete sentences than we speak.

But the fact that your writing has to be different in some ways from your speech doesn't mean that you have to sacrifice your voice, your individuality. As you read the many examples of our students' writings in this book, notice how different each is from the others. These writers all pretty much manage to conform to the conventions of standard, edited English (except where they break the rules on purpose, for effect), they all manage to establish a tone that is not what we'd normally identify as "street" talk, and they manage to avoid falling into empty, generic "essay" language such as "In today's modern society. . . ." To get back for a moment to our music simile, you'd never mistake Arrested Development for the Beatles. We love it when our students learn to develop their own voices so that we can tell whose paper we're reading before we even look at their names. As you look over the examples in this book, you won't find "in today's modern society" anywhere.

So part of our purpose in this book—part of the reason why we'll push you so hard to do a lot of exploratory writing and to see eventually how much of that writing can actually make its way into your drafts—is to invite you to establish your own voice. At first your own written voice may sound odd to you, and no wonder, since so many of us are conditioned to remove ourselves from our own work. As you practice and experience using your own voice, however, we think you will be pleased with the results.

Beyond your writing course, you see, what your professors and employers want and need from your writing is clarity—that you say what you mean as clearly and effectively, and sometimes as efficiently, as you can. "In today's modern society" isn't clear or effective. Good, clear writing in a conversational tone will work most of the time, and we hope that as you explore the writing process you'll be able to produce this sort of writing most of the time.

IT'S A LOT EASIER TO BE A GOOD WRITER. . . .

This is an important point to stress here, in a chapter that has compared good writing to good music. While only a handful of artists among the thousands of garage bands and great pretenders who take up guitars and drums to play music will ever make it and be elevated to stature as "good" musicians, most of us can learn to write well. You don't need to give up writing, even if you've been plagued by frustration, poor grades, and red-inked papers. You can improve, become consistently competent, and even capable of moments of great power in writing.

That's really what this book is all about. Agree with us to consider yourself a writer, at least for the duration of this course and of using this book. Be willing to experiment, to improvise, to challenge and change some of your notions of what good writing is and isn't, to challenge and change the ways in which you've gone about writing in the past.

WHAT GOOD WRITING ISN'T ALL ABOUT

RULES WERE MADE TO BE BROKEN; MISCONCEPTIONS NEED TO BE CORRECTED

Mark, a winter term writing student, explained to Jennifer one day why he hadn't been in class all week. He had been offered an opportunity to play junior hockey in Canada and went there to orient himself to the program. When he got up there, he was amazed at the lives these young men lead. There were five and six of them to a room; the bathrooms were rat-infested; the team practiced until they couldn't move, and they barely had time to eat. We talked for a while, and he began to pack up his work. "By the way," he said, "I can't think of what to write for my experience versus expectations paper."

Jennifer was stunned. He had told her this colorful and compelling story about expecting the best and experiencing the worst, just the parameters for the assignment she had given. Why couldn't he see that he had the basis of his paper? She knew Mark had been listening to the assignment. It wasn't that he hadn't listened to her, but as he drew his story out, he wasn't listening to himself as a writer.

It is amazing how many students can tell the most fascinating stories but draw blanks when asked to write about them. Perhaps this comes from an inability to think of writing as a natural way to communicate. Many students get so bogged down in conforming to fancy rules about writing that they neglect the most important elements. Mark had a great story to tell and a passion to tell it, which was more than half his battle.

A Writing Exercise

We have some ideas about some of the "rules" that keep writers from being good storytellers, but as in the previous section we think your ideas should come first. Freewrite about a time when you wrote something that you thought was pretty good, but somebody corrected it to death. How did that make you feel? What problems did they have with the writing? As you look back, how did that affect the next piece of writing you produced?

We are all for writing that presents itself well. We just don't think rules that inhibit students from writing are necessary. We're not really sure how some of these beliefs became rules—maybe because of now-outdated notions about what good writing is really all about. The problem with sticking strictly to these these rules is that good writers break them all the time.

Here are some of the "Rules" our own students have come up with in the past:

The "Rules"

Never begin a sentence with "I."

We can't begin to tell you how many students still enter our courses thinking this is a rule. This rule stems from very old notions about the formality of academic prose. Just as our spoken language has changed much in the last decades, our written language has as well. Now, even the most formal written work often uses "I." If you don't believe us, just look through this book at the writing we've given you as examples of good writing.

Now it's true that in some cases "I" is inappropriate, for example, in some forms of journalism. But because there are so many exceptions to this "rule," we've included it here.

Never begin a sentence with "and" or "but."

Wrong again. Sentences beginning with these conjunctions may not be the most common things around, but sometimes beginning a sentence with an "and" or a "but" is perfectly all right. Some writers do tend to start too many sentences with these conjunctions because their writing is choppy. (You can refer to the section on sentence-level revising for a discussion of working on your writing at this level.) But that doesn't mean that ands and buts need to completely disappear from the beginnings of sentences, as this sentence shows.

Never address the reader in the text.

Wrong again. What better way could there be to draw your readers in, to invite your readers to be more involved, to ask your readers to identify more closely with your writing? Ask them questions; prod and poke until they are intimately involved in your work.

Again, as with the "I" rule, sometimes the "you" might not be appropriate. But for the most part you needn't worry about such occasions for now; we haven't included the sort of rigidly defined writing assignments in which "you" and "I" are inappropriate.

Never write in fragments.

Oh, so wrong. But we'll need to qualify this rule a bit more. Much good writing contains sentence fragments (incomplete sentences) put there by the writer for their effect. In fact, when writers use dialogue or attempt to recreate thought (stream of consciousness), which a lot of good writers do, they use quite a number of fragments. We speak and think in fragments, as we've discussed elsewhere, and often fragments appear in even the most serious and academic of essays.

Here comes the qualifying part, though: Control is the key. Good writers learn what fragments are and use them effectively. Great chefs often don't follow recipes; they improvise. But they do so only after they have mastered sticking to a recipe. Once you know how to do something, you can understand when and where you can make your own choices. If you're a writer who has sentence fragment problems, you need to learn to recognize your problems, correct the ones that need correcting, and recognize the ones that may be okay because they work well in that particular place.

All papers must have five paragraphs.

What a dull world this would be if that were true. Five-paragraph themes are one kind of paper but not the only kind, and they may very well not be the strongest kind. Write paragraphs that are direct and meaningful. When your text feels complete, go ahead and test it out on someone to see what he or she thinks. If it is wonderful, we'll bet nobody will even notice how many paragraphs it has.

Never use slang in papers.

This rule often needs to be broken. One reason so many papers written by students sound the same is because the writers aren't speaking their own language. Try telling a story the way you would tell it to a friend. Use that language (within reason, of course). It is also the writer's responsibility, however, to remember the audience. Will those people understand a particular phrase? Will the expression "seriously strung out" be misinterpreted? If it may be, think about how you can compromise between your language and the language of your audience.

What other notions about what is "correct" make it hard to just get on with writing? What did you come up with in your own freewriting? Sharing these as a class can significantly add to your list. Perhaps your instructor wants to hear your lists, compare them to ours, and explain her or his own ideas about what might keep you from being a better writer. And, if you have a chance, drop us a note through our publisher so we can start thinking about your ideas and about more rules we still may be conforming to.

To go along with the rules that are often broken, we've compiled a list of notions that many of our students enter our classes with. If we get them out of the way, we can get on with the work of writing. We always find it helpful to have our students read these and respond to them in writing. Can you add to or take away from our list?

The Misconceptions about Good Writing:

Good writing comes easy.

As we've mentioned elsewhere, this one's a killer for beginning writers. Writing is difficult. As many of you will discover when you begin to explore the writing process, there are many false starts, many ideas just won't work, and much writing will never make it into any final drafts of your work. As the great American short story writer Flannery O'Connor said, "I write for months and months stuff that I simply have to tear up—but I don't know what I can do until I have found out the hard way what I can't do." Now it's true that a student with a limited amount of time and deadlines won't often take the sort of sustained "months and months" to write something that O'Connor did. But be prepared to make false starts, to cut from your drafts much of what might be there, and to add to drafts what is not yet there. Be prepared for good writing not to be "easy."

Good writing comes out right the first time.

This is also one of the killers for writers. If you believe this to be true, you had better disbelieve it as quickly as possible, or your writing will probably never improve.

Good writers don't expect their writing to turn out "right" the first time through. As Henry Miller, author of *Tropic of Cancer* and *Tropic of Capricorn,* two very famous novels, once said, "I never do any correcting or revising while in the process of writing. Let's say I write a thing out any old way, and then, after it's cooled off—I let it rest for a while, a month or two maybe—I see it with a fresh eye. Then I have a wonderful time of it. I just go to work on it with the ax." Good writers generally spend at least twice as much time revising something as they do composing it in the first place. As you explore the writing process with us here, be ready to revise each of your papers three, four, or more times. Be ready to have your final version resemble the original draft only slightly, which happens quite a lot. Writing is revising.

Good Writing is "fancy" and "formal."

This misconception causes students to write phrases such as "in today's modern society," which we've discussed before. Good writing can often be simple and straightforward. Say what you mean. Don't go rooting through a thesaurus trying to replace simple, concrete words with multisyllable wonders. Improving your vocabulary is a good goal, but this isn't the way to do it. You'll be surprised how often the simplest way of saying it is the best.

Good writing requires lots of research and facts.

You won't find a single piece of "good" writing in this book that required any special research or that relies on statistics and obscure facts for its effectiveness. This misconception is responsible for a lot of the plagiarism that students find themselves doing both intentionally and unintentionally. It's true that in college and in many careers you'll need to do research and use outside sources in your writing, but that's not the business of most writing and composition courses or of this book. Figuring out how to structure and expand an idea is most of writing any paper, so that's what we'll concentrate on.

As a writer you can explore your own experience and feelings, no matter how limited you might think they are, and find plenty to write about. Your own experiences can be your "research."

Good writing equals correct writing.

While most good writing is done by a writer in control of the conventions of standard, edited English, "correctness" of grammar, punctuation, and spelling does not ensure good writing. Correct writing can be pretty lousy, in fact.

You can't expect that learning grammar and mechanics will make you a good writer. (A lot of research done in the last twenty or so years confirms this.) That's why this book doesn't concern itself with teaching you grammar and mechanics. When we deal with grammar and mechanics, it'll be in the context of what you've written, of what you want to say, to whom, and for what reasons. Nobody ever finished reading a paper, then looked up, and said, "Well, how amazing. All the commas were in the correct places." This kind of thing goes best unnoticed. If the grammar and mechanics are handled fairly well, then readers can concentrate on the real meat of the writing: the language, the ideas, the message.

Good writers write well all the time.

Donald Murray, a professional writer and teacher of writing, says that he can tell how good a piece of writing is going to be by how much he throws out. Good writers write a lot of things that they don't like, but they give themselves the freedom to do just that. They write lots and lots of bad stuff because they know that writing poorly can teach a lot about writing well. How could you better figure out what works than by seeing what does not?

You can learn to write well without doing much reading.

In *The Writer's Way,* Jack Rawlins calls this one of the "blinders" that guarantee that you won't write well. One thing that seems to be true about many student writers is that they haven't read much and don't read very much. That's something you'll want to change if it's true of you. You won't ever be able to achieve whatever full potential you have as a writer unless you read a lot.

We've talked about what good writing is, through an analogy to music, and talked about what good writing isn't, by going over "rules" and popular misconceptions. It was important for us to share these ideas with you before you begin to explore your own writing process so that as you begin to write—particularly as you begin to use writing as a process of thinking—you'll be able to avoid the sorts of barriers that have been so counterproductive to student writers in the past. Even more important is your ability to add your own ideas to those that we have presented. Think and write about what we have said—refute, extend, amend our statements—as a way to spur thinking and writing.

INVENTION

WHERE DO I START?

■ ■

Thomas Edison came up with a great idea. He wanted to read his books after the sun had set and his house had become dark. He had a real problem, so he set about finding ways to solve it. He considered, he planned, he rejected ideas, he talked to others about his problem, he changed his wish, and he came up with the beginning of an idea. You know the rest, especially if you're reading this now under any kind of artificial lighting. This is how inventors work. They locate a problem and then go about imagining ways to solve it.

As you can see from Edison's plight, there are really two distinct parts to the invention process. First, people need to imagine a true problem that needs a solution. Once that problem is identified, the process of solving the problem can begin. Beginning to write has many of these same characteristics. Understanding the relationship between scientific and technological invention and the invention portion of the writing process can bring you much closer to understanding how to succeed in writing.

When writers begin to write, they do much the same thing as Edison did. Often, they begin with finding a purpose, a reason to write. Then they go over it in their heads: reject some ideas, plan, think, test those ideas out on others (hey, what do you think about this?). They begin, often are dissatisfied, and begin again. Other times, they may not have their purpose all that clear, but they begin to explore their thinking by letting their writing lead them through the many possible things they could write about. This is all part of the process of invention, of trying to find an idea worthy of exploration. And that is what invention is all about, exploring your thoughts to come up with an idea to be further explored.

Because you are part of a writing class, you are in an interesting position relative to invention. Writers often write only when they have already been through the first portion of the writing process: finding something to write about. They have a purpose, much as Edison did. They have a problem to solve, an idea to communicate, a relationship to explore; they have a reason for embarking on this project. You need that reason as well. Imagine if Edison had been given an assignment: "Okay," his teacher might have said, "go invent something." It is hard to imagine that this would have resulted in something as magnificently important as the lightbulb. This is an artificial assignment. Less thoughtful students will approach it as that, simply an assignment, which is very different from approaching an assignment as a problem to be solved. If you can do this, you will make each writing task more rewarding.

In this same way, you need to take every writing assignment and find a way to make it something that needs to be written. You have to take something that may or may not be relevant to you and turn it into something that is. Otherwise, you can only go through the motions of being a writer.

WHERE TO BEGIN

Often, you are asked to begin with an assignment. Your teacher will ask you to write on a subject, a topic, a question, an image, a past event, a future hope, anything, or maybe your teacher will give you many choices to select from. Maybe you will even be given the freedom to write about anything that occurs to you.

Later in this section we will give you lots of ideas that our students have found revealing or rewarding to write on, but for now let's take a word—*freedom*—and imagine we are going to write a paper defining that word (not an uncommon essay topic for a political science or history course). If you are like most people, you probably have no idea where to begin. And if you are like most people, you will have very little patience for sitting with a pencil in your hand or in front of a keyboard attempting to write a paper on a word that you did not choose and that you might know or care almost nothing about. That is why it is so important to learn a range of invention strategies that will allow you to go about developing an idea.

The surest way to get writer's block is to sit down with a blank piece of paper and say to yourself, "I'm going to write this paper. I will start with a brilliant idea, move to an engaging middle, close with a meaningful anecdote that will stun the teacher; okay, let's go." This is too difficult even for experienced writers. Instead, you need to develop a set of strategies that will help you find an idea that motivates you to continue.

A wonderful teacher and writer once told us that good writers never know where they are going when they begin to write. If they do, she explained, they have no reason to begin their project. She went on to argue that the writing process should be able to take the writer somewhere surprising. We think this is a very liberating idea. How many times have you tried to begin writing, only to find yourself worrying about the end? How many times have you abandoned an idea because you couldn't see where it might lead?

Think instead about finding a start—not a beginning, just a start. What's the difference? A beginning has permanence; it sounds as if it will be there at the end. Not so for a start. A start is just a way to get you moving. In writing, moving somewhere, anywhere, is progress.

SEEDS

We like to use the term *seed* to describe what writers look for when they are beginning to consider a writing project. A seed is just the start of an idea. It is a small speck and may seem and feel insignificant (so insignificant that you might miss many, many of them). Discovering this seed can be the most difficult and rewarding part of the writing process.

Let's go back to our assignment for a moment. Mythical teacher #1 has given you this topic: Define *freedom*. Here are some strategies you can use to try to find your seeds.

FREEWRITING

Research has shown us that a lot of students' problems with writing occur early in the process and are caused by worrying too much about correctness. Freewriting lets you explore ideas that you might not have found if you had worried about convention and correctness. The very purpose of a freewrite is to find out something you may not have ever come up with. Oftentimes, students find connections between ideas that they never would have articulated if they'd started more formally.

To freewrite, simply put your fingers on a keyboard, or grip a pencil or a pen, and begin writing, unconcerned about spelling, organization, grammar, mechanics, or even if the writing is making much sense—none of this matters now. Just write. The only rule is to keep writing for a given period of time, say, ten minutes to start.

If and when you draw a blank, keep writing. There's an actual physical connection between the acts of writing and thinking, so you've got to keep the writing moving. If nothing else, write about not knowing what to say, or write about all the other things that are in your head at the time that are keeping you from being able to freewrite about something—paying the rent, being hungry, concern about an upcoming exam, anything.

You might say, "What good does writing about that do? How will I be able to use that?" Well, writing about it will do a lot of good, even though you won't necessarily be able to eventually "use" the writing. You may write yourself through whatever it is that was keeping you from writing. Once you've gotten other distractions at least temporarily off your mind, your writing may turn to topics that will be useful for your drafts. Or maybe not. Freewriting doesn't come with a guarantee. What it does do is help writers free up ideas. Though it may feel awkward at first, we ask you to try to do it whenever you are first given a writing task. As you become confident as a freewriter, you'll see that there are lots of times throughout the process of writing that you will stop formal drafting and go back again to freewriting. (We'll discuss freewriting middraft later.) Many of our students find this sort of writing to be among the most valuable and the most fun kinds of writing that they do.

Half-Focused Freewriting

Since you could do pure freewriting forever, you may want to try to focus it some. To focus your freewriting just a little, write the word *freedom* (or any "topic" or "idea" that you may have been given or arrived at) at the top of your page. We call this a half-focused freewrite. But don't let the term *focused* restrict you. The word or idea at the top of the page is there to prompt you, but the idea is to go anywhere that your writing might take you.

Josie took the word *freedom,* put it on the top of her paper, and came up with this:

FREEDOM

```
I'm as free as I want to be when I want to be as freee as
I can. free trade free association free coupons for free
foodstuffs. There is nothing about this word that appeals
to me accept I really do like to spell it!! I really do
like when my kids are asleep and I am free to do the things
that help me. They think they have no freedom and I am free
because I am a grownup, that is a bunch of bs they can do
whatever their little minds want them to and I am stuck
mopping it up. Freedom? I'm as jailed as a murderer by the
circumstances of my divorce and custody of my kids. I got
free food stamps when I was really down and out. That was
real freedom. They even told me what kinds of cereal I
could and couldn't buy. . . .
```

The first thing you might notice is all the inconsistencies and jump-arounds of this piece of writing. Obviously, it is not something that has been "corrected." That is the point of freewriting. Freewriting breaks down writers' inhibitions and allows them to unload.

The best part of this piece of writing is that it is totally "free." It sounds like Josie; it is her; it is what she might say if we had asked her. This isn't the only value in this piece of work, though. Josie came up with some interesting connections and ideas concerning the word *freedom*. She could now take any of these lines and see where they might take her (see the next section on loops). She might imagine which is the most interesting part for her to continue to explore. Maybe she would want to think more about the idea of free food stamps, of government "giving" you something and then legislating what things you may purchase with it. Maybe she would want to further explore the idea of adult versus child freedoms, or maybe something about divorce. Instead of facing this assignment blank, Josie has many ideas to consider pursuing.

Her final draft, as you can see, has many of the ideas that were originally generated from her freewrite.

FREEDOM

When most of us hear the word "freedom" what do you think of? Doing what ever you want when ever you want? Or not being tied down with children? Or no responsibilities? Yes those things are freedom: physical freedom. I have experienced a different kind of freedom. The freedom of forgiveness.

I grew up with four brothers and three sisters, myself being the oldest girl. I had a lot of responsibilities. I babysat, cleaned house, and was a peacemaker. My brothers were hockey players. My father was always busy with them, if it wasn't a practice it was a game. The hockey practices and games went on season after season, year after year until my brothers were in colege. During the summers it was baseball. Season after season, year after year.

My mother was always busy doing something especially with seven kids. If she wasn't grocery shopping, or getting her hair done, it was housework, laundry and doctor visits.

I used to get up early on Saturday and Sunday mornings to wash my dad's car, and to mow the lawn in hopes my father would notice and give me the attention my brothers got. Most of the time these things were completely unnoticed. I would keep trying. Years passed. What little did I know that I built up an enormous resentment towards my father. Not receiving the attention from him I didn't think I was good enough, good enough for what? I wasn't really sure myself.

I can remember going out to dinner and ordering the least expensive thing on the menu even if I wanted something else, and it wasn't because of the lack of money. I just wished he would insist I get the more expensive item. My mother and I would go shopping and instead of buying the silk blouse I would choose something much less expensive. Hoping that she too would insist I get the more expensive clothing. I just didn't feel I was worth it, and I really loved silk. I pitied myself from the lack of attention from my father. I felt sorry for myself, therefore I just didn't feel worthy of materialistic things.

The self pity was getting me no where but feeling depressed. I put myself in therapy to deal with this weakness. Only to discover that my dad did the best he knew at the time and I needed to forgive him, not that it was going to change the past nor did I blame him, but rather to forgive him put it behind me and move on.

The day finally came and I was ready to confront him. I called him on the phone and said "Dad I need to talk to you about something, can ya spare a half hour or so?" he said "yea sure come on over" As I was on my way I thought, "He had no idea what I am about to say to him" I was trembling and scared.

I walked in the house and went to the kitchen where he was sitting at the table. I was silent for a few minutes with a lump in my throat. We both said Hi. I took a deep breath and said "Dad I want you to know that what I have to say to you isn't going to change the past, nor do I blame you, but this is for me." "I want you to know how mad and hurt I am that you never gave me your time, or encouraging words, and praise like you did my brothers." Wasn't I worth it to you? "You never gave me the time of day and I want you know how much that hurt my feelings and effected the way I felt about myself" the tears just rolled down my face, my heart was pounding. My dad just sat there for a minute. He put his face in his hands, then looked up at me and said "honey I am so sorry, I wish I had to do it all over again. He flet so bad that he cried to. "I wish

I would have given you, and your sisters all the things your brothers had. I did the best I knew." I told him I knew that. We hugged each other and he told me "Please let me do for you now what I didn't do then, whatever you need, you just let me know" I felt like a thousand pounds was lifted off my shoulders that afternoon.

This brings me to my point, for me to forgive my father was a way of telling myself that its time to be responsible and to not let a persons actions determine how we feel about ourselves and to put the past behind. Now when I visit my father I can leaving feeling good about myself, because I know I was a rejected child, but that was then and this is now and only I can be responsible for how I feel. Being able to forgive and move on is an emotional freedom I think that I will always live by.

Not every freewrite will yield as much rich material as Josie's did. As with anything, it takes practice to be a good freewriter. If you do it often, you will find how valuable it can be.

Perhaps your teacher will want you to freewrite often as part of a journal. This kind of freewriting is helpful for many reasons. It is great practice for the more focused kinds of freewrites that you do when you have a specific assignment; it also can yield some material that may be valuable for a more open-ended writing assignment.

Students who do lots and lots of freewriting are often able to draw from several freewrites as they go about getting their first drafts together. They take an idea from here, one from some writing they did in class, and one from some ideas they jotted while in line at the grocery store, and they pull them all together and begin to explore and connect the things they have already written. Often, students are amazed at how much good writing they already have before they officially "start" composing a draft. (We'll go into this idea with you more in part 3 of this book.)

Much of the advice we're giving you comes about as a result of extensive studies of "good" writers at work; this is the way most "good" writers work. As Flannery O'Connor, a great American short story writer, reported, sometimes writers produce "pages and pages" of stuff that ultimately ends up in the garbage; the important thing to accept is that none of that was "garbage" because all of that writing led to the writing that eventually became the final product.

Think of freewriting as a way to keep you sharp as a writer. Some freewriting will seem to get you nowhere, but that's not so. Everytime you exercise by freewriting, you are improving your skills as a writer.

Focused Freewriting: Loops

Another valuable form of freewriting has been variously called *focused freewriting, loop writing,* or *loops.* It is particularly good for writing courses when your instructor is leaving your choice of topics totally up to you, as we sometimes do with our students. A good session of loops can give you enough material for an entire semester.

Writing in loops is a process of doing a series of freewrites. The first session is the wide-ranging ten minutes of letting your writing take you wherever it may. Next, read over that freewrite. Write out in a sentence—or two or three sentences—the most interesting point in that freewrite. Then, using that sentence or sentences as a starting point, do another ten minute freewrite. Carry out this process several times— five, six, as many as you can. Then relax, read, and see what has happened.

Often, you will find that your writing has "looped" back to its original point and that in between you've covered a lot of ground that would need to be covered in a paper on that topic. Sometimes your loops will end up suggesting five or six or more separate topics, each of which could then, after more focused freewriting, become topics for your papers. And sometimes in the process of looping, you lose track of time and end up doing so much writing on a given loop that you very nearly end up with a rough draft by the time you're finished.

One student, Pamyla, was sort of following along wherever her writer's nose led her, looping along somehow into a vacation she had taken in Toronto, when her focused freewriting took off into this form:

SHOPPING SPREE

There we were my girlfriend Darice and I on vacation together in Toronto. Street after street there were little stores to shop at. Darice and I had been friends for 14 years and had never been shopping together. We were excited and ready to go. We had a lot of money on us and our main objective of the day was to spend it.

This was my first time in Toronto and I didn't know what to expect. As we headed down the first street I couldn't believe all the strange, shady looking characters rushing by me. Every inch of the street was occupied by a person. It reminded me of new York City. Half shaved heads, men with make-up, girls with rings throught their noses and all sorts of wild clothing. I felt like it was a movie of the future and somehow we were starring in it.

It was cool outside and there was a dark gray overcast. The grayness nade these people look even shadier to me. I very seriously looked at Darice and said: "Whatever you do today hold on to your purse!"

We went on our way, in and out of small crowded stores. Darice was buying one thing after another. We had been shopping for hours and I hadn't bought anything. I still had a purse full of cash that I held close to my side.

We were approaching our last stop of the day. It was a huge mall with three levels of stores. I had never seen anything like it, or so many people in one place. We spent two hours shopping in the mall. I almost bought this and I almost bought that but the bottom line is I never bought anything. Before leaving the mall we noticed that there was a liquor store in it. We stopped and bought some Canadian beer to take back to the hotel. I spent a whole ten dollars after shopping all day.

We headed for the exit doors, having a great time, walking, talking and just enjoying being on vacation. Tons of people were pouring into the mall and another ton were pouring out of it all at the same time. Darice and I were walking closely together side by side. My purse was still close at my other side with my arm through the shoulder strap and my hand in my pocket so noone could grab it from me. Halfway through the door some guy pushed Darice out of the was to get through the door next to me. He bumped against my side. My first thought was how rude, what is he in such a rush for?

My next thought was that man just took my wallet. It was just like you see on television. I didn't feel or see anything, but I knew shat had happened. I yelled,Hey, get over here, and turned to go after this man. He was gone, out of sight, lost to the crowded street.

Darice and I looked at each other stunned. We both felt so helpless. Where should we turn? How could we get my wallet back? We both knew we couldn't. I felt so invaded upon.

We started along the six block walk back to the hotel. I was thinking about all the terrible things I wished would happen to the "pickpocket." All I could remember from my glimpse of him was a long dark coat he wore and a clean cut look. How does anyone grow up to believe that they can just walk up to someone, and take what they've worked for. I actually felt a little sorry for him. Who knows, maybe he had a drug problem. I didn't know what his deal was but I prayed for him.

We saw a police officer on the way to the hotel and flagged him over. I told the officer that I had made it through growing up in Detroit without getting robbed and couldn't believe I had to come to another country to get robbed. I was trying to find a tiny bit of humor in the situation. I wished that I would have bought everything that I had almost bought that day, but no. I saved my money for the pickpocket.

The police took us back to the hotel and we told the guys we were vacationing with what had happened. I told them, "This man already got my money. I'm not going to let him steal my fun from me too!" I said, "Let's go out somewhere really nice tonight because I know I am not footing the bill."

> The main concerns I had were my checkbook and credit cards in my wallet. Of course I canceled everything. When I canceled my checks I put a code word on my account in case he ever came to Michigan and tried to get money out of it. My code word is TORONTO.
>
> This man had also used my calling card and I tried to track him down by that through the Canadian Police Department. That didn't work because he used a pay phone near the mall that he had robbed me at. When my Visa bill came in we had to laugh. This pickpocket ate at the same restaurant as we did the night it happened and used my Visa. I fantasized about seeing him in line in front of me and nabbing him.
>
> What I've learned from this experience is to use a waist purse when carrying cash. Always take traveler's checks for the majority of your spending money and if you are robbed don't let the theif steal anymore from you that he or she already has.
>
> Hey, I should be a commercial for traveler's checks. what do you think?

Pamyla worked this way throughout the semester: stopping, starting, moving around, before finally happening upon a focus that allowed her to write a lot and led her into a first draft. As with Josie's freewrite on freedom, the real strength of this first draft is that it sounds like Pamyla; it's an interesting subject that she's deeply involved in, and it's a subject that she was able to make work for something.

Notice that this first draft is a little short on purpose; there's no carefully defined thesis or main point, though Pamyla does begin to explore the event's meaning, what she may have learned from it, in paragraph fourteen. As you will see in her final draft, the "don't let the thief steal anymore from you that he or she already has" ended up taking on great significance for her.

Understand that Pamyla received a lot of feedback, twice from groups, and once solely from her instructor, to arrive at this final draft. But because we want to keep the idea of the entire writing process always in your minds, we include the final version here so that you can see where her original focused freewriting led her.

SHOPPING SPREE

There we were, my girfriend Darice and I, on vacation together in Toronto. Street after street there were little
stores jammed together to shop in. Darice and I had been
friends for 14 years and had never been shopping together.
We were excited and ready to go. We both had about $300 in
cash, and our main objective of the day was to spend it!
I had no idea that by the end of this day I would be a
candidate for an American Express travelers check commer-
cial. Though something told me from the minute we stepped
out on the street to hold on to my purse.

This was my first time in Toronto, and I didn't know what
to expect. As we headed down the first street, I couldn't
believe all the strange, shady looking characters rushing
by me. Every inch of the street was occupied by a person.
It reminded me of New York City. Half shaved heads, men
with make-up, girls with rings through their noses, and
all sorts of wild clothing. I felt as if it was a movie of
the future and somehow we were starring in it.

It was cool outside and there was a dark gray overcast.
The grayness made these people look even shadier to me. I
very seriously looked at Darice and said, "Whatever you do
today, hold on to your purse!"

We went on our way, in and out of small, crowded stores.
Darice is 5'6" and weighs 120 pounds. She has long legs, a tiny
waist, and she looks totally hot in everything she puts on.
The two black stretch dresses she bought clung to every fine
curve of her body. Darice convinced me to try on some of them
and gathered a cheering crew of sales people to tell me how
good they looked. I almost bought one until I caught a glimpse
of the rear view. My butt looked like a pancake mix poured
into a large pan. Big and flat. Two creases at the bottom were
the only sign of where it ended. I decided to pass!

I still had a purse full of cash as we approached our last stop of the day. It was a huge mall with three levels of stores. I had never seen anything like it or so many people in one place. We spent two hours shopping there. I almost bought this and I almost bought that, but the bottom line is I never bought anything. Before leaving the mall we noticed that there was a liquor store. We stopped and bought some Canadian beer to take back to the hotel. I had spent a whole ten dollars after shopping all day.

We headed for the exit doors having a great time, walking, talking and just enjoying being on vacation. Tons of people were pouring into the mall, and another ton was pouring out of it, all at the same time. Darice and I were walking closely together, side by side. My purse was still close at my other side, with my arm through the shoulder strap and my hand in my pocket so no-one could grab it from me. Then it happened; halfway through the door some guy pushed Darice out of the way to get through the door next to me. He bumped against my side. My first thoughts were, what a rude guy. What's he in such a rush for?

My next thought was, that man just took my wallet. It was just like I've seen on television. I didn't feel or see a thing, but I knew what had happened. I yelled, "Hey, get over here," and turned to go after this man. He was gone, out of sight, lost to the crowded street.

Darice and I looked at each other, stunned. We both felt so helpless. Where should we turn? How could we get my wallet back? We both knew we couldn't. I felt so invaded.

We started along the six block walk back to the hotel. I was thinking about all the terrible things I wished would happen to the pickpocket. All I could remember from my glimpse of him was a long dark coat he wore and a clean cut look. How does anyone grow up to believe that they can just walk up to someone and take what they've worked for? I actually felt a little sorry for him. Who knows, maybe he had a drug problem? I didn't know what his deal was, but I prayed for him.

We saw a police officer on the way to the hotel and flagged him over. He listened to me politely and gave me a hopeless smile, as if he had heard this a thousand times before. From the tone of his voice and the look in his eyes, I gathered that I would probably never recover my wallet. I jokingly told the Officer that I had made it through growing up in Detroit without getting robbed, and I couldn't believe that I had to come to another country to do it. I was trying to find a tiny bit of humor in the situation. I wished that I would have bought everything that I had almost bought that day. But no, I saved my money for the pickpocket!

The police took us back to the hotel, and we told the guys we were vacationing with what had happened. I told them, "This man already has my money and I'm not going to let him steal my fun from me too!" I said, "Let's go out somewhere really nice tonight because I know I'm not flipping the bill!"

The main concerns I had were my checkbook and the credit cards in my wallet. Of course I canceled everything. When I canceled my checks, I put a code word on my account in case he ever came to Michigan and tried to get money out of it. My code word is "TORONTO."

This man had also used my calling card, and I tried to track him down by that through the Canadian police department. That didn't work because he used a pay phone near the mall where he had robbed me.

When my Visa bill came in we had to laugh. This pickpocket ate at the same restaurant as we did the night it happened and used my Visa. I fantasized about seeing him in line in front of me and nabbing him. In the next three weeks he used my Visa about six times. Most of the charges were at restaurants. I had an eery feeling when these charges appeared on my statement. I wanted to be in control of the situation, but it was out of my control. I think I would have spent another $300 just to watch him get busted!

I was relieved to find out that I wouldn't be held responsible for any of the charges.

I've read alot about the power of the human mind. Some people believe that we think our experiences into being before they ever happen. It seems strange to me that I was doing the warning all day and clutching my purse; and it was my purse that was picked.

What I've learned from this experience is that I don't look good in stretch dresses, and the next time I talk myself into getting robbed I'm going to spend all my money first!

So try focusing your freewriting and looping around, especially when you can pick your own topic or you have a wide subject area to narrow down to a topic. You could end up with as entertaining and meaningful a paper as Pamyla's.

BRAINSTORMING

Brainstorming is a close cousin of freewriting. You may have heard the term *brainstorming* in the context of a business problem. Executives use brainstorming sessions to pump through as many ideas as they can in a short time. Maybe company A is having a problem marketing a new snack food and needs to know what kind of advertising would best suit this new product. A group of individuals might get together to come up with lots of ideas for solutions to the problem. These ideas are not rejected or accepted at this point; they are only acknowledged. The idea is to get as many as possible out onto a written list; usually it is one member's responsibility to write down everything that is said.

As does freewriting, this method frees people from many of the constraints under which they usually look at things. Because every idea is recorded, ideas that once might have been dismissed as too radical or too expensive or too whatever get considered closely. It isn't a concern how odd or unusual the idea might be. The point is to think freely, drawing ideas from the ideas of those around you.

Writers can also use this technique very effectively. This can be done as a preliminary step to freewriting or as a way to generate ideas from a freewrite. Some students have had success brainstorming on ideas to gain focus and then going right from this list to a tentative draft.

Writers can brainstorm in groups or alone. They take a topic or a word and record anything that comes into their minds about it. Brainstorming often takes the form of lists, as people struggle to write down their ideas as fast as they come to mind.

Here is a list that an English class came up with—twenty-three students participated—when again given the word *freedom* and asked to brainstorm:

Stayfree	Free as a Bird
Free my brother	freestyle wrestling
freestyle swimming	free range chickens
free falling	liberty
peace	America
Statue of Liberty	Congressional Medal of Honor
Free fighters	freedom fighters
free reign	free love
free as a bird	justice and the pursuit of happiness
Kraft-free salad dressing	fat free
sodium free	Jorge Freedman
Mandela freedman	

This list was taken from the chalkboard, where someone furiously wrote down everything that was yelled that way. Many of the students came up with many different ideas for topics to write on from this list, even though many of the items were also thrown out. Nobody knew who Jorge Freedman was; nobody was very intent on using Kraft-free salad dressing in their papers; nobody really knew what it meant to "free my brother." But there were lots of ideas generated.

Some students chose to write about symbols of freedom like the statue and the medal. One picked up on the idea of free love, deciding at the end that love was never really free. Many of these papers were begun in that very rough and preliminary brainstorming session. You can brainstorm alone, with friends, whatever. You just need to get a long enough list so that you can go back, throw a lot out, and still have enough to work with.

Brainstorming with your instructor may be very useful, especially if you're "lost," hopelessly locked in writer's block, and such. After all, writing instructors have a lot of experience in writing and helping students write. So seek them out, go by during office hours, or call to make an appointment; use them.

We do a lot of brainstorming with our students on a one-to-one basis, time after time watching students who once thought they had nothing to write about walk away with a good topic or topics in mind. We usually begin in pretty much the same way, by asking our students various questions, many of which you'll find later in this chapter: What are your interests? What has made you angry in the past week? Have you seen a good or bad movie lately?

When students come to us to brainstorm an assignment that we've given some focus to, we often ask them to bring all their rejected ideas. Discussing why they have decided not to write about a certain subject often helps. This can be the start of a brainstorming session on what they do want to write.

As we talk, we jot down ideas, and we often begin to push students to focus more. When students answer "sports" to what they're interested in, we begin to dig around into their reasons for liking a particular sport. Sometimes this jogs memories of an incident that will yield fruitful material for writing: the first time I watched a hockey game, the day my team lost the championship, skating instead of studying. Sometimes it will lead toward an idea that needs exploring through writing: How can violence be curbed? Why don't more women play ice hockey? Should there be a salary cap? These conversations are often interesting and fun for both student and instructor; more importantly, they tend to unblock writers. Students can then continue to brainstorm or begin a half-focused freewrite or two with any of these ideas.

A brainstorming session on what had made Virginia really mad lately produced quite a few things, but she concentrated mostly on people who were rude in one way or another. Of these, an incident that occurred while she was chaperoning a field trip for her son's first-grade class caught her attention the most, so she decided to follow through on it.

LIFE WITH KIDS

SECOND PAPER, FOURTH DRAFT

LIFE WITH KIDS

Life with kids is not something someone can know by growing up around little brothers and sisters. It's not something that one can get to know by babysitting a lot as a
teenager. It's not even something that can be learned in
child psychology classes. I know because I did all of these
things before I became a parent. I was as prepared as anyone could be to be a parent. Still none of that prepared
me for what it's really like to have a life with kids of
your own. I am no longer the person I've always known myself to be; I am a MOM.

I was a room mother by my son Cody's first grade class. We
had been on numerous field trips during the school year . It
was summer and school was almost over. We had just received
notice about our last and biggest field trip of the year. We
were going to an indoor roller rink, Bon-A-Venture. As I
read the flyer to my son-free pizza, pop, roller skates, and
our own private ticket window (so we don't have to wait in
long lines with the other skaters) -he was bubbling over
with excitement. We had never been there before, but Cody
had heard all about it from some of the older kids at school,
and he couldn't wait to go.

After a few days of waiting impatiently, the big day was
here. At the school, all the parent chaperones were
assigned five kids from their child's classroom to be responsible for. I worked in my son's classroom every morning and was a great help to his teacher, so I was allowed
to have first pick of the kids I wanted in our group. Of
course I picked all of Cody's best friends. We were all

briefed on our responsibilities as chaperone or student, and were anxiously, almost uncontrollably, waiting to board the busses. Everyone was in such a good mood at this point that even the bus ride over was packed full of song, laughter, and good spirited fun. Believe me, this is not always the case on field trip bus rides.

When we arrived at the roller rink, my group was the first to pour itself out of the busses. We had to maintain our composure until the rest of the kids were off the busses and lined up behind us. Finally, we entered the building and saw the lines of would be skaters winding on and on forever. "Not to worry," I exclaimed in a most optimistic voice; "We have our very own private ticket window." So with flyer in hand and my kids behind me, I made my way through the crowd, explaining my intrusion as I went. I was sure people were wondering what I thought I was doing, but I was confident that once I reached the front of this line our school would be ushered to some other line and all would be satisfactorily explained .

As I approached the front of the line, I saw the attendant of the rink already in conversation with another person. I politely waited to speak but did not get the opportunity. As I stood there waiting, an impatient mother who was next in line spoke to me. "Who do you think you are busting to the front of the line?" I turned my attention to her, knowing full well she was referring to us. I smiled widely and started to explain that I wasn't cutting to the front of the line. "We are from Eisenhower school, and we . . ."

She cut me off with; "Why don't you take your fat ass to the back of the line where you belong?"

Boy, wasn't I surprised? I don't suppose I hesitated too long before I responded but the possible responses were running through my head so fast and furious that it seemed an eternity. I was so angry I don't know how I didn't explode. My first thought was to swear something back at her. That thought was quickly replaced with a thought to deck her square in her FAT mouth. I must have just stood there with my mouth hanging open while these thoughts ran through my mind. Then I thought of my kids who were standing right next to me the whole time. I looked down at my son and he was staring at me wide-eyed with his hand covering his mouth. He was muttering something I could not understand ,but I knew it meant he was shocked by her behavior. His reaction brought me back to my senses, and finally I responded. Calmly, and with composure I said, "I'm sorry, you're mistaken. Please don't use that kind of language in front of the children. You're setting a very bad example as a mother."

She hastily pushed her kids ahead of us, and said, "Go on in kids, and don't go near that lady, she's crazy! I'll pick you up at five," and out the door she ran. I vaguely remember her shouting something about being in a hurry, and what a so and so I was, while I was struggling with trying to get my temper back in check.

Meanwhile, the rink attendant explained to me that I *was* in the party line and that I needed to be at the end of it. "Fine, no problem," I said and went to the back of the line where the rest of the school was waiting. All anyone could talk about the rest of the wait in line was the incident. I felt real bad because the cheerful mood of the day was ruined; or so I thought. Just then my son squeezed my hand and said; "Mom, I thought you were going to punch her; your face was real funny looking."

I said, "Son, I wanted to. But that wouldn't be a very Christian thing to do , would it"?

He smiled and said, "Mom, I was really proud of you. You must be the best Mom in the whole world. The moral to this story is about realizing morals, and a lot of other qualities that make up the personality hiding under who I thought I was all my life.

Though we've only given you the final version here, which she arrived at after three other versions and feedback from groups and her instructor, we want you to see that the final version of Virginia's paper doesn't really end up being much "about" something that made her mad lately. It is more about both her and her son's learning something about her. Although she initially thought she was writing about rudeness, her paper took an unexpected turn. Far from being wrong, this was an exciting process for Virginia. She took an assignment and put her own thumbprint on it.

CLUSTERING

Many of us are visual learners; we learn best when we're able to see or create some sort of visual representation of our ideas. This is why many writers use outlines all the time. Clustering is an invention activity that helps people represent their ideas in visual form *before* they begin to write and *before* they need to make up an outline.

Clustering, as you can see from the example that follows, is pretty simple. You place your main idea or topic in or near the center of the page, and then in corresponding bubbles you follow out on the subtopics or other ideas related to that main topic or idea. You then end up with a cluster of interconnected and interrelated ideas; you can now look at them to determine which belongs with which and which are or are not a part of your main topic. A good cluster can help you determine where to begin focused freewriting.

In the following clusters, our student, R. J. Raymundo, used a special computer program, Inspiration, created for this sort of invention activity. You could, of course, do the same thing with pen or pencil and paper. What's important to note is what a range of ideas and options R. J. explores in his clusters. Of course, not all the ideas in a cluster end up in eventual drafts of papers. Remember, a cluster is a good place to discover that such and such a subtopic really doesn't belong in the paper at all.

We need to reinforce here that once you've brainstormed or clustered, your next best step is to begin focused freewriting or looping on

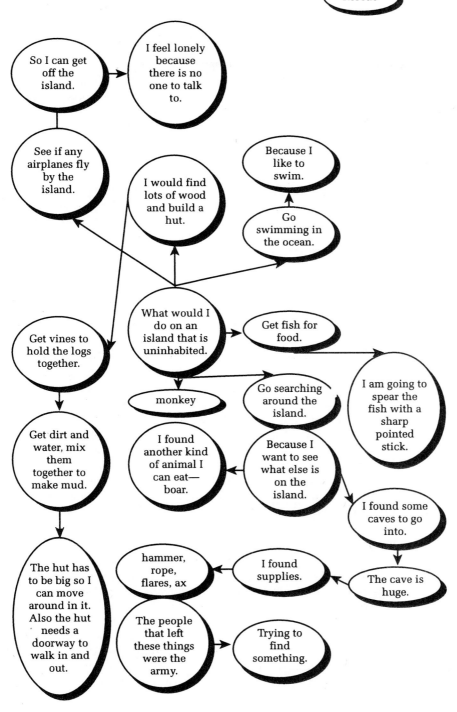

Rescue

So I can get off the island. → I feel lonely because there is no one to talk to.

See if any airplanes fly by the island.

I would find lots of wood and build a hut.

Because I like to swim.

Go swimming in the ocean.

What would I do on an island that is uninhabited. → Get fish for food.

Get vines to hold the logs together.

monkey

Go searching around the island.

I am going to spear the fish with a sharp pointed stick.

Get dirt and water, mix them together to make mud.

I found another kind of animal I can eat—boar.

Because I want to see what else is on the island.

I found some caves to go into.

The hut has to be big so I can move around in it. Also the hut needs a doorway to walk in and out.

hammer, rope, flares, ax

I found supplies.

The cave is huge.

The people that left these things were the army. → Trying to find something.

the topic or topics that emerged from your brainstorming or clustering sessions. These invention activities are often preliminary to freewriting; they don't take the place of it for most writers.

So we hope you'll discover that brainstorming, clustering, and freewriting are very useful tools for you. Practice with all sorts of ideas. The more you do, the more useful these activities will become. Many instructors will ask you to do a lot of practice in these activities before you begin writing. Understand that practicing invention techniques will allow you to use them more productively when you do begin to write.

One more thing to think about as you go about inventing your work: The more raw material you have to work with, the more ammunition you have given yourself for actually writing the paper. When you get to a topic that you are pretty focused on and comfortable with, don't think your inventing days are over. You may want to continue to brainstorm, freewrite, or use looping or clustering to further refine and gather as much information as possible. Subjects, even very narrowly focused ones, have many different facets. You can always find new angles, connections, and things you would not expect. Continue to freewrite and brainstorm until you have much more material than you could possibly use.

Let's say you have decided to write a paper on your dear, eccentric Aunt Mary, a topic you arrived at because you were working through (in writing) some fears you have about becoming as odd as the rest of your family. You come to realize that this very close aunt has planted many of these fears in your mind. Maybe now is the time to list all the fears. What about writing for ten minutes on all the differences you see between the two of you, then all the similarities? You can look at her and at yourself physically, emotionally, intellectually. Maybe you could compare the language that the two of you use. You could go on and on with this. Don't worry if you begin to go down a track that you hadn't intended or aren't comfortable with; go with it and see where you arrive. Just because you have a topic already (or were given one) in no way means your inventing days are over.

In the next chapter especially, we'll talk about writing as recursive. This means that it doesn't proceed in any natural order. At times you are revising before you have finished inventing. Sometimes you go back to freewriting just as you begin a conclusion. If you find yourself doing this, feel good. True writing is messy and goes back and forth in this way. If you stop and start a dozen times, you may be surprised to see how much nice work you have done in between. What all this means about the invention strategies we've talked about is that they come in at many points in the writing process.

Perhaps you've been through quite a lot of freewriting and such to come up with a topic you are focused on and happy about. Maybe after writing several strong paragraphs, you have no clue about where to go. If you are proficient at invention strategies, you have many options. You can go back and read over all your clusters and freewrites to find a place that might give you material to continue, or you can take a word from what you have written and start freewriting again. These strategies will allow you to continue in the writing process when otherwise you may have thrown up your arms in frustration.

USING COMPUTERS DURING INVENTION

Using computers during invention, as during all parts of the writing process, makes your brainstorming, freewriting, and looping that much easier. Also, many programs designed to help you invent ideas have come on the software market. You may want to check with the staff in your learning lab, writing center, or tutoring center. They may be able to let you experiment with some of these tools. Generally, these programs prompt you to take a word or group of words and manipulate them into all sorts of potential ideas. They help you narrow down a general subject such as freedom to a potential topic.

We can learn a lot from these programs even if we never use them. One thing so many of them do is *ask questions about the topic.* Once we know this is a useful technique, we can do it with or without the actual program in front of us. For instance, when we entered the topic "freedom" into the Writer's Helper program, which was designed to help you explore possible topics, we were prompted to explore three ways of seeing freedom: to think about freedom in isolation, to think about how people's attitudes toward freedom have changed over time, and to think about freedom as it relates to other ideas. In order to explore how people's attitudes toward freedom have changed over time, you might ask yourself how your own attitudes toward freedom have changed, what caused you to change those attitudes, and what you think your future attitudes might be toward freedom.

We think you can see that focused freewriting on each of these questions could produce lots of material and many possible focuses on the more general idea of freedom. What this particular program is really doing, you can see, is taking you through a focused brainstorming session much like what you might do with your instructor or classmates. This and other programs can help you narrow down broad subject areas into manageable writing topics while you're actually writing about them.

Other parts of Writer's Helper and other programs ask you to construct metaphors for your subject and to construct analogies for it: What is it like and why? What is it unlike and why?

These programs also prompt you to explore your audience's relationship to your subject: What do they already know about your topic? What don't they know about it? What are your readers' attitudes toward your topic? Given all this information, what is your purpose? How do you wish to affect your audience? Do you wish to entertain them, teach them something, persuade them of something? (All this and more we'll talk about further in part 4, "Revision.")

The Primary Value of Inventing on the Computer

You can accomplish the same thing that these computer programs are designed to help you do by brainstorming with your peers and your instructor. You don't *need* any fancy software to make invention on a computer a useful activity, so if you're not using special software, why use the computer to do your early writing or brainstorming?

We run into students all the time who insist on doing their early writing with paper and pencil or pen and only later retyping actual drafts of their papers on the computer—in effect, using the computer as a glorified typewriter. And we're constantly asking them to at least try to freewrite and compose directly on the computer. Why?

There are a lot of reasons, but before we get into them we'll deal with the primary issue our students cite for not composing at the keyboard: "I'm a lousy typist. It takes me twice as long." Our answer: "Bad excuse. Become a better typist."

Let's face it: It's a computerized world, so you're going to have to improve your keyboarding skills, at least until the *Star Trek* world of talking, interactive computers becomes an everyday reality. You are going to need keyboards for just about every profession, so improve your skills now. There are computer programs that are inexpensive and that will teach you how to properly keyboard; check with your learning center or writing center on campus; many carry these programs. A lot of colleges offer keyboarding classes; they are often tutorial, self-paced, and inexpensive. So check them out. One way or another, develop those keyboarding skills so that you'll be able to use computers efficiently.

Typing skills aside, then, there are some strong reasons for learning to compose and invent at the keyboard. The most important reason is speed. Once you're a half-way decent typist, you can write faster at the keyboard than you can on paper. And since your mind moves much more quickly than your fingers can, you want to use the fastest method available to you—that's the computer keyboard.

After all, we're urging you to explore freely and quickly during the invention portion of your writing process. Many of the problems student writers have early on in the process can be directly attributed to the difficulty and slowness of transcribing by writing with paper and pen or pencil. If something is long and laborious to write, it is hard to part with, even if it isn't what you wanted to say. We've made the point that good writers write lots that they never put in final versions of anything, so writing quickly is valuable. The computer is the fastest possible way to work.

Another thing that slows student writers down—and slows down most typists—is error anxiety. Because errors are so easy to correct on the computer, you can write without worrying about them so much. We have spelling checkers, so you needn't take the time to look up words while you're writing to find out what you have to say. Don't break your chain of thought; type the word any old way and keep going because you can easily correct the spelling later. Appearance doesn't matter, and neatness doesn't count when you're sitting at the computer during your invention time; you can easily make your paper look great later on by changing fonts, fixing margins, underlining where necessary, and all that, *after* you've felt free to ignore all that and concentrate on figuring out what you want to say.

And as you'll discover when you get to part 3, "Composing," putting together your first draft can be a matter of *assembling* bits and pieces of what you've already written into some sort of coherent whole. Without the computer, this process involves going through your freewriting with a highlighter to mark sections you'll use and then recopying those sections as you write your first draft. This is a time-consuming process. If you've done your freewriting on the computer, though, you can cut and paste from your freewriting file(s) into the new file you've created for your first draft. A typical cut and paste from one file to another takes all of forty seconds, tops, and in that forty seconds you can have cut and pasted a page or two of material. How long would it have taken you to recopy the same amount of material? And you can double that if you're a slow typist.

So the ease of transcribing, of cutting and pasting, means for most students that they end up writing more, more quickly. And the more you write, the faster your writing will improve. Using a computer throughout your writing process is just a smart way to improve your skills.

Chapter

SO WHAT DO I
WRITE ABOUT?

■ ■

Every weekday the morning team on the classic rock station in our city, Detroit, does a comedy bit called "Learning to Spell with Darnell." In this bit, the deejay, who is white, puts on an African American voice and presents the audience with a word, which he spells and then says he will use in a "sennence." Of course, the word is used entirely out of context, and the gist of the bit is often some lame, sexual innuendo.

This routine is pretty tiring. It's racist and insulting, and we can't understand how they get away with it so unchallenged in a city such as Detroit, where a majority of the population is African American. So now R. J. has something to write about, which he'll do later. In fact, a columnist in one of the city's two newspapers is soliciting readers' ideas about their least favorite, most obnoxious comedy schtick being put out by the deejays in this town. So not only does R. J. have something to write about but also he has an audience, a forum for what he wants to say.

The point is that stuff to write about is all around you every moment of every day. As a writer, you need to pay attention to the various stimuli that affect you every day and then establish the discipline to sit down and write about them. This will be beneficial for you when you come into a class where one or more assignments are quite open-ended. Perhaps your teacher will see great value in allowing you to write on a topic of your own choice. We like to have students select their own topics at least once or twice during a writing course.

Still, we know it can be hard to have that much room to move around in. We hope that what follows in this chapter and the next will give you some advice and direction that will help you choose meaningful topics.

"ACADEMIC" VERSUS "PERSONAL" WRITING

There has been much debate in recent years about what sort of writing students should be doing in their composition courses. On one side of the debate are voices that say a main purpose of college writing courses is to prepare you to write for other courses. By this view, the papers you write in your composition course should be "academic" in nature—essays that summarize or synthesize research, essays that argue a side of an ongoing debate, or essays that compare or contrast concepts or events. We've read wonderfully witty papers comparing television shows of the 1970s with those of the 1990s, moving papers on the danger of animal abuse, carefully constructed arguments on the rights of hunters or smokers, you name it. Academic writing need not be stuffy or dull. Once you find a topic that compels you, chances are you can compel your reader as well. Your own instructor may guide you toward the more academic writing assignments in this text or may provide you with some of her or his own.

On what would be roughly the other side of the debate are those voices that value writing's unique virtues as a process of discovery, of self-discovery quite often. Many of these teachers give no assignments at all and let their students' writing dictate what their students will write about. Assignments that are given are often more "personal," or expressive in nature, leading to essays that recall and analyze personal experience, essays that are highly descriptive and visual. Indeed, some students find writing such a powerful act of discovery that their writing starts to border on the highly personal or confessional. We've had students write about their struggles with anorexia and bulimia, drug and alcohol addiction, about being raped or about having been an incest victim. We've also had wonderful papers on seeing a sunset, buying a first car, and traveling through Europe. Personal writing need not be private; it is personal because it is based on an individual's unique experiences. You may have an instructor who leads you to the more "personal" sorts of writing assignments in this text or who wishes you to write about whatever you discover.

Despite the fact that there are sides to this issue, the fact is that many, many writing teachers land somewhere in the middle. They wish their students to experience writing as an act of discovery, *and* they wish to prepare their students for the other writing they'll need to do in college. That is why this book gives you both academic and personal assignments to choose from. The fact is that good academic and personal writing share most of what we've discussed good writing is all about.

AUDIENCE FOR ACADEMIC AND PERSONAL ESSAYS

Very often, a main difference in academic versus personal essays, at least as they're practiced in college settings, lies in the relationship between the writers and their readers. In college writing classes, you are quite commonly asked to write for an audience wider than your instructor—a general, educated, academic audience represented by your instructor and your peers in class.

In more traditionally academic courses outside the college writing classroom, your audience is often limited to just one person—your instructor. Your purpose is often to show your professor how much knowledge of the field you've absorbed and can put into practice, what your research indicates, or what side of the issue you can argue logically. When you're writing for an instructor, an expert, you'd be able to use a lot more technical jargon and you'd have to explain fewer basic concepts than if you were including the more general audience of your writing classroom.

If you're doing an academic sort of assignment for a college writing class, your instructor may wish you to approach it in such a way that a more general, nonspecialized group of readers will understand it. (See Greg's essay on gravity waves later in this chapter.) Many of the same skills will be called on in either instance—summary, synthesis, logical argument—but as we've indicated, there will be differences in the level of the discussion.

Different issues arise when you consider your audience as you construct a response to a "personal" writing assignment. As we said before, personal doesn't always mean private. Your instructor isn't necessarily asking you to bare your soul by asking you to relay an experience that happened to you. You need to determine which kinds of experiences you can comfortably share with your classmates and your instructor. It may be that you would like to write about breaking up with your first love; it may be that you just can't imagine sharing that. Nobody should make you feel that you have to share certain parts of your life. Then again, you may welcome the opportunity to write about issues that you are still trying to figure out. Maybe it will be a relief to detail the injustices you faced at the hands of your high school principal. It may feel great to get this all out on paper and share it with a captive audience. Our only advice is to be wise. Think about the needs of your audience and your own needs.

One last word on your audience. Be fairly sure that anything you say will need some forms of expansion. Don't select a topic that has boundaries you aren't comfortable exploring with a group of people in your class. We remember a student who wrote a paper about an underground club she frequented. The paper was interesting and confusing, so a group of students and her instructor asked questions to try to find places where she could expand and explain. The conversation went something like this:

"So, where is this place?"

"Can't tell you that."

"What goes on there? Can you give us a clearer picture of what you do that is so enjoyable that you go back every weekend?"

"No way. I would be betraying the trust of all who go there."

"Oh."

Clearly this student wasn't thinking about her audience when she decided to begin a paper on a place that she wasn't comfortable describing. Since she wasn't about to clarify or add detail, she decided to begin a new paper.

So as we go on to give you some ideas about the sorts of things you can write about, we'll often tell you how you could take the ideas in more academic or personal directions. And in chapter 5, which gives you some specific, detailed writing assignments, we'll have the assignments divided up into roughly academic and personal categories.

WRITING ABOUT CONCEPTS OR EVENTS YOU'VE STUDIED IN OTHER CLASSES

If you think of it, one of the *best* things about an undergraduate education is that your college or university has a lot of requirements you need to take outside whatever your major happens to be. Think of this as an opportunity to learn a little bit about a lot of interesting things. Say you're a computer science major, but you *have* to take another English class beyond the composition requirements, so you figure you'll take a literature course. Look at it as an opportunity to find out about something you wouldn't have known otherwise, and, hey, if sometime in the future you're being chatted up at a cocktail party by some English major, maybe you'll know who T. S. Eliot is and why *The Waste Land* is such an important poem.

At any rate, your other courses can be a wonderful source of material for your composition class; they also provide you with the sort of "academic" topics that you're going to need to learn to write about anyway and that a lot of English instructors prefer.

Greg was not an astronomy major; he took astronomy to fulfill his lab science requirement and in the process learned about a lot of interesting things. In this paper, he pursues gravity waves and constructs a good academic treatment of a technical subject that is written for an audience of readers he can't assume will be familiar with the concept or with the jargon; notice how he defines terms he knows his readers will most likely be unfamiliar with, terms he wouldn't have to define if he was writing this essay for an astronomy course.

GRAVITY WAVE

Right now, the field of cosmology, which is the study of the universe, is about to take another giant leap in what astronomers know. As in the leap from the naked eye to using a telescope and the creation of the radio telescope, the detection and measuring of gravity waves will be this next big leap.

To understand what a gravity wave is, let's review what gravity does. Gravity is the attractive force between any number of objects. The larger the object, the more powerful the attractive force. A star, for example, is one of the largest objects in the universe, and our sun in 1.3 million times larger than the earth. These massive bodies indent the space around them, just like a bowling ball sitting on a soft mattress. Placing a golf ball on this mattress would be like the attractive force planets feel from stars. The golf ball would roll down the incline to the bowling ball. Next, let's move the bowling ball up and down, and as you can imagine, anything on that mattress will be jostled. As in the bowling ball example, stars do the moving, which causes a vibration in the space-time mattress. Vibrations travel out from the star, just as waves travel our from where a stone landed in a calm pond. Gravity waves are these vibrations that the astronomers want to measure.

To measure gravity waves, astronomers use the same technology as geologists do for measuring earthquakes. Yet, the space quakes are so small that measuring is very difficult. Some gravity wave telescopes are cylindrical bars the size of trucks, and when a big space tremor is felt, the cylindrical bars will ring like bells. Other gravity wave telescopes have two big, suspended masses that appear to move as the gravity wave travels through the space between them. The amount to be measured between these two masses is very small, roughly a thousand times smaller than the nucleus of an atom.

Having a network of gravity telescopes set up all over the world will allow astronomers to determine exactly where the gravity waves originate, just as geologists knew right where the epic center of the last California earthquake was. By measuring how big and how often gravity waves are felt on earth, the astronomers can tell the size, location, and what direction these very large heavenly bodies are moving.

The gravity wave telescope will allow astronomers to verify some objects and locate more of the rare ones. Black holes are only thought to exist, because radio telescopes only show the swallowing of light and matter by what looks to be a hole. With the gravity wave telescope, astronomers will hear black holes and know where they are. In addition, when a star goes super nova (is a star that runs out of fuel and collapses into a very small, dense star, which is called a neutron star) a loud clap will be heard by the gravity wave telescope, which will allow astronomers to pinpoint exactly where these new neutron stars are located.

To get a better understand of how much gravity waves could possibly tell astronomers, let's look at the last big leap. When the radio telescope was invented, astronomers discovered pulsars, quasars, and neutron stars. All three words people have heard, but may not be familiar with by themselves. These words we run across everyday in Pulsar Watches, Quasar Televisions, and Neutron Stars. Astronomers believe this leap with gravity waves will be even more productive. As sound was to the silent pictures, gravity wave information will be to cosmology. What wonders await us when astronomers finally get everything worked out? We might even hear from celestial beings.

WRITING ABOUT WHAT YOU'VE READ, SEEN, OR HEARD

Many, many academic writing assignments ask you to read an article, a textbook chapter, whatever, and then respond in some way to what you've read. Similarly, you may often be asked to observe a lab experiment, an opera, or the stars, and then write about the experience.

Even if you're left on your own as to what you're going to write about, what you read, see on television, or hear on the radio are good sources of ideas for writing both academic and nonacademic essays. How many times do you find yourself speaking aloud to the television, radio, or newspapers? We all do it because it is so often frustrating to hear views completely different from our own. Next time, try writing these responses down: See what comes of putting your ideas onto paper. There is plenty to respond to by picking up a newspaper or magazine. Or go ahead and respond to something we have said in this chapter. Maybe you completely agree with the disk jockey who so offends us. You could certainly turn that into the beginning of some kind of writing.

Beyond those things that prompt some sort of emotional reactions in us, we also read books, see movies or television shows, or hear CDs that we love or hate. We've all blown six bucks or more on a movie that turned out to be bad, and we've all seen good movies. So write about them. Most newspapers from good-sized urban and suburban areas have movie reviews. They're also published regularly in *Time, Newsweek,* and the *New Yorker.* Read some of these, and then write your own.

WRITING ABOUT PEOPLE, PLACES, AND THINGS

Here's another rich source of material for both academic and nonacademic essays. Many of our ideas come from the things and people we see or experience around us. An object like an empty Diet Coke can sometimes bring a wealth of material to mind. It may remind us of something funny or sad that happened, it may make us wonder why we drink diet soda at all; it may make us remember a good friend who hated drinking her soda out of a can, or it may make us wonder how the soda got into the can in the first place, prompting a visit to a modern bottling plant.

Similarly, the people around us can prompt wonderful ideas and responses. We are naturally interested in the comings and goings of those around us. Why not turn those musings into a paper? See that woman with the pierced tongue? Could you interview her, find out how much the piercing cost, why she did it, how she eats? Maybe this interview leads you to think that you, too, should get this sort of piercing. What about watching a group of children playing? What sorts of memories from your own childhood come rushing to you?

It's helpful to look at the objects and people around you through the eyes of a writer. Writers are in constant search of material that might be grist for their mill. Think of all the millions of things that you pass throughout the day without really seeing. Once you start looking, you will find that you can't keep up with all that is around you.

Writing about People

Writing about other people can be most gratifying because it so often yields much about ourselves. Why we like, hate, or admire particular individuals really shows more about us than it does about them. Imagine a student writing a paper about a controversial figure, a conservative radio personality prone to outbursts of antigovernment propaganda. If this student began the paper in this way—"All of my life I have been searching for someone who understands me. I was switching through my radio dial the other day and I finally heard the voice. No, it wasn't the voice of God but it was close. It was the voice of someone I have since come to call my greatest hero"—you would know a whole lot about the writer just from those brief recollections of his first experience listening to a radio personality.

Similarly, see what you can determine about this writer from the way she speaks of her grandmother's hands: "My grandmother laughed when I told her all the *Vogue* models have freckles now. My grandmother's freckles are only on her hands and they are all in one big mass, almost like a suntan. My grandmother, is wonderful and wise: that is what I see in her hands."

Of course, learning about the writer isn't the only good reason for writing about other people. Sometimes you may write to try to understand why a friend betrayed you. Sometimes writing helps you see parents as people, superstars as fallible, or simple people as extraordinary.

And, of course, as you well know from having come through as much school as you have, teachers often ask you to read and write about people by reading and writing their biographies or through personal interviews. In many academic fields, we study the *people* whose work has helped to define the field: Freud, Madame Curie, Einstein, Mozart, Martin Luther King Jr., and on and on.

After a brainstorming session, Nicole began freewriting about her grandmother. She went through about everything she could say about her grandmother, from physical description to her family history to memories of and with her grandmother throughout the years. When Nicole weighed everything she had done, she discovered what she felt was the most fascinating angle on her grandmother.

INSANITIZED

If cleanliness is next to Godliness, then look out God, here comes your replacement. What I'm about to share with you is the absolute truth. After hearing about it you may just want to see out my grandmother, for fear she needs a straight jacket. I must admit I've had similar thoughts, but I love her dearly and couldn't imagine life without her. You must realize that besides being obsessively clean, she wouldn't hesitate to move a mountain for you. Also I can't condemn her too much, for I'm told I'm not a far cry behind her. I tell you, there goes that gene thing again!

Let's start with a formal greeting. My grandmother is known as Nanni. She's 100% Irish, extremely petite, can you imagine that, very fair skinned, has blonde hair, and that huggable appearance that doesn't camouflage her sharp as rack hilarious wit. With all of this, she is overall one of the most giving people I know. Of course that is next tom my grandfather, Poppi, whom she has taken upon herself to title, "Dirty Butter." Together they have devoted their lives to doing for others. However, at the same time she's about driven everyone, and herself (although she won't admit it) crazy with her cleaning.

I don't think there is such a thing as clean enough in her eyes. It controls her life, limiting time for the enjoyable things she could be doing. This fetish is carried over into not only her house, but the laundry, food, and going out to other people's homes, or out to eat, is a major hassle. She doesn't say too much when out, but I just know her eyes are doing the once around sanitation check. She lives to clean, and she even has to carry our her crazy rituals when she's moved into brand-new homes.

Regardless of this all, though, Dirty Butter has willingly stuck beside her for the past fifty or so years. Or should I say Nanni has stuck to Dirty Butter. Nanni has a special way of sticking you with her masking tape device. She religiously wears a tape ornament on her shoulder. This is used to remove lint, hair, or any other frivolous speck of dirt off of, mostly, Dirty Butter. So in a sense she is sticking to him. Together they stick to a strict regimen of cleaning!

A day in the life of Nanni: Her eyes fly open by 5:00 am. She lives by the saying, "You'll have plenty of time to sleep when you're dead." The bed is immediately stripped while my Poppi is forced out of the bed so as not to be rolled up in the bedding. Then it's taken outside to be shook. Why, I have no idea. It could be that air or other foreign particles have been shed off exclusively by dirty butter. When the sheets have been rid of any skin flakes or hair, and it's not washing day. She continues on to make the neatest bed I've ever encountered. It could without fail pass the Army's quarter-bounce test.

Next task is dusting the entire house. This must be done twice a day. You will never find a dust mite at Nanni's. Then comes vacuuming the carpet, walls, furniture, and my Poppi if she sees a flick of lint on him. In this area she has relaxed, though, and manages to make due with twice a week lint removal. I say relaxed because she used to vacuum, and wash floors on her hands and knees, daily. Maybe age does slow you down? In this case I would never give her Geritol.

Other insane tasks she takes part in to thoroughly sanitize her home include: wall and window washing, polishing the furniture, and ready? The four vacuum cleaners she worships are polished too. She also has the need to pull out the stove, refrigerator, washer, and dryer to clean them and behind it. Nothing escapes her dirt finding radar eyes. And yes, her basement is also a sterilized vision. It is cleaned all the way up to the pipes and rafters on the ceiling. Also, you really could eat off the floor. And the furnace you wouldn't believe. It shines so bright it resembles a trophy. I really think she takes pride in performing these ridiculous, unnecessary feats.

With all the fuss, our family refers to her house as the white house. It's very fitting considering that white is the prominent color, and you can't find a single flaw, including foot prints on the carpeting. I still can't figure out how they accomplish that. Maybe in between their cleaning rituals they've mastered the fine art of levitation. I must admit it looks better than the homes in *House Beautiful*, but they don't live in or enjoy their home. The profess to be relaxed in their home, but I know first hand how uncomfortable I and the rest of the family feels when we visit. You're afraid to move in fear of making a foot print or the deadly deed of creating dust. Can you imagine growing up like that?

I remember when I was little how restricted I felt. My Nanni never told me I was restricted, but I just knew to be on my best behavior when at the White House. I had many moments I was dying to jump on the couch, sneak in with my shoes on, or wrestle and play with my siblings and cousins. Not in the white house, though. We all learned self control out of necessity. All I can say is thank God. Even though my mother is very clean, we still could be children and live in our house.

I just have a couple more bubbles to stir up for you. Nanni in the kitchen. Again she has chilled out to some degree, for she used to make her family ill by washing all the meat and produce with soap. She had to take my mother to the doctor to find out why she was getting sick. The Doctor came to the diagnosis, informing her, "You are plain and simply too clean causing your daughter not to have enough germs in her system." Well, that's a whole other paper. I just wanted to give an idea as to why eating out is not worth the coaxing that goes on to convince her the food's not contaminated. Plus, it's so embarrassing to see her washing off the silverware in her water glass.

Finally comes the public restroom rules: Nanni's toilet etiquette. As a child I was actually afraid of going to the bathroom because she used to repeatedly remind me, "Don't touch it's dirty," "Did you put paper down? It's dirty" and "Wash your hands, they're dirty." Oh, and you must remember to keep the paper towel in your hand to open the door with because, you guessed it, it's dirty. Can you imagine what the people in the stall next to us thought?

So now you think my Nanni is as neat freak. You're right!
Still, I love her dearly. I could write a book about all
the wonderful, uninsane things she's done. Unfortunately,
though, cleaning seems to be what everyone remembers most.
It makes me look at myself when I go to clean foolishly
and remember what my Nanni did to herself and others. It
has taught me a lesson I must use when I find myself emu-
lating her. The dirt will be there when I'm gone, but the
time to enjoy life won't!

Writing about Places

What about places? One of our favorite assignments is to send people
back to a place where they haven't been in many years. Once there,
they are asked to reflect on the changes in the place and changes in
their view of the place—did it once seem elegant, and now is shabby?
was it once big, and now is smaller?—and contemplate if those changes
were actual physical changes over time or if the change is a product of
their new perspective. It is amazing to go back to, for instance, our old
elementary schools. When we do this, we often learn remarkable things
about how our memories have preserved our past experiences.

Place assignments are quite common in psychology classes; R. J. was
required to visit and write about a state hospital for the criminally insane. And in graduate school, he observed and wrote about the teaching of English in a state school for the deaf and blind. Of course, writing assignments in geography classes require you to write about a place
and its people, and many art and music classes ask you to visit museums and symphonies and report on these.

In response to the place assignments, Angie revisited the house she'd
grown up in, and after several drafts she came up with this account:

MY OLD HOUSE

It is Friday afternoon. I am sitting at the corner of Ventura
and 13 Mile Rd, in Southfield, right in front of my old house.
I lived in this house for about four years, till we moved to
my Grandmother's house because we were supposed to move to
California. But that never worked out. So we are stuck here
for the time being.

For as long as I can remember, our house has been the same color (beige). My father loves nature, so I remember him decorating the trees, bushes, flowers, and his favorite, the garden. In the summertime he would always bring me and my two younger brothers outside to appreciate the fruits and vegetables of his garden. He would sometimes bring us out at night, if he got home from work late, and look through the garden with a flashlight. My younger brother, who at that time was five, would get the advantage of picking the vegetables. I can remember how good the fresh cucumbers and tomatoes tasted.

Not only did we have a garden but a variety of flowers all around the house. My father planted them for my mother because he knew how much she loved flowers. So my mother would walk around outside with an empty vase in her hand and she would come inside after five minutes with the most beautiful bouquet of flowers. The aroma was like none other; it was sweeter and more pleasing than any other flowers. My mother would set the vase on the kitchen table, and whenever I would walk in the house I would be greeted by the fresh smell. That would be the first thing my eyes laid on when I walked in the house. That's all I needed to make my day.

It is the beginning of October, and the grass around my old house is covered with rust-colored leaves. It is about six o'clock and the sun is still shining. The rays of light pass through the tree on the side of the house. When I look at the tree with the gleaming sun shining upon it, a feeling passes through my body of warmth and love. The sight is so beautiful that I don't want to look away. As my eyes are fixed on the tree, I remember when my grandfather used to trim the tree and I would help him. He passed away the year we moved in, and I always remember him by looking at a tree. As I turn my head away from the tree, I look at my old house, and I never missed it so much till now.

Across the house there is aluminum siding. There is one particular part where there was a big hole on the side of the house. My mother was going to get it fixed, but my father wouldn't allow it when he noticed that the birds made a home of it. This was about four years ago, and as I look at the hole now there are birds who still live in it. I wonder if it's the same birds. I geuss I will never know.

The sound of dogs barking reminds me of the many animals we had over the past years. If I remember correctly, it was about two cats, two hamsters, and a lot of fish. I can remember the smell of these animals, which is why we don't have any now and will never have again. My favorite animal was Snoopy, a white cat who was adorable. In winter he would play in the snow, and sometimes we couldn't even see him because of his pure white color. Snoopy was always a cheerful and playful cat, which always got him into trouble with the other neighborhood cats. He ran away, and I miss him a lot.

As I look at my old house I can see the many changes. They painted the garage; it looks a lot better now. All the flowers are gone. They threw all the flowers away, and they gre grass instead. That is very disappointing. The house looks a lot bigger now, I think because now we live in a smaller house. I go up to the door and I knock; Tommy opens the door and he lets me in. I've known him for several years because are mothers are very good friends. Now I go inside and I see many different minor changes: They painted the house gray, they changed the tile, and many other little things.

I begin to climb the stairs, and I remember how my little brother used to slide down the stairs. All the rest of my memories in this house came back, and that makes me smile. My room looks very different because now it is a boy's room. In my closet where my clothes hung now hang boy's clothes. I remember where I had pictures of my friends, many different posters, and several little different knick knacks are hanging there. And now posters of cars and girls are hanging there. I can feel a tear going down my cheek, so I go downstairs, and tell Tommy I will talk to him later, and I leave.

Now, the sun is setting, and it is beginning to get chilly outside. I can feel a cool, sharp breeze, which makes my hair fly back and gives me goosebumps. Ths sound of the birds chirping, the dogs barking, and the children playing outside creates the perfect mood. The sight of the sun setting and the sweet memories of my past experiences in my old house leave me with only one thought in my mind . . . it feels wonderful to be alive.

Another variation, one we've borrowed from sociology classes, is to visit a place you've never been before but have always been curious about. Go a couple of times and record everything about the place—describe it, describe the people in it, describe what goes on inside, describe your impressions of it, and describe how what you've found out about the place either matches or contradicts your preconceived notions about the place. We've had students write about funeral homes, nude bars, state asylums, mosques, baseball parks, amusement parks— you name it.

WRITING ABOUT EXPERIENCES

The stories of our lives, the things that have happened to us, can be the most interesting of places to begin writing. Remember a night when you finally felt your parents were treating you as an adult. Talk about a time when you understood the real value of money. Examine a time when you first played a sport, acted out a part, created art, aced a test— when you understood you were truly good at something. (Notice that many important events in our lives involve "firsts," and also notice that the events don't have to be traumatic to be meaningful.) All the trivial and not so trivial moments in your life may be fodder for your writing. Don't worry that at first glance they don't seem like the beginnings of a masterpiece. Start with a small story and build.

As you may have noticed, many of the sorts of "place" assignments you might get from college professors contain a huge element of your experience of the place—what happened to you there, what your reactions were. We hardly think anyone could visit the National Holocaust Museum and then be able to write about it without sharing emotional experiences about it. So you can see that often the lines between what constitutes one kind of assignment and another are blurry at best.

ESPECIALLY FOR INTERNATIONAL STUDENTS (OR AMERICAN STUDENTS WHO HAVE LIVED IN OTHER COUNTRIES)

If you have come here from another country or have lived in another country, your knowledge of another culture can be especially fertile ground for things to write about. Just about everyone admits that we Americans are inexcusably ignorant about the rest of the world—its cultures, religion, geography, and so on. And one of the things that our American students regularly like the most about our writing classes is the chance to interact with people from all over the world and to learn more about their countries and their cultures. So why not consider writing some papers informing us about your countries, your cultures, your customs and traditions? Or, if you're American but have firsthand experience with another culture, why not write about that?

Perhaps you'll wish to discuss the social life of your country and ours or the family values that each country represents. Perhaps you can focus in on a particular custom, tradition, or institution and explain it to us. Whatever way you do it, you will probably have an appreciative, interested audience.

Jyoti began writing about marriage traditions in her country, India. Her first draft for the group was a model of an informative, well-structured essay that would have been wonderful for any number of college classes. Her group in the writing class, however, quite naturally asked her if she was married and what her own wedding was like, which she hadn't included in the first draft. Here is the paper that eventually evolved and that was one of our students' favorites of the semester:

MY WEDDING

In India there are different kinds of weddings. Every region has its own traditions, customs, and marriage ceremonies. But the basic system of finding a partner is the same. A few generations ago, elders used to decide the wedding and the life partner of their kids; the bride and groom were not allowed to meet and select their own partners. Nowadays, we also have love marriages, but those can usually take place only with the elders' blessings. Mine was a love and arranged, as both our mother's (Mayank's and mine) were friends. I had seen his photographs, and knew him through his mother but had never met him in person, but he looked handsome in his photographs and from what his mother had said most of his hobbies and style matched mine and therefore I thought he was the right person for me, and therefore was in love with him since then. But he did not know me (as he was in America at that time) until we met officially, for an arranged marriage. Both of us were lucky as we had the freedom to select our own life partners, and each decision was left to us. We had a grand wedding on 16 May 1993, in Bombay, India (the west coast of India).

We had approximately six to seven ceremonies that took place about five to ten days before the wedding. One of the main ceremonies was *Varnu*. On this day, my mother-in-law came home (at my parent's place) to give me jewelery and clothes (which all mothers-in-law prepare for their future daughters-in-law). In *Mosadu,* another ceremony, my uncle (mother's brother) came home to give me "paneter and chudio," a red and white colored sari and bangles which the bride wears on her wedding day. When my uncle gave me the saree in my hand, it made me feel so special, as I used to always see the dream of being a bride myself whenever I went to weddings and saw other brides and finally the time was here when I was going to be a bride myself. Next was *Kariyawar*. In this ceremony we invited women from the friends and family to see the clothes, jewelry and all the other things that my parents had given me for my wedding. All my clothes were wrapped and decorated in different ways with bows and ribbons. Then they were placed in the bedroom in a very artistic way. Almost everyone loved the clothes, jewelry, and the decorations on them. *Mehendi,* is also called Hena. This was one of the best ceremonies, as I love having mehendi put on my hand. On this day we invited all my friends and cousins to have mehendi put on their hands along with me. Mehendi is a plant of which you make a pste and put on your hands and legs, and it gives a temporary color to you hand s and legs. While the mehendi was put on my hands it felt really cold. It is said for the bride, that the darker the color comes, that much more your husband will love you. All my wedded cousins and friends were jealous of me as I had darker color than them when they were brides. Usually ther are also some musical and dance programs during these weddings. We had a *Gazal Program,* which is is musical program, and *Dandiaya-Raas* a (folk) dance program. A few days before the wedding day, both the families signed a written document that serves as a formal announcement of the marriage. The document included the names of the bride and groom, their parents' names, signatures by both sides along with the witness, and the day, date, and time of signatures. Once this document was signed, we (the bride and groom) were not allowed to meet (except for the functions) until the day of the wedding.

On the wedding day Mayank (my husband) comes on a horse like a prince to get married and take me away forever. This is called *Varghodo,* which literally means groom and horse. Friends and family dance along with the band playing music in front of the horse. Mayank was not allowed to enter the hall until I came and made him wear the garland of flowers.

The whole ceremony was performed by a *Pandit* a Hindu priest. The main part of the ceremony was to take *Fera* which means: with the sacred fire as our witness, we, the bride and groom, walked around it four times as we took our vows. Once we took these feras, we were announced as husband and wife; then Mayank put *Sindoor in my mang; sindoor* is a red powder; *mang* is the partition of your hair; and he made me wear a *Mangal sutra,* a chain of black beads with a locket in it; both these things signify a woman is married. During the feras both of us were really excited, and specially me. I was really happy as I was finally getting married to the guy whom I was in love with since years.

Toward the end of the ceremony is the *Vidai,* which means to part. This was the most crucial moment for my parents, as they will be giving their daughter to someone else forever. This is the time when everyone in the bride's family becomes very emotional and usually breaks down in tears. At this time I had mixed feelings going through my mind, as I was sad living with my parents and happy as I will be starting a new life with the person I love and I will be sharing my life with.

Right now, I am still newly married (I have been married 11 months now), but when I look back on my wedding day it all seems like a dream, as time is passing by fast. I will be completing one year of married life in May, but my wedding seems as if it was yesterday. Right now my life is perfect and I am a happily married woman.

A SORT OF MENU OF WRITING TOPICS

We hope this list will be particularly helpful to those of you whose instructors are asking you to choose your own topics for one or all of your writing assignments.

As you have undoubtedly come to understand, writers are limited only by their own imaginations. Virtually all you can imagine can become alive and meaningful on a page. However, one of the writer's most difficult jobs is to arrive at the beginning of an idea. To help you, we've compiled a list of ideas or topics that our students have found revealing, challenging, meaningful, frustrating, gratifying, or all of the above to work with as a writer. Feel free to put your own mark on any, or your teacher may wish to help you select.

We are sure that you have seen by now that finding a topic for your paper doesn't mean you don't need to do any of the brainstorming or freewriting we discussed earlier in this book. Once you have some kind of direction, either from an instructor or your own choices, use those techniques to further narrow your ideas. I may know I am going to write about going camping in northern Michigan, but I have no idea where this thought might take me. This is where I return to invention strategies like those discussed in chapter 3.

We've broken these ideas into categories to help you:

Negatives (These are things or events that made you mad, sad, frustrated.)

A lousy meal at a restaurant

A really bad movie you blew six or seven bucks on

Rude people that you can encounter just about anywhere

A tax hike or insurance rate hike you feel is unjustified

The too-high salaries of sports stars

The worst teacher you ever had

The thing that bothers you the most about the college or university where you are taking this course

Why things were so much better when you were a kid

Almost everybody I know feels absolutely the opposite of me on this issue. . . .

Positives (These are things that made you happy or satisfied.)

A really great meal and great service at a restaurant

A really good movie

Examples of people who may go out of their way to serve others

A really important friendship

The best way to spend a Sunday morning (or Saturday night)

The best place to live in the world

Why you absolutely love Italian food, Nikes, or snowstorms

Experiences

A time when you did something, even though your peer group was against it

A time you did something because you were pressured into it, often by peers

A time when you stereotyped something or someone incorrectly (you misjudged a book by its cover)

A time when you proved yourself wiser than someone older or more experienced

Take a word that people use all the time and show a "new" definition for it based on your experience

A time when you learned something more than you ever could have in school

A time when you did something wrong for a good reason

A time when persistence did not pay off

A time when truth was stranger than fiction

Talk about a place where you felt like an outsider

A time when you did something for truly selfless reasons

A time when you did something that still horrifies you

What are you doing in school?

A really good date

The date from hell

An experience you had built up too many expectations for and were disappointed

Almost any event that has made you sad, frustrated, or angry in the last few days

An experience you thought would be negative but turned out to be positive

Something really funny that you witnessed or participated in

The best day you ever had

Things that interest you from other classes

A concept or theory from the hard or social sciences

The life of an author or historical figure

A great book or poem

An interesting historical incident

A debate being carried on in a certain field

Why your readers should really be interested in ———

Why what's going on in another part of the world is relevant to us

Why you chose your major

Comparisons

Compare your best personality trait with your worst

Compare this time in your life to any other

Compare a friendship that you have now with one in the past

Compare something that happened to you with a similar scenario from TV, a book, a movie, a song

Compare a person to an animal: Are people better listeners, better companions?

Compare two choices you made at different times in your life

Compare yourself to the person you admire most

Abstractions (And of course, you can begin with any number of abstractions, freewrite and loop about one or more, and try to narrow down to a focused topic. Following are a few; you can add to the list.)

Freedom

Friendship

Love

Lust

Greed

Honesty

Anger

Compassion

Hope

Fulfillment

Faith

Especially for international students (You can write papers that discuss things in your country and the United States or papers that explain various things from your own culture on a variety of topics.)

Educational systems

Family values

Social lives

Television shows

Food and diet

Dominant religions

Histories

Economies

Transportation systems

Cities

Marriage traditions

This list should serve you well as you freewrite, brainstorm, and begin formulating topics. Keep coming back to it as the book progresses and as you are given even more opportunities to think and write.

5

FIFTEEN DETAILED WRITING ASSIGNMENTS

■ ■

What follows are fifteen writing assignments that we use quite a lot with our students. They are more detailed treatments of some of the topics in chapter 4. You might want to use some of these, or your instructor may ask you to use one or more of them. We do suggest that if in your writing class you're being allowed to choose your own writing topics, don't rely completely on these assignments. Use your writing to explore your thinking and arrive at your own topics whenever possible.

We've split these up into roughly personal and academic categories. Realize, though, that these boundaries are dotted lines. Many of these assignments could be taken in either direction, could be hybrids, or could end up as essays that would be hard to put into either category.

"PERSONAL" ASSIGNMENTS:

Writing Assignment: A Writer's Self Assessment (Adapted from Jack Rawlins's The Writer's Way)

So here you are in a college writing class, and you may not know what to expect. Perhaps you're an adult returning to school after many years, and you haven't done much of any writing since high school. Or you might have a first language other than English, so writing in English is a real struggle for you. Or maybe you just weren't the best student in high school, you didn't really apply yourself or try very hard, and so you find yourself entering college nervous about writing.

Some of you have had very bad experiences with writing and with writing classes in the past. Your papers have been marked up time and again by English teachers who would write end comments you really didn't understand and give you bad grades for almost everything you did.

Maybe you've had some good experiences—written some successful papers, some decent poetry, a good love letter or two, gotten some good grades or received praise for your efforts. Whatever your feelings as you begin this writing class, we'd like you to begin the semester by exploring your experiences as a writer. Do some extensive freewriting; you might write about your English teacher(s) from hell, about learning English as a second language, about a paper you did for school that went really well, whatever. In your freewriting, explore everything that might affect you as a writer now.

Your goal will be to produce a paper that touches upon:

Everything you've done or had done to you that has helped form your writing or your view of yourself as a writer.

What has helped?

What has hurt?

Where do you think you stand now, as you begin this writing class?

Writing Assignment: Why I'm in College (adapted from William E. Coles Jr.'s Seeing through Writing)

Why are you in college? Presumably, no one is making you attend, not like you had to in elementary and secondary schools. So why are you here instead of doing something else? And what would you be doing if you weren't here?

What's in it for you to attend college? What do you hope to get out of it? Do you have anything more in mind than mere practical, material goals?

What are you going to have to sacrifice to get through college? (Money? A social life?) What is it that's going to make these sacrifices worth it?

We want you to do a lot of thinking and freewriting about just why you're here and just what you hope to accomplish with this thing called a "college education." Challenge yourself to go deeper in your freewritings, to go beyond the sorts of clichés you might expect to hear just about any beginning college student utter: "I want to better myself"; "I want to become a better thinker"; "I want to have a better career." While all of these things may be true, challenge yourself to go beyond the surface assumptions to the *why*s that are particular to you. What will that career do for you? How will being a better thinker improve your life?

Write a paper in which you explore these three things:

Single out and describe at least one positive change that you expect or hope your experience with college will make possible.

Explain what you think you're going to have to pay for this change, for your moving from your point A (wherever that may be) to your point B (wherever that may be). We're not only talking about what you'll have to pay financially; what other sacrifices will you have to make?

Say what for you, in spite of what you think you're going to have to pay, makes point B worth shooting for, what makes it worth it to you. When the change is effected, what specifically do you think you'll have gained?

Above all, be yourself. We want to hear *your* voice, know about *your* life.

Writing Assignment:
Writing about a Valued Object

We all surround ourselves with stuff, objects, possessions. Indeed, we know people whose lives are a virtual clutter of stuff, so much stuff they can barely move around in their homes: TVs, VCRs, knickknacks, photo albums, CDs, clothes, toys. . . . You could add endlessly to this list.

What's *really* important to you, though? Out of all that stuff, what would you really not want to lose? What really means a lot to you, and why? We're asking you to think of something that we wouldn't normally associate with having much value: If you have a seventy-thousand-dollar automobile, it's pretty obvious why you'd value it. We're talking about the sort of stuff that has no *real* value to anyone but you. It may be a rock, ticket stub, an empty bottle, or a dried flower. Look for something like that.

Next, you want to write about that object in such a way that you communicate its value to us, but you want to do that by *showing* more than by *telling*. Try not to be too sentimental; too much sentiment usually means a paper that's too abstract. By *showing* the object's value, you give us concrete associations with it. A stone or an empty bottle may be meaningful because of the person you were with when you found them or who gave them to you. If that's the case, you can show us the story of finding or getting the object, let us see the place where it was found, and let us hear the things you and the other(s) said to each other. Or an object from your childhood may be so valuable to you because of the memories it brings back; if that's the case, then draw out some of the memories the object invokes.

No matter what your object, then, here are a few of the things your paper will attempt to do:

Describe the object concretely and in some detail.

Let the concrete description carry much of the weight of the object's importance to you.

Share in some detail anecdotes, memories, and the like that the object invokes for you.

Writing Assignment:
Writing about a Place from Your Past

For this assignment, we're asking you to write about a place that was important at some time in your past. Your job will be to describe this place and through your description convey your feelings or attitudes about this place.

If possible, go back to a place where you haven't been in many years: a school, a church, a home, a neighborhood, a bar. Once there, reflect on the changes in the place, the changes in your view of the place—did it once seem elegant and now is shabby? was it once big, now smaller?—and contemplate if those changes were indeed more connected to actual physical change over time or if the change is a product of your new perspective. By writing about this, you can learn remarkable things about how your memory has placed your past experiences.

If you can't revisit the place (perhaps it's too far away), then your job will be to recollect it in as much detail as possible, showing us how it played such an important role in your life. You will not only be exploring the place itself, but the qualities of the memories you have about it. You'll be looking at and trying to communicate to your readers *why* the place has such a significant place in your memory.

Whatever your choice, do a lot of freewriting about this place. Concentrate on sense details: Let us see, hear, smell, taste, even feel the place. Think, for example, of how all of your senses are active in a movie theater: the smells and the taste of popcorn, candy, pop; the sights and sounds of the film; the feel of the theater seats or the stickiness of the floor beneath your feet. If there are people in the place, let us see and hear them: the people who gather in the neighborhood bar, the things they say.

Writing Assignment:
Writing about Experience versus Expectations

Have you ever looked forward to something—really looked forward to something—for a long time, only to have the actual experience be a big disappointment? This happens a lot; first dates, prom nights, weddings—there are all kinds of experiences that we build up in our minds only to be disappointed by the actual event. The first date turns out to be a real bore; the wedding turns into a disaster; prom night is more sad and melancholy than fun.

Have you ever been surprised by an experience—that is, surprised because it turned out to be so different from what you had thought it would be? This usually happens when we're expecting the worst, when we're expecting to dislike something, and then the actual experience turns out to be not so bad. This happens a lot as well; summer camp, summer school, a family event, a move to a new place, a new school—there are all kinds of experiences we dread, only to discover that they weren't so bad after all. Summer camp or summer school turns out to be a lot of fun; the calculus class is pretty easy and pretty interesting; the move from place to place or school to school means a new start, new friends, positive change.

In this paper, we're asking you to recall and analyze your experiences, turning your writer's eye toward those experiences that somehow turned out to be not as you expected. One thing that helps many of us learn to write well is becoming proficient at re-creating our experiences and then stepping back to see what those experiences taught us or teach us about our lives, so we want you to figure out how this experience affected or still affects you.

Do a lot of freewriting about several experiences in order to narrow them down to the one you're going to compose into a draft. Whether you choose an experience that turned out better or much worse than you planned, we want your paper to do at least the following things:

Draw out, in detail, what your expectations were prior to the event. How did you have it built up in your mind? What contributed to these expectations? Had you heard about this from other people, read about it, seen something on TV? How much time did you spend thinking about it, looking forward to it, dreading it? You'll want to give us a clear indication of just how you felt actually entering into this experience.

Draw out, in detail, the actual experience. *Show* the story as it unfolded. This usually means that you will use description of the place and the people involved, that you will use dialogue, and that you will order the event in time.

Clearly show how the experience turned out to be so different from what you expected.

Come to some sort of conclusion about what you learned from this experience.

Writing Assignment:
Writing about a Person Who Has Influenced You

We have all been influenced by many, many people in our lives. Just about everything about us—the way we talk, dress, think, believe—has been influenced by parents, other relatives, peers, or friends. It's pretty easy to see how people this close to us affect our lives.

It's also interesting to think about how our lives have been altered by people we didn't know well. We have all been affected by strangers or by people we barely knew. What we'd like you to do is write a paper about one of these people. Let's get away, for the moment, from people the rest of us would *expect* to influence your life—parents, siblings, relatives, clergy, coaches—to explore some of the more surprising influences.

A person you knew for a very short time, who walked in and out of your life, but you've never forgotten

A person you never have met but have observed closely, perhaps a co-worker or someone in a class you once took.

A person you have never met that you've come to know through the media: books, television, film. Beware, though, of turning this into an adoring fan paper.

After extensive freewriting, focus in on the person you're going to write about. You want to work toward a paper that will do at least these three things:

Describe the person and the circumstances by which you came to know him or her.

Show *specifically* how this person has influenced you: Is it the way you dress, the way you eat, the way you think, the way you believe?

Analyze how this change in yourself has been for the better or for the worse. Some role models are positive, some negative; what has this one been for you?

Writing Assignment:
The "Figure Eight" or "Double Experience" Paper

Did your parents haul you screaming and kicking onto a roller coaster when you were a child? And did you find yourself as a teenager at an amusement park suddenly petrified, unable to get onto the biggest coaster in the park?

As a child, did you ever break off a relationship with a good friend? As an adult, have you broken off a relationship with a significant other?

These and many other experiences, though they take place far apart in time, may have solid connections in your life. That bad experience on a roller coaster may explain something about your fear of them now. Breaking off a relationship with a friend may have taught you something about breaking off adult relationships. As you begin to think about the disparate experiences of your life, you may find some amazing connections you haven't thought about before.

This paper calls upon a couple of your thinking skills that have often been taught as types of essays: (1) cause and effect and (2) comparison and contrast. As you approach writing this paper, you use these modes of thought to consider two separate experiences in your life. Because of the form these papers usually take, we call it a "figure eight" assignment; some students have preferred calling it the "double experience" assignment.

What you need to do is come up with two experiences in your life: one that happened quite a long time ago and another one that happened more recently. You will try to figure out—and your paper will attempt to draw out—how they fit together, how living through one experience somehow changed or determined the way you lived through the other. The experiences don't need to be exact replicas; in fact, that would be nearly impossible. They only have to have a similar choice or set of circumstances implicit in them. Think about it this way: You are taking two apparently disconnected times in your life and showing how the first was a building block for the second.

Whatever experiences you choose, here are some of the things your paper must do to be successful. After extensive freewriting about each event, you will wish to:

Recall each experience in some detail. Remember, you are telling stories, so you'll want to *show* each experience as it happened. You will probably need descriptions of people and places, as well as some dialogue.

Provide a transition between times. You won't be able to just end one story and begin another. Remember the figure eight—8—the two circles are joined together in the middle. So must your paper be.

Make the connection between the events fairly clear. There are a lot of ways to do this: in the introduction, in the conclusion, or implicitly in the rendering of both experiences. Most writers find that a strong conclusion is the clearest way of connecting the two experiences in their lives.

Writing Assignment:
The Antimaxim (Taken in part from Jack Rawlins's
The Writer's Way)

You can't judge a book by its cover.
Absence makes the heart grow fonder.
Good things come to those who wait.
A stitch in time saves nine.
He who laughs last, laughs best.
All work and no play makes _____ a dull boy or girl.
The pen is mightier than the sword.
Beauty is in the eye of the beholder.
A penny saved is a penny earned.
The grass is always greener in someone else's yard.

This list of common maxims can go on and on; we're sure you can add more to it.

Now, you've all had experiences that can disprove these maxims. Perhaps you've had a long-distance relationship go kaput, or you know of others who have. Perhaps you've waited quite patiently for something good to happen, and then it never did. Perhaps you know someone who *never* works and is still the dullest imaginable human being. Whatever the case, each of us has knowledge or experience that can prove these maxims untrue.

So for this paper you should set out to disprove an old maxim; use your own experience or the experiences of others you've known and observed. Tell whatever stories you have to tell in detail. If you've got more than just one story to disprove the maxim, that's even better.

Writing Assignment:
Proposing an Alternate Definition
Freedom is just another word for nothing left
to lose. . . .

This song lyric from "Me and Bobby McGee," written by Kris Kristofferson and sung by Janis Joplin, defines *freedom* in a way much different from any dictionary definition of the word. *Webster's College Dictionary* defines *freedom* as "the state of being free or at liberty rather than in confinement or under physical restraint" and "exemption from external control." Which definition is more meaningful to you? Why?

What the song "Me and Bobby McGee" does is tell a story that exemplifies its definition of *freedom*. It goes on to support its view in some detail. And that's what we're asking you to do now.

Think of a word you use all the time but usually don't think too much about. Write a paper where you give a *real* definition from your own experiences. Don't rely on the way you have always thought about the word; instead, challenge yourself to rethink old conventions.

Here are some words to think about; you can probably add many to this list:

love	relationship
freedom	family
education	goals
happiness	work
loneliness	dependency
destiny	independence
faith	success
fun	parenting
friendship	competition

You will want to start this project by freewriting about some of the notions you have about the word or words you select. (Even though you'll eventually focus on one word, don't limit your freewriting to only one; use your freewriting to explore possibilities.) No matter what your word, eventually your paper should do the following things:

Introduce the concept and its traditional definition. You don't have to use the dictionary definition; it's better to illustrate the definition through an anecdote.

Introduce *your* definition of the term.

Support your definition with specific examples taken from your own experience.

If we were going to do *freedom,* for example, and we wanted to use the Kristofferson-Joplin definition of the term, we could construct a detailed paper profiling several of the people in our lives for whom this alternate definition of the word turned out to be true: people who weren't truly happy or free until they lost nearly everything, including jobs, money, and family.

Writing Assignment:
Writing a Personal Essay about a Film

Easy Rider	*Rumble Fish*
Midnight Cowboy	*Apocalypse Now*
Forrest Gump	*Reality Bites*
Stand by Me	*The Breakfast Club*
The River's Edge	*The Big Chill*
The Outsiders	

These films have at least one thing in common: They elicit very strong personal reactions from many of their viewers. Each of these films in some way touches many, many people's lives, and so they attract a loyal following in a way that other very popular or very brilliant films don't; they are loved because of what they say about the viewers' lives as much as they are because of whether they're "good" movies.

For your next paper, we'd like you to write about a film that in some way touches you on a personal level, that you have a strong emotional reaction to. (Your strong reaction to it doesn't necessarily have to be positive, although most students do choose to write about films they "like.") It can be a first-run movie that you see in a theater, or it can be something older that you rented on videocassette or watched on TV. Video versions are often a good idea, so you can view it more than once while figuring out what you're writing about it. Don't merely write about a movie that you liked because it was entertaining—many action adventure movies fall into this category. Write about one you in some way identify with.

Freewrite about the movie, then, and about how the movie connects with your life. Write a lot about each—the more the better—so that you have a lot of material to work with when you start to assemble your draft. Once you begin composing, here are the things you need to make sure your draft does:

Summarize and analyze the movie. You can't assume everyone in your audience has seen this film, so you need to tell us the name of the film and who's in it; you'll need to do some plot summary, some character description, some analysis of the film's themes. We should come away knowing what the film is "about," at least in terms of what happens in it.

Connect the film to your experience. Do you have an uncle who's just like Forrest Gump? Do you have a friend or relative who has been out to the river's edge? Does *Reality Bites* capture a lot of the same questions and frustrations you're feeling in your own life right now? Does *The Big Chill* help you understand your parents a little better? Whatever the case, you will want to relate your experience in detail. Tell us the story or stories; let us see and hear the people. Show.

Come to a conclusion about the parallel between the film and your experience. You'll probably be saying that the film somehow captured some essential truth or truths about your own or someone else's life. You may even be saying that the film somehow changed you or taught you to see something in a new way.

Writing Assignment:
Arguing from Experience

Has anyone cut you off in traffic lately, or tailgated you?

Has anyone cut in front of you in a grocery store line, or gone into the "10 items or less—No Checks" lane with a full basket and then written a check?

On your job, have people been unnecessarily rude to you?

Have you had to put up with a salesperson's bad attitude?

You can probably answer yes to more than one of these questions; in fact, you can probably answer yes to most of them. And you can probably start to add other behaviors to this list that all fall under the general category of rudeness or of people's lack of civility toward each other.

If you were to begin doing some freewriting about times such as these, you'd probably find that you were exploring reasons why people act the way they do sometimes, and you may even find that you started writing about reasons why we shouldn't act in these ways. In doing so, you'd be coming up with some sort of argument: "This is rude because. . . ." "People act this way because. . . ." "You shouldn't treat people this way because. . . ."

For this paper, we'd like you to construct some sort of argument, and we'd like you to argue strictly from your own experience. You don't need any specialized knowledge; you don't need to do any research; you don't need the opinions or support of "experts" in any field. Your own experience will do for this paper.

There are any number of things you can argue; what we've suggested is only one example of how you can begin to explore experience in order to figure out what to write about. You can argue something about child rearing by questioning your parents' policies for you. You can argue something about music lyrics based on your experience as an avid music listener. You can argue something about school policies because you have been and are a student affected by those policies. Issues everywhere affect you, and you can effectively argue about them because they affect you.

So do some freewriting about those sorts of things that you already feel very strongly about. Test out several different ideas, and let your freewriting help you determine if you've found a topic that you can draw out in some depth and detail. Once you have settled upon a topic, next consider your readers. How do you wish to affect us? Are you trying to change our behavior, or our opinion? Are you simply hoping to convince us of the validity of your viewpoint?

Once you have settled upon a topic, here are a few key things to keep in mind as you compose your paper:

Know the counterarguments, if there are any. It's important to know what people who would disagree with you would say and when, so that in your paper you can meet those objections and try to refute them.

Don't attack people who disagree with you. You may see this done in the "real world" a lot, but you want to avoid it. So avoid railing at "liberals" or "conservatives." Remember, you are targeting issues, not the people who are on the other side of the issue from your own.

Try not to overgeneralize. Watch out for words like *all, every, none,* and other such inclusive terms. "People" aren't too rude these days; "many people" might be.

When appropriate, make it clear to readers what you want them to do. If you're arguing that we're all responsible for the damage being done to our local environment—the litter floating around campus, the pile of junk dumped along the river—then you'll want to be sure you make clear to your readers what you want them to do about it.

Be specific, and use many clear examples. We could go on for quite a while with examples of unthinking rude behavior today, and we'd want to do that in our paper.

"ACADEMIC" ASSIGNMENTS

Some of these are variations on the previous assignments. With some subtle changes, their focus has become more traditionally academic, and they resemble assignments you can expect from other classes.

Writing Assignment: An Argument

Tuition costs are rising at colleges and universities, while financial aid is becoming scarcer. More and more students are being forced to greatly lengthen their time in college while they attempt to work their way through.

Politicians are once again making Americans' fear of crime a major campaign issue. Congress has passed anticrime legislation providing for longer prison terms, more prisons, and more cops, while doing little to provide for the sorts of programs that may get at the roots of crime.

Television, newspapers, magazines—all the media have had much to say recently about the so-called generation X, much of it negative. Generation X'ers, it seems, have short attention spans, few loyalties, little incentive, and grim futures.

While politicians and the public sometimes violently debate what role, if any, sex education should play in the schools ("just say no" versus "safe sex," for example), birth rates, venereal diseases, and even AIDS are on a steady rise among teens of all ages and socio-economic classes.

Do you have any feelings about any of these issues? If you do, chances are it's because one of these issues has directly touched your life. Perhaps you are a working student, one who is looking at many years, many dollars, and many student loans to get through college. Maybe your parents make a bit too much money for you to qualify for help. Maybe you're on your own.

Perhaps you've been a victim of crime, live in a crime-plagued neighborhood, or have a friend or relative who is or is becoming a habitual criminal. You might know firsthand just what goes into the making of some criminals, and you might feel that no amount of jail time is going to change anything for this person.

If you're a generation X'er, which many of you are, you might really resent being stereotyped as uncaring, misdirected, and lazy.

If you're a single parent or know single parents, maybe you know something about what might do some good to curb teen birth rates.

Of course, these are only a few among hundreds of possible issues that affect you and that you may have strong feelings about. What we're asking you to do with this assignment is to identify an issue, do some reading on it, and build an argument about it; in addition to what you learn about the topic through your reading, you will be able to use your experience. We want you to write an argumentative paper in which you interact with the issue directly. So our guidelines are these: Don't argue handgun control unless you have had firsthand experience with what you feel is the need for it or reasons against it; don't argue about national health insurance unless you can show from your experience how it is desperately needed by someone; don't argue about intensely emotional, moral issues that are already overargued, such as abortion.

We're asking you to write an argument about something that you relate to personally so that you write with more conviction, so that you can offer many specifics, and so that you can avoid the sort of overgeneralizing common to so many arguments. So do some extensive reading about your issue. You may eventually wish to construct your own essay as a response to someone else's, someone on the other side of the issue, perhaps. Start freewriting on several possible issues; weigh and judge which one you seem to have the most material on, which one you think you can present to an audience most effectively, and then narrow your focus to that one issue. As you begin to compose your paper for your readers, keep these things in mind:

Consider your purpose. Are you trying to get your readers to *do* something? If so, be specific about what you want us to do. Or is the core of your argument more to get us to change our way of thinking?

Know the counterarguments, if there are any. It's important to know what people who would disagree with you would say and when, so that in your paper you can confront and try to refute those objections. If you're constructing your essay in response to someone else's, you'll need to give a fair and accurate picture of that other person's viewpoint.

Don't attack people who disagree with you. You may see this done in the "real world" a lot, but you want to avoid it. So don't rail at "liberals" or "conservatives" or "that fool" you're writing in response to. Remember, you are targeting issues, not the people who are on the other side of the issue.

Try not to overgeneralize. Watch out for words like *all, every, none,* and other such inclusive terms. "The media" aren't too negative in their portrayal of generation X'ers; "many portrayals of generation X'ers by the media" may be too negative. Perhaps you can find many such overgeneralizations in your opponents' words; if so, point these out.

Be specific, and use many clear examples. If you're going to quote from other sources, don't forget to use quotation marks and the proper documentation form: Ask your instructor about MLA guidelines for documentation of your source(s). If you have a story to tell, tell it in detail. If you have people to tell us about, let us see them, hear them, and know their stories.

Writing Assignment: Writing a Review

Writing good reviews can be a tricky business because you need to have some specialized knowledge of the field you're reviewing. But we know that our students have or are gaining that sort of knowledge when they're in our classes. We have students who know a *lot* about all sorts of music, about dance, about film, about theater, and so on. When you know a lot about a given field, you're in a position to know the criteria by which people in that field judge the quality of a given performance, a given CD, and so forth.

If you take a music appreciation class, you'll likely be asked to attend a concert or two and review them. In any number of classes, you may be asked to read one or more books chosen from a reading list and to write reviews of them. Many students at our college take a very popular film course and write reviews of first-run movies.

So for this assignment we ask you to choose a movie, concert, play, or dance performance to attend, a book to read, or a new CD to listen to and to write a review. Your instructor may even specify what she or he wishes you to do.

The best way to learn how to write good reviews is to read them. As we've mentioned elsewhere, most large newspapers have all sorts of these reviews in them, and even if you live in a rural area you probably have access to national magazines that contain these sorts of reviews, so find them and read them. We generally bring some into class to discuss with our students; you may wish to bring some in for large- or small-group discussion, or your instructor may ask you to find some or bring some in. Read them, discuss them, use them as models, and, recalling what we've been telling you about good writing, look at how different writers put their unique signatures to their own reviews through their writing.

Writing Assignment: Responding to an Essay

This is a common sort of "academic" writing assignment. You read and then respond to an essay of your choice or, more likely, one your instructor has provided. This is the sort of writing you will do in many content area courses, especially those that deal a lot with abstract ideas: literature, political science, sociology, psychology, economics, and many others. Writing in response to assigned reading calls upon many important skills: your ability to analyze and synthesize information from your reading, your ability to formulate a cogent response to your reading, and your ability to offer specific evidence in support of your reading.

After reading and engaging in class discussion about the essay you've been assigned, you should begin some focused freewriting about the essay. Let your freewriting explore what you feel is the main gist of what you've read—the author or authors' implied or stated thesis—as well as the many ideas raised through class discussion and your own ideas. In response to your reading, then, craft a paper that does at least the following things:

States the main point(s) in the essay. What is this piece "saying"?

Formulates your own thesis. Do you agree or disagree with the main point(s) of the essay?

Provides evidence in support of your reaction. This may take the form of a closer reading of the essay itself, your responses to the evidence or claims the essay makes. And often you will provide evidence from "outside" the essay, from other reading or research you've done, as well as from your own experience. (In many classes, what form of evidence you offer may be carefully defined by either your instructor or by the rhetorical situation.)

Writing Assignment:
Writing about a Place

You can find a lot of essays about places in magazines such as *Time, Newsweek,* and *George,* as well as in the Sunday magazines of large metropolitan newspapers. Readers are interested in experiencing new and different places.

For this assignment, we're asking you to visit someplace new and then write a profile of that place. Now how will you decide what place to visit and write about?

Use your other courses for ideas: If you're taking a comparative religions class, as many students at our college do to help fulfill their humanities requirements, perhaps you'll be moved to visit a mosque, a synagogue, an ashram, a Catholic or Baptist church— whatever is beyond your own realm of experience. Perhaps you're taking a history course, reading, say, about the many skirmishes and wars fought between America and the British. If you live in our area, you are anywhere from less than an hour to a four-hour drive away from many historic forts, both British and American. In many places there are historical museums that you probably haven't ever been to. Go. If you're taking an art history course and have never been to an art museum, what better time to go? Any of these places can make a wonderful paper for your English class as well as for your other courses.

Visit a place you've always been curious about but have never taken the time to go to. Factories, farms, funeral homes, dance clubs, sporting events—there are all kinds of places that may have aroused our curiosity but that for one reason or another we've just never gotten around to going to. Go.

When you choose a place, go there as a writer; be ready to observe and record; be ready to analyze. Record in great detail the sensory experience of the place: the light, the sound, the smells, the people and how they dress, speak, and move. When you get around to freewriting about the place, include everything, a lot more than what you may eventually use. You'll want to let the writing help you figure out exactly what you have to say about the place, exactly what dominant impression of it you want to leave in the readers' minds.

As you begin drafting your essay, remember: For this essay, showing is worth a lot more than telling. You'll want to create images in our minds and let those images do the work of carrying your message. It's best to avoid too much blatant editorializing about your opinions; let your descriptions communicate to us.

3

COMPOSING

6

THE FIRST DRAFT

As we begin to talk with you about composing your first draft, we'll re-iterate that we're talking about something different from what most of you have done in the past. We're *not* talking about a first draft as the first piece of writing you've done on the subject. We're *not* talking about those hastily-assembled-the-night-before-they're-due monstrosities that have earned so many of us such poor grades in the past. We're *not* talking about something you write on a McDonald's napkin on your dashboard on the way to school. We're talking about taking your freewritings, focused freewritings, clusters, loops, and whatever else you've already done and using those elements to now "compose" a focused, unified piece of writing. As far as we're concerned, if you haven't done the invention piece of the process, you're probably not ready to write a first draft.

So composing the paper is not a process independent of other phases of the writing process. Writers can rarely compose a word without the absolute assurance that anything they write has the potential to move, change, go away. No idea will vanish if it is refined. No word is so precious it cannot be moved or qualified. No example is so sacred it can't be expanded. We do all these things in the act of revision. This knowledge casts a far different light on composing the paper than the misguided belief that what we write today is set in stone by to-morrow.

HOW TO USE RAW WRITING TO COMPOSE: WHERE DO I START?

You've freewritten, you've brainstormed, you've used a computer program to find an idea, or you've listened to the radio to mark down idea after idea that makes you mad. Maybe you've done all these things and have several really potent ideas you would like to write on. Now what? Before you can know where to go, which one to pursue, let's remember back to the first chapter of this book. Remember, good writing is like good music. And what does good music have? A message and sound, a voice, a purpose. Although these seem like concerns for much later in the process—after all, we revise to work on all these things—really they can give us clues very early as to how a certain topic can or cannot pan out. This is where the work that we did in invention becomes so crucial.

Let's go back to our freewrites. Remember Josie's, the one she wrote as she struggled with the idea of freedom? Remember what we noticed about some of the lines in that very rough and unformed freewrite? They sounded like her. That's good. Don't let anyone tell you it is not. That's voice. Often, going through a freewrite or talking with a classmate about a topic, you will find that there are certain parts that stick in your mind or in the mind of someone else who is helping you to form your ideas. Often those stick out not only because of what they say but because of how they say it. These are the lines that can start a paper—and when we say start we don't necessarily mean put at the beginning—they can jump-start your ideas.

The invention notes, ideas, and the like that you worked with while trying to find or clarify your topic can be a good place to begin the process of composing. Maybe you see a few words that, when strung together, feel like a rhythm that you are interested in continuing; for some reason they just sound satisfying. Start there. Or maybe you know that you have found a central idea, a message, a place to center a text around; then go with that. You have to begin somewhere; why not begin with something you have already created? Remember, freewriting, brainstorming, and looping allow you to get your ideas out free from the rigidity usually associated with writing in school. This is the kind of writing that has the most potential for success. Try to find places and passages in the work you have already done that will enable you to continue working in a style that sounds a lot like you.

Consider these central things as you review all the writing you've done and begin to assemble it into your first draft.

WHO IS MY AUDIENCE?

This is really a central concern. How can you possibly imagine how to write to someone if you don't think about who they are, what they know, and what their views might be? Obviously, you can't know every thought and feeling of any other person, but you can make a meaningful guess about how they might respond to one thing or another. It is as simple as being considerate. It is as clear as thinking through your strategies.

If your readers haven't understood you, then ultimately you haven't done what you needed to do. That's why you have to put yourself in their shoes. Think about them carefully as you compose. If you were talking to someone from another generation—your grandmother, for instance—you would use different language than if you were talking to a friend your own age, even if you were communicating the exact same sentiment. Let's say you are at the dinner table with Grandma and your best friend. If the ketchup was on Grandma's end of the table, you might say, "Please pass the ketchup, Grandma." When she did just that you might respond, "Thank you." No misunderstandings there.

However, let's say the ketchup wasn't quite enough to perfect this burger. You need the mustard, and it is on the side of the table nearest your friend. You might look at your friend and say, "Mustard." Your friend would know exactly what you wanted and will pass it on down. Try this trick with your grandma, though. Say, "Ketchup," and see if you get the results you wanted as effectively as by using the magic *please* and *thank you.*

See the difference? Same message, different audience; got the results you wanted. It is just being smart.

The same thing goes in writing. You want to be smart about whom you are talking to. If your readers are the people around you—your classmates and your teacher, for example—what generalizations can you make about them? If you refer to MTV, will they understand what you are talking about? If you talk about our esteemed ninth president of the United States, will they have knowledge of who that is? If you discuss "the problem" with your younger sister, will they know that she has a lisp? These are all questions that writers ask themselves as they go about writing for an audience.

It also goes much deeper than that. An awareness of audience is also a great way to keep yourself expanding where you need to expand, cutting where you need to cut, and defining where you need to define. As you go about composing your first draft, keep the voice of your audience in the front of your mind. If you write, "It was the perfect day to bring out the old pitching wedge and practice getting them to the flag," ask yourself what questions your readers might have. Do they know what a flag is in this context? Why was it such a perfect day for this? Pitching what? Continually seeing your work as your readers might has enormous benefits.

Another thing these imaginary readers in your mind can do is help you stay within your topic. One of the biggest problems student writers have is that they don't have confidence that one small idea, given proper expansion, will be enough to sustain an entire paper. So what do they do? They go off on many different tangents to try to fill space and gain some credibility by the sheer volume of what they wrote. Skilled writers can take a topic and reveal it from many different angles, can discuss it in such vivid detail, and can draw their readers into their feelings so well that they have the energy and space for only one line of ideas. Imagine that your audience keeps drawing you back to your topic, that they want to know, "Well, what does that have to do with your main point? Isn't that really about something completely different?" This will curb the temptation to go off in lots of different directions.

A Social Perspective

Primary among your responsibilities as a writer is to take a social perspective of the needs of your readers. Here are some questions you need to ask yourself about your readers as you begin to compose. (Basically the same questions will appear in part 4, "Revision," as you will again need to consider your audience carefully as you revise):

1. What do my readers already know about my topic? What don't I need to tell them?

2. What don't my readers already know about my topic? Are there key concepts or terms that I need to explain or define? What are the key events that I need to include?

3. What do my readers already know about my topic that I need to repeat in order to make my point clearer? What needs to be repeated or stressed for me to make my point?

4. What are my readers' opinions and feelings about my topic? Taking those opinions and feelings into consideration, how can I effectively present my topic to my intended readers?

Try answering all these questions about your readers as you begin to compose your papers. Remember, most failed communications, written papers included, fail because the writer fails to anticipate the needs of readers.

Next, then, you need to move on to asking yourself about your purpose, about just how you wish to affect those readers.

WHAT IS MY PURPOSE?

Purpose is one of the most basic elements in the struggle to write what others will want to read, so once you've carefully considered who your readers are, what they know or don't know about your topic, and how they feel about your topic, it's time to carefully consider just how you want to affect those readers.

Many writing students don't think of the work they are doing as something anyone would actually want to read. And honestly, if that isn't a concern of the writer, then the paper usually becomes a text that isn't desirable for reading. When we think about writing with purpose, we think about producing a text that will teach, inform, amuse, anger, elicit emotion, or explain something about what one person (the writer) thinks or feels. Maybe this sounds like a simple order to you; maybe not. What we mean to do is have you think, in this early draft, about what this piece of writing will achieve and how it will affect its readers.

A student presented Jennifer with a paper idea early in the process. He wanted to write a paper arguing that pepperoni was his favorite pizza topping. They talked about it for a while, and she finally asked him if he could convince us to care what kind of pizza he preferred. He thought about it and decided that he could. He read the first draft of this paper to a group of students. At the end, one of them asked if he wanted to convince them to eat only pepperoni pizza. He said he didn't really care what kind they ate as long as they saved enough pepperoni for him. "Then why do we need to hear this paper?" asked this same student.

It's a very important question. We don't always need to write in order to try to change someone else. We do, however, need to give the reader a purpose to identify with. We need to share the stories of our life with another because there is a reason to do so. Re-creating our experiences provides lots of benefits to our readers: understanding of our common actions, identification with one another, education about various cultures. But discussing a trivial detail like food preference without a context that provides a reason for the importance of the detail isn't purposeful. It's useful to draft for a while and then sit back and ask yourself, What is my purpose? Why will my reader care? Who will want to know this?

We're not saying that a paper about pepperoni pizza couldn't be good. Indeed, a main purpose of many a paper or essay about such stuff is to be entertaining and make us laugh. But the best humorists do more than merely make us laugh. They get us to identify with their love of that pizza by appealing to our own experience with pizzas or with something else we love as much as they love their pepperoni pizza. Maybe their real purpose is pointing out how much of our energy and devotions can be wasted on an object such as a pizza.

Possible Purposes

You've probably heard or seen some of these before. We can write out a brief list of some possible purposes for your papers, a list that you could add to:

To instruct

To persuade

To argue

To define

To compare

To contrast

To critique

There are many possibilities.

It's important as you begin to compose a draft, then, to consider what you know about your audience and ask yourself what your main purpose for approaching this topic with this audience is. We say main purpose because you could well have more than one; you could wish to entertain and to argue at the same time, but most likely the argument would be the thing you'd wish to focus on the most. Given your audience and your purpose, then, you need to scour your raw writing for that material that best fits each, and you may often need to return to raw writing in order to provide more material.

Take a scenario such as this: You're an avid rollerbladder, and you know a heck of a lot about rollerblading, so you figure you'll do a paper on it. After reading through your raw writing, you've decided that your audience is your classmates and instructor, and you've carefully thought out what they know and don't know about rollerblading; that is, you figure they'll probably all know what rollerblading is, and you figure that at least some of them have tried rollerblading. Your purpose, you decide, is to explain why this is such a great sport, and you realize that you may even be trying to persuade the people who haven't tried it to give it a chance.

So, okay, now you begin to highlight or take out chunks of the raw writing that seem to serve this purpose and this audience. You pass over a definition of rollerblading that you'd done because you've decided your audience doesn't need it. But you highlight and use a section of your freewriting where you'd talked about the different kinds of rollerblades, their prices, and their relative quality. This is information your readers will want if you're successful in convincing some of them to try it. You use a section that talks about the thrills you experience on a good downhill; even your already-rollerblading readers will identify with this, and those senses of thrill and adventure are good hooks for some readers who may be thinking about trying it. And you decide to keep a couple of anecdotes you've told about your own difficulties learning to rollerblade; they're funny, for one thing (it's almost always good to make people laugh), and you can show your readers that everybody will have a problem or two that can be overcome. You decide not to include some fairly graphic freewriting you'd done on common injuries; hey, you don't want to scare people off, so you decide instead to be sure to tell people what safety equipment they should be sure to have in order to prevent injuries. You see?

Your paper would be different, though, if the audience you'd defined was made up of avid rollerbladers; it would have a different focus and purpose. Perhaps that paper would be an examination of the quality of different rollerblades or a profile of a good place to rollerblade. Much of what would be in your first paper, you wouldn't put in the second: different audience and different purposes.

So the clearer the picture you have of your audience and your purpose as you begin to compose a draft, the better off you may be. We realize, though, that you may still be struggling with the topic, with your purpose; don't let any of this cause paralysis. Go on and begin composing; you may discover your purpose as you go along, and you will certainly be able to deal with your readers and your purpose further as a part of your revision strategies, especially if part of your process will be presenting your draft(s) to a group or groups of readers.

Take a look at the following paper, "Attitudes." As you read through it, realize how much Greg had to have known about his readers, and pick up on how he makes his purpose clear to his readers:

Greg Voorman
English 131
Dr. Willey

ATTITUDES

Picture this: you're outside jogging on a wooded dirt road. It's early June, 60 degrees, the sun is slowly peeping up over the horizon, you're listening to birds and watching small animals scurry away as you pass by. Above all, you hear the constant rhythmic sound of your breathing and your shoes crushing the dirt beneath them. Among all this stimuli your mind is relaxed, thoughts of yesterday slowly pan across your mind's eye, or thoughts of what might happen in the near future.

Now picture this: you're outside riding a dirt bike on a tight, wooded trail, it's mid September, 50 degrees at best, you're traveling at 18 mph and standing on two pieces of steel the size of a match box car. All of a sudden, the sight of the trail making a right hand turn pops into your field of view. Instantly, you brake hard on the front wheel, let off the gas, ease the rear brake on, and move from standing on your foot pegs to sitting well forward on the gas tank. You also decide if you have the proper speed to lock up the rear wheel, push the left hand grip, and lean slightly forward and to the right. Then, waiting that 1/100 of a second to know if putting out your right foot, pushing down hard on your left foot peg, pulling slightly on the left hand grip, turning the gas on hard, and releasing both brakes, worked, It did! You came out of the turn slightly sideways, front wheel four inches off the ground, rear wheel spinning, accelerating you back to your comfortable 18 mph.

You're asking, "What do these two events have in common?" They both get you outdoors, both serve as a way of getting exercise, and both relieve stress and relax their participants. Then you may wonder, "How can riding a noisy, two wheel death machine be relaxing?" I believe that all the fast movements, quick decisions, and just plain reactions allow my mind to forget the big and little stresses of the week. On top of all this, you also receive a good physical workout that not only makes you feel better mentally, but you also sleep like a rock.

Today, ever one of us knows that if we want to live long and prosper (the greetings of Vulcans) we have to eat right and exercise, no ifs, ands, or buts. Yet fitting a regular exercise program into your weekly schedule and keeping it there is difficult. This got met to thinking that obviously there are different ways people relax, which could have a big influence on your preferred choice of exercise.

My favorite sports and/or exercises are ones that move quickly and usually have little time for thought. Some of these are racquetball, volleyball, dirt biking, karate, and golf. A few of them, such as golf and volleyball, have slow movements, but when you get down to the actual move you're not thinking, you're just doing. On the other hand, my wife enjoys running, biking, swimming, walking, and hiking. These activities would have me climbing the wall in fifteen minutes because the entire activity is one slow movement.

I believe if you sit down right now and decide if you are like my wife or me, you could choose an exercise program that fits you better, thereby saving you time, money, and lots of frustration. It shouldn't take you long to figure out where you stand, but this quick test might help if you're unsure. Would you rather go for a run or watch grass grow? Would you rather go for a long walk or watch paint dry? If you're having a rough time choosing what you would rather do in both of these questions, you would love to go dirt biking with me. On the other hand, if you didn't hesitate to choose the run or the walk, you would enjoy most of my wife's choices of exercise.

For the person who has the unfortunate problem of not being able to do all the action packed activities for their regular exercise program, there is little choice but to struggle through the boring exercises that they can do. So you ask, "How do I make these types of exercises I find boring, fun and exciting?" I'd love to tell you that I have the answer, but alas, I'm stuck just like you. Hopefully, recognizing the problem will help us put out the extra effort needed to get our exercise programs a little more user friendly. Yet how and where to put this effort is important. Using a quote from Mosha Feldenkris, from his book *Awareness through Movement*," For only those activities that are easy, and pleasant will become part of a man's habitual life and will serve him at all times. Actions that are hard to carry out, for which man must force himself to overcome his inner opposition, will never become part of his normal, daily life." In my own words, put the effort towards any part of your program that will increase your pleasure and ease. Applying the right effort will make an exercise that otherwise is a little on the boring side for you easier and more enjoyable.

To accomplish this, try to make it an event, do it with another person, wear headphones, join a club or a group, think positive thoughts, and always try to have fun. This will allow you to "get over the hump" as my wife would say, from mental pain and suffering to tolerable and pleasant.

```
So don't feel bad if you have to watch Star Trek reruns
while you Nordic Track or take an aerobics class just for
the view. Feel good because you're doing what it takes to
get over the hump.

 One day (may not be in the near future) with time and
lots of effort, I just might be able to say in all hon-
esty, that I enjoy running. In the meantime, though, I will
enjoy the activities I find easy and pleasant to do.
```

Greg knew that physical fitness is very much a hot topic today, and he can safely assume that all of his readers have at least thought about their own fitness. He could also assume that many of his readers would be those who are too busy or too lazy or whatever to cram a regular fitness routine into their weekly schedule. He knew there probably wasn't much more he could do than anyone else has already done to convince those folks to start exercising. So he took a different approach by identifying more directly with us on that level and trying to figure out how to make the necessity of exercise more palatable.

IS IT ME?

Thousands and thousands of students sit in writing classes like this one every year. Chances are, your teacher will have read more student papers than he or she can ever recall. So how do you set your writing apart from the writing that everyone else has done before you? Remember, in writing, conformity is not always the rule. You want your writing to do something that other people's writing could not possibly do; you want it to sound like you. We've highlighted this before, but it bears repeating here.

Poor writing has no feelings; it sounds as if it was written not by a person but by a computer. It's the elevator music of composition. We know you have read lots of stuff like this. (In fact, English textbooks are often the greatest offenders.) However, the fact that many people feel the need to write this way does not make it good writing. Good writing—the kind of writing that we all want to read—has personality. If you submit a piece of good writing without your name, your teacher should still have a pretty clear idea whose it is.

Consider the first and second versions of the first paragraph of Darcy's paper on living together before marriage:

FIRST

In our society there is a big problem with people living together before marriage. People try to fake a marriage and it never works out, besides it is immoral. People need to pledge themselves to one another before their church and their family in order for any union that they have to be truly what it should be. I think that living together before marriage causes more divorce than anything.

SECOND

My sister and her husband had the greatest relationship. I was so jealous because they were always together, affectionate, and always declared their love. Then the worst thing ever to happen to them did. They decided to move in together. "Why not get married?" my mother asked. "Just get married," I demanded. But NOOOO. They wanted to do the "in" thing—live in sin.

There are two significant differences in these two drafts. The second one uses specific details that give the story some texture, and (partially because of these details) it sounds as if a living, breathing person wrote it. Darcy's mistake while composing her first draft was writing out the sort of introduction she mistakenly thought sounded smarter and ignoring this passage from her freewriting, which you'll probably agree is a better piece of writing because it sounds like Darcy. So here's another case where freewriting provided better writing. You can probably also see how this paragraph might make an interesting, engaging beginning paragraph for her paper.

When You Might Want to Sound Less Like Yourself

Of course, we'll need to add some qualifiers. For one thing, different writing situations call for different levels of formality. A letter to a friend is a different thing from a lab report. And most often a story will be less formal than an argument.

For another thing, how much like yourself you'll wish to sound depends a lot on how you sound. Some of us have voices that are . . .

colorful. Our everyday language is filled with expletives, slang, and street talk. We think you can see how that sort of language might be inappropriate in an academic, argumentative paper. But we also think you can see that it might be okay to include some of it as actual dialogue in a narrative paper where the people who are doing the talking are using that language. Here you have to learn how to judge what's appropriate and what's not, and you have to adjust your language accordingly. If you don't know what's acceptable, ask your instructor.

And for a last thing, there are house rules, which we'll discuss fully in part 4, "Revision." In academic writing there are certain conventions and expectations, matters of correctness to consider, and "house rules" that good players will abide by. Again, your instructor will be your ultimate guide about how much like yourself you should sound in a given paper.

But we can tell you that generally, in composition courses, striving to capture your own voice is a good thing to do. So as you compose, try to make your writing sound like the kind of person you are. Use your voice to tell your story. This isn't just a matter of style. It is a matter of sheer communication. When we mask our voice, we mask our true relationship to our topic.

As you create your first draft, try to get used to the idea of privileging the concerns of your readers, of sharpening your purpose, of letting your voice come through—then go to it. Besides, you already know that this first draft of your paper will not be the last; you will be able to revise your language as you go along.

AS YOUR PAPER BEGINS TO TAKE FORM

You've got your audience well defined, you've got a purpose in mind, and you're going to try hard to make your writing sound like you. We hope you've done enough freewriting that you've got chunks of it you can use. If you haven't, you'll need to do some raw writing now that's directed toward your purpose and audience. Once this is done, we can now talk with you about outlining and about putting together various parts of your paper.

TO OUTLINE OR NOT TO OUTLINE?

Some writers use outlines a lot; others will rarely, if ever, use one. But as we mentioned in part 2, "Invention," most good writers outline only after they've done enough writing to discover where they're going.

So if you're going to outline, now is a good time. With purpose and audience in mind, you can read over your raw writing, begin to highlight the chunks you think you can use, and sketch an outline of the order that material may take in your paper. We suggest using full sentences and a sort of listlike structure rather than the more formal single word, capital- and small-letter, and numerals sort of outline.

An outline for the rollerblading paper we talked about might go something like this:

ROLLERBLADING

1. Intro—use first-time story as a hook. Tell how difficult that first time was.

2. Tell how I overcame the difficulties quickly, how it became fun.

3. Talk about what a high rollerblading is—good downhills.

4. Talk about what great and fun exercise it is—compare to jogging or going to the gym.

5. Talk about equipment, courses, etc. Tell them to use safety stuff.

6. Conclusion?

This is only one form an outline might take, and don't mistake the six numbers for any suggestion that you'd limit this paper to six paragraphs. Point number five, for example, could take several paragraphs: one on safety equipment, one about different rollerblades, one about different places to rollerblade. This sort of outline is a technique for organizing your thoughts; it covers what you think your main points ought to be and the order in which you think they'll go. It doesn't dictate the number of paragraphs or anything else.

If you're going to outline, then, now's a good time to do it. Then you'll need to move on to putting the paper together.

THE INTRODUCTION

■ ■

Have you ever slept with your husband's boss? Are you a woman in love with a man behind bars? I could hear the announcer say as I was getting out of bed, "If you are willing to share your experiences with our viewers, please dial this number." Viewers today are drawn into the gloomy world of TV talk show trash. Flooding our networks today are a growing number of television talk shows. From Rush to Springer, Vicki to Ricki, Joan Rivers to Bertice, Oprah to Jenny, Donahue to Geraldo, the list goes on. In addition, talk shows are becoming a growing part of radio. What concerns me most is why people appear on national television and confess their bizarre actions to millions of Americans. Furthermore, I wonder, really, do these illogical, irrational people exist in our society, or were they beamed down from another planet?

We all giggled as Patricia read her introduction to a draft on the preponderance of talk shows. This is a grabby, clever introduction that was really pretty simple to put together. It also shows that Patricia knew her audience: Her readers recognized many of these talk show hosts' names and were aware of the abundance of talk shows on the air. And the intro gives a pretty clear indication of her purpose and scope: She's going to explore the whys of talk show trash.

Most students find it logical to start a paper at the introduction. Most students also find this one of the most difficult parts of a paper. Because it is so difficult, sometimes it's best to put it off until you have drafted some other parts. You can start in the middle, working backward or forward, whichever best suits you that day. In fact, a lot of writers write their beginnings last, after they've gotten the paper pretty much put together the way they want it and have a clearer idea of exactly what it contains. But, whether you write this piece first, last, or somewhere in between, the special concerns of writing introductions need some discussion.

GRAB 'EM

Yes, you have to generate interest. No, you shouldn't do it at the expense of clarity (no needlessly long sentences with too many polysyllabic words), consistency (I bet I could get you really interested in my paper by using a shocking statement that I don't really believe), or coherence (the introduction does have to lead somewhere). Try to think of it as a part of the whole paper, not a separate entity. The best advice we ever got about writing introductions was to just start the paper. Forget about thinking of the introduction as something other than the paper. Just start writing. Chances are, by the time you are done, you will have an introduction already sitting there. When that doesn't happen, at least you've got the paper pretty much written, you've seen what it is you've said and how you've said it, and writing an intro might be much easier now as a result.

THESIS STATEMENTS

Many teachers like you to clearly communicate your purpose in a thesis statement in your introduction, often near the end of the first paragraph. Sometimes this is the very best place for such a statement. Putting it there can help to keep writers and readers focused on their purpose. If you stray away from a clear, early thesis statement, your revision process will usually put you back on track.

The following introduction, written by Chris, does not have a clear purpose in the introduction. How do you feel when you finish reading it?

When I was in High School I had a very good friend, her name was Sandra. Everyone called us Mutt and Jeff because she was a towering 5'11" and I was under 5'. Sandra and I had everything in common, we liked the same type of boys, hobbies, sports, the list went on and on. We also had both applied to South East Oakland Vocational Education Center. This was a school that High School students could attend to learn a trade and collect High School Credits at the same time.

Are you curious? Dying to go on? Most likely not. While Chris has started a story and given us some nice detail, she hasn't yet given us a reason to want to continue reading this paper. She hasn't offered a purpose for continuing our relationship with this text. She hasn't built any suspense. And while ultimately this paper turned out to be a very interesting story about betrayal and reaffirmation of friendship, there is nothing about these events yet in the introduction. Chris may be assuming her readers are more patient than they might actually be. Don't imagine your readers will automatically be interested in your paper. It is up to you to set up that interest.

Jon's paper on the meaning of spirituality does have a thesis statement:

When you think of sprituality you probably think about going to church and praying. To a lot of people this is what spirituality is all about. When I go to church it seems to me that I'm sharing my time with other people more so than sharing time with God. It seems that every time I go to church that there is a disturbance. Like children fighting, or people coughing. These disturbances take away from what I get out of church. I'm also in a place that man built. I feel a lot closer to God in a place that he created. To me true spirituality revolves around going out into nature fishing.

Jon builds this introduction by first telling us what he doesn't believe in and then going into his beliefs about where he can find true spirituality. This is a classic introduction form. He starts broad and then narrows to his main point. Knowing this form is useful.

Your best indicator of whether you should use a thesis statement and where it should go is your instructor. But we do wish to tell you that opening thesis statements as clear as Jon's, while sometimes considered a norm for academic writing, are pretty rare in most writing. Thesis statements, when they can be found, will sometimes be in the middle of a paper or near the end. Sometimes there's no thesis statement at all; the thesis is implied and then made clear by the details the paper offers. And there's no rule that states your introduction has to be only one paragraph long; your intro may run several paragraphs, with your thesis statement coming at the end of your intro, in the fifth paragraph.

SUSPENSE

Your intro may also create some suspense, although not the kind of suspense you see in detective movies; that kind of drama is usually overdone in introductions. The kind of suspense that writers look to create is the kind that leaves readers with a nagging thought after the introduction: What might this writer do next? If you have gotten your readers curious, then you have done a lot in an introduction. But this is hard. You want to be subtle. You don't want to hit your readers over the head with a bunch of mysteries. Just make them wonder.

What do you wonder after Chris's first paragraph? Probably not a whole lot. But how about this one?

```
The phone-ring and the siren started almost at the same
time. I picked up the phone almost without thinking, par-
alyzed, Who is it? What now?
```

There is a lot to wonder about this short introduction. What is happening? Who is on the phone? Had this happened before? It would be very difficult to stop reading this paper right here. In fact, this paper goes on to discuss Haya's reaction to the beginning of the Persian Gulf War as she sat in her apartment in Israel on January 16, 1991. The introduction really works. She hasn't overdramatized but just immediately put us in her terrified shoes.

Haya's introduction also doesn't have a classically presented thesis statement, but you know where it is going. You can predict it will go on to explain the pain and fear that occurs in the mind of this writer when confronted with an incident that is largely unknown. In a way, Haya tried to mimic her experiences for her reader. Since she was unaware of exactly what was happening at this time, she gave her reader that same glimpse into her experiences. She re-created a feeling.

Think about the suspense in Jon's intro as well. While we aren't looking to find out what his paper will be about, we are still curious why he would say such a thing about finding spirituality in fishing. This is not something we hear everyday, so we want to go on to see how it pans out.

Experiment with different ways to create introductions. Maybe write two versions, and ask some classmates to tell you which they like better. Weigh the needs of your reader: Is it more important, in this paper, that they know what to expect, or that they are surprised? Remember that there is no formula to any part of writing. You will need to possess a wide range of strategies to approach all parts of the writing process.

As we've said before and will say again in this book, read a lot; look at the different ways different writers do intros in their nonfiction work. Mimic some; it's okay. That's a good way to learn. Look at the way a certain writer has done something; then try it out yourself.

8

ORGANIZING THE BODY

▪ ▪

Here is a passage from Sean's paper, "Getting It Right":

> I put my heart into it. It was everything I ever wanted to
> say about this friendship. I had never written a paper that
> meant anything like this had before. My teacher returned
> it a days later. All that was written on it was DIS/O. What
> did that mean? When I asked her she said my paper was dis-
> organized. I still didn't know what she means.

Sean wrote this passage as part of a paper he was drafting on a
painful writing experience. And guess what? This paper was disorganized too. We talked about what that teacher might have meant and
how he could rethink the order of information. We also talked about
the many good things he had written in the paper. Yes, it needed to be
organized. No, that did not mean it wasn't a strong early draft.

Student writers are often terrified that their writing will be disorganized, probably because the task of reorganizing can be bewildering.
What does it mean to relocate information? How do you know what is
out of place and where it might go?

Our best advice is to try to remember how simple changing the order
of things may be. In the past, when a student went to reorganize lines

or paragraphs or sections of a text, they had to spend hours in tedious transcription, retyping *everything* to move around just a few things. With computers, it's now simply a matter of cutting and pasting text. What this means is that you have the freedom to fail. If you have a draft that doesn't quite "flow"—a term often used to describe the sound of a disorganized draft—you have lots of opportunity to experiment with changes. Sean was able to make many attempts at changing around his work, testing it out on others before he submitted it again. When he was finished working through this paper, he had learned a lot about moving around information. He may always struggle to get his ideas into a logical order in the early stages of writing. That's okay. His process of revision takes him closer every time. So the best thing to remember is to get feedback on your structure to determine if it works for your reader.

We're getting ahead of ourselves, though, talking really more about revising. There are also some strategies you can use right from the beginning, as you're organizing your first draft, to help clarify your thinking on what it means to organize information.

RETURN TO INVENTION

Remember, we never stray too far from any phase of the writing process. Though you may be well into what you perceive as the composing phase, invention can still aid you. All that stuff that you wrote when you were getting ready to refine your ideas or choose your topic can gain new life when you are ready to organize a chunk of your paper. For instance, say you did some freewriting on a significant event in your life, something that you always remember because it was "a first." You may have written a bit describing the event, some on how you feel about it now, some on any other people who were involved with it, and some on your feelings immediately after the event took place. You may have whole sheets of paper recounting some of the dialogue that took place that day. If you have any or all of this, you are lucky.

You can begin sifting through and organizing what you already have. When done with care, invention can piggyback into composing in helpful ways. You aren't facing blank pages or computer screens; instead, you are drawing connections from writing that already exists. Some students like to draw a tentative outline from some things in their freewrites. Others go through with different-colored highlighters and mark yellow for the parts that may need to go early, pink and purple for parts near the end, and green for the middle. Still others type their raw paragraphs in the computer randomly and start experimenting with putting things in different places.

REMEMBER YOUR READERS

Keeping your readers in mind will help. You want to organize your ideas, but you aren't sure how. Think about how your readers would perceive the points you make. What will they need in order to get from idea to idea? If you change locations, ideas, or time frames, have you given your readers enough warning? Think about organizing your work so that you take your readers through your own journey. Of course, the best way to account for all the things your readers need is to ask them. You will have ample opportunity to do this. For now, though, try to anticipate their needs.

SOME USEFUL PATTERNS OF ORGANIZATION

For much of the writing students do in composition classes, we've been able to identify several of the most common organizational patterns associated with that writing. We'll highlight a few here. Realize, though, that it is your material and your readers' needs that will ultimately determine how you organize your work; you can't usually determine the organization before you do the writing.

Chronological—A lot of narrative papers get organized in this way: as events happened in time.

Degree of importance—Least important details first, followed by increasingly important ones. This is often used in argumentative papers, where you save your most convincing or strongest arguments for last.

Point-Counterpoint—Also common to argumentative writing, you begin each section of your paper with what others say, and then you respond to them.

Comparisons or contrasts—Each section of the paper gives one difference or similarity between two or more things.

Spatial—Descriptions of places are often organized as the reader would experience them when first walking through the door or arriving at the place.

Cause and effect—You examine what causes "A," or you examine what effects "A" has on "B."

These are only a few of the more common among many possibilities.

Of course, ideally you have already discovered the order of your paper as you assembled the chunks of your raw writing, or you have outlined based on that raw writing. Often, as you see what you have and really begin to think about how to put it together, a form emerges for you. The best test, though, will be to actually put it together and then see how it works on a reader.

THINK ABOUT PARAGRAPHS

One of the kindest things you can do to help your readers is to use paragraphs thoughtfully. This means you don't just create a paragraph break because it is convenient, your paragraph looks a little too long, or you are getting tired, but for reader-helping reasons. Using paragraphs in meaningful ways is one of the easiest ways to organize a text.

Think of it this way: one main idea per paragraph. At the end of a paragraph (as at the end of a sentence), your readers should have learned something and be somewhat satisfied with that piece of information, yet they should be eager to learn what comes next. Every time you switch locations, arguments, or trains of thought, you should think about beginning a new paragraph.

As you get more comfortable with writing, you will see that sometimes the things we have just said don't hold true at all. Sometimes it is effective to write very long and complex or very short and abrupt paragraphs, but this is only with the knowledge that you are doing this for a good reason. Don't make them long and windy because you don't know exactly where to stop; instead, think about and experiment with all sorts of ending points. (This is one of the beauties of writing with computers; you can move paragraph boundaries almost effortlessly.)

SAY IT WELL, SAY IT ONCE

Often, student writers are taught the five-paragraph essay form as a way to organize their thoughts. This can be very useful to develop strategies to sort out ideas. Its biggest drawback for college-level writers is that it is a defensive form. It assumes that the writer will not be able to communicate the point effectively enough to need to say one thing only one time. The form relies on the formula "Tell me what you are going to say, say it, tell me what you said." Essentially, this form asks a writer to make a point, reveal the support for that point, support the point, and then repeat support and point again. There is very little room for misunderstanding in this form; that's its strength.

Its weakness is that it can be dry, predictable, or formulaic. Increasingly, people who evaluate writing done on admissions tests and such look at five-paragraph themes as indicative of students who aren't ready for college-level writing. So think about taking the good parts of that form and incorporating them into a new, more sophisticated way of presenting ideas. If nothing else, think hard about why you would ever need to repeat a point. If you say it once, clearly and fully, it will stick with a reader. If you spend the rest of the paper supporting that point, they won't forget it. You should draw your power not through repetition but through effective use of language the first time.

SOME OTHER THINGS TO THINK ABOUT WHILE YOU DRAFT THE BODY

Show, Don't Tell

Remember the game "show and tell"? In writing, it's a new game. We call it "show, don't tell." Instead of *telling* about feelings, scenes, events, you actually paint a picture for your reader by putting them in the action. This is one of the keys of writing that is hard to teach and perhaps even harder to learn. When a writer does it with skill, though, we know something wonderful has just happened. We'll take our own advice now and show you what we mean.

Two students wrote papers about friendship. Here is how Wendy described the special relationship she had: "We instantly bonded. We had so much in common even interest in guys. Over the years we became better and better friends sharing everything you could share with a best friend. She was like my sister."

Now, read Lisa's description: "We've always remained very close. . . . I let this guy basically take over my life, so I ignored all my friends. When he dumped me I was completely crushed. Even though I had ignored Linda for the past nine months, she bought me an ice cream and listened to me cry."

We hope you notice that Lisa's description is more vivid. There is nothing wrong with what Wendy says; it is just that she has described her friend as millions of us could describe our friends. There is nothing in the description that acknowledges that their friendship is different from anyone else's. In Lisa's passage, we can see what the nature of the relationship is. She has drawn us a picture with her language. Writers want to bring their readers as close to their own experiences as possible. Showing with clear detail will aid in this.

Look at the difference: If Antonia is writing a paper about her best friend and she says, "I couldn't belive how anxious she was to get to the party," you might say, "Okay, I completely understand what you just said about your friend." But what if Antonia shows you her feelings instead of telling you about them? What if she says, "She ran about ten red lights and almost plowed over a small child as she sped through the night to get to the party"? More personality? Definitely. More visual details? Obviously. Every time you are able to show instead of tell, you have allowed your readers a glimpse into a specific experience of your own or of someone else you may have been with.

This also works in more academic papers. What if you were describing the effects that home computers have on your life? You might tell about them by saying: "I have so much more time now that my computer does all my paperwork." Or, you could show: "Now I can watch all the reruns of *Star Trek* that I want, for I just pop some numbers in my machine and hey, my checkbook is balanced." See the difference? As you go about showing as much as possible, you will begin to see that not only is this good for your readers' understanding of your work but also it is a lot more enjoyable for you as a writer.

Use Dialogue

A great way to do some real showing is by using dialogue to let people talk. When there is a significant conversation (significant either in language choice, content, or drama), you may want to think about presenting it in dialogue form, just as it occurred. This is the difference between Kris's presentation of an argument in his first draft—"My father told me I was not good enough to be his son anymore. I responded with begging and pleading"—and the conversation as it appeared in his final draft:

"If you are going to behave like that then . . ."

"What, Dad?"

"Then you aren't my son anymore."

"I am your son. Yes I am." Then there was silence.

Dialogue can be very powerful. Use it when the words speak for themselves better than you can speak for them. Mundane conversations are probably better off summarized, but if there is significant emotion attached to the actual words, go ahead and let people speak.

Use Specific Detail

Actually, showing, using dialogue, and being specific are all part of the same idea. The more ammunition you can give your readers to be where you are, the better. Writers of nonfiction have learned much about this from fiction writers they admire. Fiction writers are often quite schooled at using texture, color, shape, and other such factors to communicate something about an object. They write about people by using details about skin tone and hair color; they describe meals by their smell; they use comparisons to help us visualize the weather. These are all good things for us to remember as well. Why talk about "a car" when you can describe "a beat-up, '75 LeBaron convertible"? Why just "a dog," when it could be "a mangy, overweight beagle"?

Of course, nobody wants to read (or write) something that is too detailed. Use details wisely. Experiment with them. This really is one of the most enjoyable parts of writing.

CONCLUSIONS

Two very different problems can be found at the end of many student papers. Either the students are so drained by the end of writing a paper that the end falls flat, or they get such an energy surge from finishing that they almost begin a new paper at the end. You may feel there is so much riding on the conclusion that you will never be satisfied. As is clear by now, there is no formula for writing strong conclusions (or introductions or bodies). But there are some strategies to consider, some things to avoid, and some models that might help you.

Remember the idea that an introduction should not be something that stands separately from the rest of the paper? It is the same for conclusions. You don't want your readers to say, "Hey, I see we've come to the beginning of the conclusion now." That kind of thought makes them too aware of the work of you as the writer. Try to be more transparent than that.

SOME *DON'TS* FOR CONCLUSIONS

Our recommendations about conclusions are largely about what not to do. Don't omit anything important, but don't stumble around either.

Some more *don'ts*:

Don't repeat your introduction: Say it once with power and precision, and you won't need to repeat it.

Don't start a whole new topic: There are all sorts of aesthetic reasons for this, the most important being that most papers should have a single, coherent main point. This isn't a soap opera or movie that could have a sequel; you don't have to try to sell your readers by suggesting you'll have more to say in the next paper.

You can think of this in practical terms as well. If you want to write about your dog's bad habits, why bring your bird into this and risk making us more interested in the bird than we are in the dog? (Note, though, that often in early drafts there will be a better main point lurking in the conclusion. Sometimes writers think they've written an entire draft about X, they come up with Y in their conclusion, and Y ends up being more interesting. We'll talk about such centers of gravity in part 4, "Revision.")

Don't become stiff, formal, or go into thesaurus-speak: Some students are able to completely control their urge to write like a textbook until they get to their conclusion. Then something inside them must snap, and they lapse into what they think sounds more "academic." We've talked about this idea before in relation to introductions. You should maintain a consistent voice throughout your paper. Don't allow the conclusion to seem like an outsider in the paper.

Don't feel you have to sum up the world: Students often try to make their introductions and conclusions too big. They have a nice story about something or a good, small argument and then worry it won't have enough significance. That's where "and that's what is wrong with the world" and "that's why it is so true that you can't judge a book by its cover" come from. Don't ruin a well-constructed paper with final thoughts that overgeneralize or are such common expressions that they have become trite. Strive, instead, for concluding ideas that are consistent with the message of your paper and are not clichés (things we've heard so many times before).

And though you may have been taught that conclusions are supposed to summarize the paper, realize that summary conclusions are only one kind of conclusion. They are really only common and necessary for very long reports, not usually the sort of thing you're doing in composition classes (unless, of course, your instructor asks you for a summary conclusion; in that case, do it).

SOME *DO'S* FOR CONCLUSIONS

With that said, there are lots of things you should think about when working on your conclusion. Many of these strategies you will remember because we have discussed them in reference to writing introductions and early drafting. But because the conclusion is so vital to the lasting impression the paper leaves with its readers, let's go over them again:

Remember the needs of your reader. What will be too much? What might be too little to leave them satisfied?

Say something new. You aren't done yet, so keep your paper going until the end.

Stop when it feels right; then ask for advice. As with all drafts and through most phases of the writing process, working in a vacuum has little value. You could sit around just about forever wondering how this draft or this conclusion is going to work on readers, sit around forever tinkering with the draft or the conclusion, and never get it done. At some point, write it and share it. You can revise your conclusion further later on.

Probably the best way to improve your conclusions is to read a lot of them and then experiment with writing all sorts of endings. Here are some that students have felt were effective:

I feel times have changed—women are working and struggling more than ever to help out in the family to make ends meet. Also, I think because couples are busier than ever, they need to set some time aside in their busy schedules to spend some quality time with their children. They are only young for a short time, and before we know it, they'll be grown and gone.

Approaching 40, can I tell you that I have it all together? Heck no! But it's so much easier than it was in my earlier years. The struggles I've conquered have left me wiser in return. With nine years of working out behind me, I'm healthier mentally and physically than I was at 25. It's extremely cool to have an idea of who I am and what I want to do. It took me a while to come around, but I sure am glad to be turning 40 to tell about it! I always say, "If you're bummed about getting older, then take a moment to consider the options!"

Well, now that you know the true confessions of a dental depressant, all can say is, if you and your dentist are best buddies...I HATE YOU!

Though you haven't read these conclusions in context, there are a few things we want to say about them. You can tell that each is quite different from the others, and you can certainly make a good guess as to what each of the papers was about. These conclusions have accomplished that much without adhering to any strict formulas. We will also tell you that each conclusion sounds like its writer; none varies drastically from the language and tone of the entire paper. In the first paper, Rosemary compared her own life as a working mother and student to that of her own stay-at-home mom and talked about how different her own life is from what she'd been raised to expect. In the second, Pamyla talked about what turning 40 meant to her and took the opportunity to reflect on how she had made it that far. And in the last one, Nicole confessed to being deathly afraid of a visit to the dentist and drew out a really funny description of a typical appointment. Each of these conclusions fit well with the papers the writers produced.

10

USING COMPUTERS TO COMPOSE

■ ■

When we talk to our students at the end of the course about the most important things they learned, these are the types of responses we get:

"I now understand that a paper doesn't have to be so good when I first write it. The class helps me make it better."

"Real writers never get it write [sic] the first time."

"I can do the paper lots of times before anyone has to tell me if it's good or not."

Our students are secure in their belief that the best tool for drafting is knowing that you can always produce another draft. This is where word processing becomes so important. When we were in college, everyone groaned when told they had to have one first draft and another final version. Why did they groan? Because this meant spending hours retyping a paper that may have had significant passages unchanged. This felt like a waste of time. It wasn't rewriting so much as it was retyping.

This is where computers have made life easier for students and teachers. Simply, computers let you spend more time writing and less time typing. You can put one draft on a screen, cut some, add some, move this and that around, erase a conclusion, move the introduction to the conclusion, and then print a copy. Then, you can go back to that same draft and change a variety of other things as many times as you like without having to reproduce the parts you want to remain intact.

USE THE COMPUTER THROUGHOUT THE PROCESS

First of all, we urge you to consider doing all your writing—raw writing, composing, revising—right on the computer. (We explained the overall benefits of writing at the computer in Part 2, "Invention.") Use one or several files for freewriting or brainstorming sessions on a given topic. When you begin to compose at the computer, then, you'll be able to access and use the materials from your raw writing without retyping them.

We remind you also that some writers prefer to do their very preliminary writing in pen and then transfer it to a computer as their work begins to take shape. Still others never touch a computer until they have a fairly formed first draft. If this is what works for you, stick with it. The most valuable use of the computer will be for revision. For this, nothing works as well.

CUTTING AND PASTING

All good computers and word processing programs, whether you're working on a Macintosh, an IBM, or a clone, allow you to cut and paste materials both within and between files. Essentially, you will cut or copy material from one file or one place in a file, as if you had cut it out of a piece of paper, and you will paste that material into a different file or into a different place in the same file, as if you had actually glued it onto a different piece of paper. Following is some advice about cutting and pasting that will make composing your draft a lot easier.

Cutting and Pasting Between Files

To cut and paste between files, you have to have more than one file active in your computer. Say you've got one file you titled "Freewrite.1" where you've done all your raw writing for your first assigned paper. Open that file; then go on to open a new file, which in most programs will come up as "Untitled" until you save it for the first time and give it a title. Now you've got two active files open in the computer: Your

"Freewrite.1" file contains all your raw writing, and your "Untitled" file will be where you'll begin composing a draft of your paper.

As you search through your "Freewrite.1" file, you come across sections you want to use in your draft. Now you need to highlight the sentence or section you want to use. If you're using a mouse, you'll need to place your cursor at the beginning or end of the sentence or section you want to use, and you'll drag across or down that section while holding the mouse button down. On computers without a mouse, most word processing programs ask you to use one of the PF keys to turn highlighting on and then to use the arrow keys to indicate the words, sentences, or section you want highlighted.

When you've highlighted the section you want to use, you use the cut or copy command: cut if you don't care to leave that material in its original spot; copy if you want to leave the original intact while still using the highlighted portion in another file. Now move back into the "Untitled" file (you may have given it a different title by now), put your cursor where you want the material to go, and use the paste command. (On computers that use mice, cut, copy, and paste are usually found in the edit menu or in a tool bar along the top or side of the screen.)

Now you've either moved or copied a whole sentence or more of text from your raw writing into the file where you're assembling your first draft, thus eliminating the need for that retyping. For an average typist, retyping a paragraph's worth of material can take anywhere from five to ten minutes or more. This cut and paste operation can be performed in about thirty seconds—really.

Cutting and Pasting Within Files

To cut and paste within a file, you perform essentially the same procedures. Now, though, there's really no reason to use the copy command, since you probably won't want multiple copies of the same passage(s) in the same file. Highlight, cut, move your cursor to the insertion point, and paste.

Now that you can so easily manipulate the text in your emerging draft, you should take advantage of that ease and do it. You can now change the order of paragraphs in this emerging draft very quickly, which means you can actually see what changing the order of the paragraphs does for your draft. Should you save your strongest argument for last or do you want to use it first, as a way of really hooking your readers? Do it each way and find out. Share each with a friend or a group to get more opinions.

Commonly, writers find that the conclusion they've written for a first draft would actually be much stronger at the beginning. So they delete the beginning, cut the conclusion, and then paste it to sculpt a new beginning. You are able to make major changes to the shape of your first draft as you're composing it. Or you can experiment with two or three different beginnings or conclusions. Again, because it's easy to do so, you should do it. Think about the power you have over an emerging draft that you never really had before.

If you do create several different versions of the same paper, you might want to save each under a different name: "Title.1," "Title.2," and so on. When you've decided which one is going to be your first draft, you may want to trash the others, or you may want to keep them around in case the feedback you get indicates that one of the other versions may work better.

The same will hold true with subsequent drafts of your papers; give them names that indicate which version of which paper you're doing. In the Macintosh world, you can give files longer names than you can in some IBM-compatible programs: "Title—First Draft," "Title—Second Draft," and the like.

As you go about drafting your first version, you have probably erased, rethought, gone back, and changed stuff. This is great. You have a good start on the most crucial part of the writing process, revision, and you will notice just how recursive the phases of the process often are. In the next section, then, we will talk about revising from draft to draft, including how to get and use feedback that will make revising easier and more productive.

REVISION

11

WRITING IS REVISING

■ ■

Here we could quote dozens and dozens of professional writers who in their own ways have said the same thing: Writing is revising. As students, though, you may have a hard time really getting a feel for what all these writers are saying. What does it mean to say that writing is revision?

It's so hard to understand because, as we've mentioned elsewhere in this book, many of us have misconceptions about what writing is all about. Too many of us have been taught or somehow have come to believe that good writing just happens—that it emerges pretty much fully formed and nearly perfect from writers who are "good" by nature of their heredity or luck or something. In fact, good writers revise their work a lot, taking a paper or a story through several or many drafts. Many good writers routinely get lots of feedback from editors, peers, and significant others and revise by using the information and advice they receive. As we wrote this book, we worked with an editor, and we also worked with the reactions of many reviewers who had seen and critiqued this book at various times during the writing. For us, the process of writing this book was truly recursive: We were inventing, composing, and revising throughout.

Just as we've made revision the central focus of our own writing courses—by requiring a minimum of four versions of each of our students' papers—we wish to make revision the central focus of this book. The better you learn to revise, the better your writing will be.

REVISING VERSUS EDITING AND PROOFREADING

First we need to define what we mean when we talk about revising; that's because we've found that a lot of inexperienced writers have a mistaken notion of what revising really is.

Chances are that about as far as most of you have ever gone while "revising" is to check your spelling, try to detect errors in grammar and mechanics (which probably didn't work too well, since you made the mistakes to begin with), perhaps change a word here or there, possibly with the help of a thesaurus, or rewrite a sentence or two. These are the sorts of revisions that we call *local* because they occur mostly at the word or sentence level.

That's not all there is to revising, though. Those sorts of concerns— spelling, correctness, word choice—are really editing or proofreading concerns and should take place after revising. (Sure, a certain amount of word-level revising goes on even as you compose, which is okay so long as it doesn't keep you from completing your paper or revising at a larger level.) Revising literally means reseeing your text. Revising means making some large changes: adding material, thus taking you back to invention; deleting significant chunks of material; moving blocks of text around; rewriting for a different or at least a better defined audience; rewriting from a different point of view; and other significant changes. This is the sort of revising that few inexperienced writers have ever done and the sort that you need to learn to do in order to see your writing improve.

WHEN TO REVISE

As we've told you, the writing process is recursive: Inventing, composing, and revising are not discrete stages that occur one after the other, forever leaving the last stage behind once you've moved on. Each of these labels merely describes the dominant activity that's going on during a given time during the process. As far as revising goes, it's almost not a stage unto itself. We're constantly revising as we write. We'll take a moment to explain.

Even when you're freewriting, the act of focusing on this thought rather than that one somehow dictates what the next thought will be;

that is, one sentence often pushes the next in a certain direction. Emerging text, even when it's freewriting, shapes the text that follows it. The thinking and the writing are being revised even during invention and composing. You see?

A bit less abstract, then, is the fact that each writer's process is different from each other writer's. As we mentioned before, as we wrote this book, we were constantly inventing-composing-revising—such was the nature of the project of writing this book. We might on a given day go our separate ways—Jennifer to work on the invention section of the book, R. J. on this, the revision section. As we worked individually, especially as we embarked on each section for the first time, we were inventing, it's true, but we were also composing, getting a feel for the shape of each section, and shaping it as we invented-composed. And during the composing of each section, the text that did emerge called for the occasional reshaping of what had come before it, and that's revising.

So what we're saying is that any time is the time to revise. It's true that we want you to put aside your critical self—the self that is always doubting and revising—very early in the writing process, especially as you learn the various techniques that we present to you in the invention section of the book. But as you get a feel for your own process, as you begin to discover what does and doesn't work for you as a writer, you may discover that you can revise throughout your writing process.

In Part 3, "Composing," we talked with you about shaping your writing into a draft to be shared with others—in essence, revising your raw writing. In this section, we'll concentrate on the sort of revising you do when you're revising from first to second to third to final drafts. We will concentrate on how to get feedback from peers, your instructor, tutors, and others; what to do with the feedback you receive; how to make the choices necessary to revise your work; and some of the many different ways you can revise your work. After we have concentrated on these more global issues in revising, we will give you some advice on how to handle the local level as well.

12

GETTING AND GIVING FEEDBACK

■ ■

Students in writing classes often don't see how lucky they really are. They have a real advantage over many writers because they have a regular, available audience for their work; that is, in most composition courses your readers are your instructor and/or your classmates, and you have them there, on hand, two or three days each week for the length of your term. You get to see firsthand how your writing affects your readers, you get to hear firsthand the sorts of questions or concerns your readers are left with, and you get to learn right away whether your readers perceive your message in the way you had intended.

GETTING FEEDBACK FROM PEER GROUPS

"Going to group" or simply "group," as we call it, is the main activity in our own writing workshops. In these groups, students read their work aloud to some fellow students and the instructor or a peer tutor. Then they can begin revision with some concrete direction. Students take the first two or three drafts of their papers to group before turning them in to us for our exclusive feedback. And you can imagine that once these drafts reach us, they're far improved over the rough or second versions.

The purpose of group is to get enough valuable feedback on your paper that you are able to resee your paper as others see it. One of the most frustrating things about writing is trying to revise when you have only your own feedback. It is difficult for you, as a writer, to become your own audience. You are too close, too familiar with your ideas and stories. It is essential to have a real audience to give you feedback for revision.

Though going to group takes a lot of time and effort, it is minimal when compared to the difficulty of real revision of your own work. Getting feedback actually simplifies a writer's life. By the middle of the term, our students are always asking the group for more and more feedback. They find that once they begin to get useful feedback, it's nearly impossible to revise without it. But getting and giving feedback take practice. We spend much time talking, practicing, and modeling feedback. Nobody should be expected to walk into a writing class and instantly get or give high-quality feedback on their writing. As with all skills, this takes guidance and practice.

In our workshops, we are also fortunate to have trained peer tutors working full-time in our classrooms; they facilitate peer group work, keep students focused and directed, and thus ensure the value of the feedback each writer receives from the group. Perhaps you will have a peer tutor in your own classroom, perhaps your instructor will choose to facilitate each group, or perhaps you will rotate the job of facilitator with some other classmates. Even without a trained facilitator or instructor, you can have productive, useful groups. What we'll give you here are some heuristics—some structured, problem-solving activities that will help to focus and drive your group. Working in or outside class, you can use these heuristics to help you give and receive much of the feedback you'd normally expect to receive only from an instructor.

In fact, the feedback you get from a group of people—when done well—will be superior to the feedback you can get from any one person. It's simply a matter of having many different perspectives available to you. No matter how skilled a reader is, one person can offer only a single perspective on a text. Multiple people allow for multiple positions.

If you aren't working with a tutor or your instructor, the first thing to do is appoint a facilitator; if you're working in class, your instructor may appoint one. Basically, the facilitator is a timekeeper and coach, ensuring that your group spends only a given amount of time on each person's paper, that everyone in the group talks, and that all important points of the heuristic get covered for each person's paper. Say you've got five people in a group and you've got a ninety-minute class; the facilitator makes sure that you spend no more than twenty minutes reading and discussing each person's paper.

The facilitator and the groups should allow for slight digressions; it can be very interesting for writers to see and hear where their writing leads people in discussion. While listening to the stories others are reminded of, writers may get a better understanding of how they're connecting with their readers—of the sorts of emotions, opinions, and memories their writing brings forth from their readers. So allow yourselves a little latitude, so long as you return, in short time, to the important issues about this paper.

What follows now are a set of guidelines for good group work and several heuristics. Your instructor may ask you to use a certain heuristic for a certain assignment or may provide you with one or more of his or her own.

We use the following for general etiquette and form in all our writing groups. We've followed up some of the guidelines with brief explanations to help you see why these rules are important to our groups. Your instructor may pick and choose from this list, add more guidelines, and modify some others. The writing group is a subculture of your writing classroom. It is important to remember that all cultures need rules and standards. Perhaps you'll spend time in class talking about how the guidelines you use will aid the group's effectiveness.

Guidelines for Group Work

1. Each member of the group will have a piece of writing to share. By photocopying or producing multiple copies from the computer's printer, the writer will produce a copy for each person in the group. (Readers need to see and hear the text in order to respond.)

2. Each writer reads aloud as the group reads along. When writers stumble over words or sentences, when they find errors as they read, they will take the time to mark these to come back to later. (Readers also should make simple marks on their copies to remind them of questions or comments.)

3. When the writer has finished reading aloud, the group may take a minute or two to review the manuscript, gather their thoughts, and jot down notes. (Let students who need a moment to process catch up to those who are ready to respond immediately.)

4. Each group member will offer comments on each paper. Comments should first focus on what's good about the paper and then move toward more critical, constructive feedback. (It is very helpful to tell the writer what does work in the paper first.)

5. For the most part, writers will remain silent, except to answer direct questions or to ask questions at the end of their time. The writers will take notes, mark up their manuscript, and the like while the group discusses. (This should not be a time for writers to defend their text. They are to listen to responses and then, later, use these responses to aid in revision.)

6. As much as possible, group members should offer comments as questions that explore possibilities: "What if . . . ?" "How about . . . ?" "Do you think . . . ?" "I wonder if . . . ?" (Responses should be reader-centered. The group is not there to evaluate the work but rather to respond.)

7. When the group has finished a paper, someone may want to summarize the recommendations of the group. Then, the writer may ask any lingering questions. This segment will end with the writer thanking the group for their input. (The group then moves on to the next paper until all the students have had an opportunity to gain feedback on their work.)

In addition to using these general guidelines for discussion, we have found that heuristics are helpful for focusing groups on specific concerns of specific writing tasks. Instead of a systematic answering of each question (yes, yes, I think so, etc.), these heuristics are used more wisely as jumping off points to get to the meat of the paper. As the term proceeds and you gain confidence in your ability to give feedback, you'll probably want to depart some from our heuristics and develop (formally or informally) your own.

We like to allow every group member to respond to each text. It is probably not necessary, though, for each person to answer each question in the heuristic. Try to use them flexibly, as conversation starters.

Six Heuristics

Heuristic #1

Here is a simple, short heuristic that's good for most papers. It asks for the paper's overall strengths, invites readers to share with the writer any questions they might have about the paper, and asks readers to state the main point they got out of the paper:

1. What do you like best about this paper? What words, phrases, sentences, or paragraphs really stand out for you?

2. What questions are you left with? What do you still wonder about? Show the writer what parts of the paper seem to need something more or seem to raise questions that remain unanswered for you.

3. What do you think the paper's main point or message is? What is the writer's central concern?

Heuristic #2

This heuristic gets a little more specific. It includes the term "center of gravity," which Peter Elbow and Pat Belanoff use to mean an idea in the paper that seems to command the most or more attention. The center of gravity may or may not be the intended main idea in the paper.

1. What do you like best about this paper? What words, phrases, sentences, or paragraphs really stand out for you?

2. What questions are you left with? What do you still wonder about? Show the writer what parts of the paper seem to need something more and seem to raise questions that remain unanswered for you.

3. What is the paper's main point? What seems to be the author's central message?

4. What is the paper's center of gravity? What draws you the most to it? (Remember, the center of gravity may not be the paper's main point.)

5. What do you want to hear more about in this paper?

Heuristic #3

Here is another heuristic that will be useful for a lot of different kinds of papers; this one may be more useful than the previous ones for more academic writing assignments and topics.

1. What do you like best about this paper? What words, phrases, sentences, or paragraphs really stand out for you?

2. What is the paper's main point? What seems to be the author's central message or argument?

3. How well is the main point supported? Point out areas where the writer uses good examples to support the paper's ideas, and point out areas where ideas aren't sufficiently supported with specific examples. Also point out those places where the points don't seem to jibe with the topic—where the paper may have gotten off track.

4. Has the writer anticipated your needs as a reader, such as your knowledge or lack of knowledge of the topic? Your opinion(s) about the topic? Are there terms or concepts that you just don't understand?

Heuristic #4

It is possible that everyone in your group is working on the same general assignment—a narrative paper, for example—either by choice or by assignment. So here are a couple of heuristics made up for more specific sorts of writing assignments.

For narrative papers

1. What do you like best about this paper? What words, phrases, sentences, or paragraphs really stand out for you?

2. Is the sequence or chronology of the events clear? Are there places where you got confused?

3. Are the descriptions of the people and the places clear and concrete? Where can the writer offer more or less description of the people and the place(s)?

4. Is there any dialogue? Too little? Too much? Where might the writer add or delete dialogue?

5. What was the significance of this event in the writer's life? How well has the writer connected with the readers' experience in order to make that significance clear?

Heuristic #5

This next heuristic works well for papers written about significant people in our lives.

For papers about people

1. What do you like best about this paper? What words, phrases, sentences, or paragraphs really stand out for you?

2. In what ways has the writer shown you this person? Physical description? Anecdotes? Dialogue? Explore the possibilities for the writer further showing the person and the writer's relationship with the person.

3. How is or was this person important to the writer? How or where does the writer most directly show this, or how or where can the writer do more to show this?

Heuristic #6

The next heuristic is a good one to use for a lot of academic writing assignments; it gets a little more specific than #3.

For argumentative, concept, and other academic papers

1. What do you like best about this paper? What words, phrases, sentences, or paragraphs really stand out for you?

2. Are there any key terms or concepts that aren't sufficiently defined or explained? Point them out.

3. Are there any places that seem to contain too much information, thus leaving you confused? Are there places where the writer has told you too much, most of which you already knew?

4. What is the main point of the paper? Do you feel that the writer has done enough to make it clear? To convince you?

5. Are there places where you might question the writer's logic? Are there any overgeneralizations? Attacks on people rather than on the issues? Phony or questionable cause-and-effect relationships?

We hope you'll find all or many of these heuristics useful as you do group work. Of course, once you've become a better critical reader, you may be able to begin to use some of these heuristics on your own as you evaluate your first drafts, before you've even taken them to group. One of the values of group is that it teaches you to anticipate readers' needs. You'll find that once you do group for some time, you can predict what readers are going to say, so your first drafts will begin to take much more of this into account.

We want to add just a word about the "positive feedback" we ask groups to begin each session with. You may feel this isn't really helpful to the writer since it is nothing they may want to change. However, giving positive feedback is valuable in other ways. For one, it tells the writer what readers really like, and if they like it maybe it is wise to do more. Also, it alerts the group members to things they may want to "adopt" or "model" from this student's paper. If you like a technique that someone else uses, by all means borrow it. Try to see how it works with your writing.

There are other values of going to group. It is not only that you learn about your paper from getting feedback on it. You also learn a lot by giving feedback. When you can identify and discuss what confuses you in someone else's paper, you have developed critical reading and thinking skills that will be enormously useful. Responding to someone else's paper teaches you what appeals to you and disagrees with you about writing. It helps you continue to clarify your own definition of what good writing is and is not.

So group is a very powerful tool. We don't believe there is any substitute for it, but there are other methods that can be useful when you can't get to group. These are especially useful when coupled with a time or two in group. The more kinds of feedback, the stronger your final product will be.

GETTING FEEDBACK FROM TUTORS

We've both tutored in the past, and we work with many tutors all the time. From this experience and these associations, we think we can give you some pretty good advice about how best to work with tutors, and we think we can make your tutoring experience a good one for both you and your tutor(s).

First of all, realize that getting tutoring is good, a smart thing to do. We're well aware of the stereotype of a student going for tutoring being somehow stupid or deficient, and that's just not true. Good students get tutored all the time in tutoring centers, with advanced peers, or from their instructors. That's just part of being a good student—using all the resources available to you to help you do as well as you can. Just about every college campus has a writing center or a learning center or a tutoring center where you can go to receive tutoring, so go and use the resources.

In most colleges, writing tutors see students one on one on either a drop-in or appointment basis. What you need to remember is that you'll need to give the tutor as much information as possible about your writing assignment, the course requirements. These tutors are likely not students in your professor's class and may never have been, so you need to give them as much context as possible for what you're writing about and why. A copy of the writing assignment, if you have one, will be helpful.

And here's another key we've learned from tutors: Show up with some writing already done, preferably a first draft, more preferably a draft that's received some feedback from a group or the instructor. Tutors can't function in a total vacuum any more than you can, so if you show up with only a vague notion of what you're supposed to do and with no writing already done, there's probably not a lot the tutor will be able to do for you. Sure, they may be able to help you do a little brainstorming to arrive at a possible topic, but if you have only the vaguest of notions of what you're supposed to be doing in the first place, the chances are good that you won't end up with an acceptable topic anyway. So go to a tutor with as much information and writing as you can.

Next, realize what tutors are there for: They are usually not experts there to proofread and edit your papers for errors; error hunting has got to be between you and your instructor. Sure, some tutors are good enough at grammar to be able to help you out with fragments, run-ons, and the like, but you can't expect your tutor to be your expert proofreader. That's just not what they're there for.

Tutors can help you the most with the global issues in your paper: support and development of ideas, the structure and organization of your paper, effective beginnings or endings for your paper. The really important words in that last sentence are *your paper;* it doesn't hurt to reiterate that whenever possible you should have a paper to show to the tutor.

Besides going with a good sense of the assignment and with a draft of your paper, you should try to formulate some specific questions you want the tutor to help you with. Say that you've received a first draft back from your instructor, and the end comments indicate that you haven't used enough specific examples to support your ideas, that the sequence of events in your paper is a little unclear, and that you've got a bit of a problem with comma splices. The best case scenario now is that you will write a second draft, attempting to use more specific examples, attempting to straighten out the sequence of events, and attempting to locate and correct your comma splices. Here is where a tutor can be of most help to you: Take to the tutor the first draft with the instructor's comments, the second draft you've written, and the following main question for your tutoring session: "How well have I addressed my instructor's comments?"

Under these circumstances you can have a really productive tutoring session. But let's say that you haven't had time to write a second draft or that you're so confused at this point that you have no idea how to proceed. Okay, take to the tutor that first draft with the instructor's comments and a list of questions you'd like to address. The list might go something like this and would be intended to help the two of you do some productive brainstorming:

1. Where do I need to offer more examples? What sorts of examples might I use?

2. Where is my sequence of events unclear? What methods can I use to clarify it for my readers?

3. I don't really understand what a comma splice is. Can you [the tutor] help me recognize them?

Any list of this sort would be most helpful.

GETTING FEEDBACK FROM INSTRUCTORS

Though we've been teaching for a number of years, and though we see it happen time and time again, we're still amazed at the number of students who don't take the time to use the greatest resource they have available to them for help—us. Quite commonly, we discover somewhere around five or six weeks into the semester some student badly floundering, confused, and discouraged, who has *never* asked us for help.

We know that many students don't seek help from instructors because they don't even know where to begin, so here are some tips.

For Help Getting Started

Our situation is similar to tutors in that we can help you most once you've done some writing. It isn't very helpful to have only questions such as "Could I do this or that?" Well, maybe you could, but we'll have to see you try before we can tell you whether it works. So if you're having trouble getting started on an assignment that we've given you, or if you're having trouble deciding what to write about, do some writing—freewriting, clustering, listing, something—and bring it to your instructor. Instructors can learn a lot and help you out a lot by looking at the raw writing you've done.

Feedback on Drafts: Markings and End Comments on Your Papers

The markings and end comments instructors put on your papers will vary widely from instructor to instructor, and they can be either fabulously helpful or completely confusing to you. Depending upon the instructor, you'll get anywhere from a sentence to several paragraphs of end comments, some of which you'll understand some of the time and much of which may confuse you.

What you do with the comments is your responsibility, though, and your primary responsibility is to come to us for advice, clarification, and help. Come with specific questions, as we told you to do with tutors. Have something more focused to say than "What's wrong here?" Formulate some specific questions you have about our markings and end comments. Here are some possibilities:

1. You say I need to strengthen my transitions. What are transitions, and where in my paper do they need to be improved?

2. You noted a problem with my organization. Should certain paragraphs be changed around?

3. You have marked several run-ons in this draft. How can I learn to recognize and correct this error before I've turned in drafts?

GETTING FEEDBACK FROM YOURSELF

In about every writing situation, you are going to have to be the final judge of something before you turn it in to your instructor. Generally, even when you've done a couple of drafts, there's going to be a "final" that's going to get graded. So at some point you're going to have to read your draft and decide whether it's ready to turn in.

Time is the real wild card when it comes to reading your own work critically and well. Many professional writers can put a piece aside long enough to come back to it—in a week, a month, or more—and look at it more objectively. It's hard to be an objective judge of your own work when you're freshly involved in it. So you'll want to work as quickly as you can and not wait until the last possible moment to write a draft; have it done a couple of days or weeks in advance of its due date so you can let it sit for a while before you come back to it more critically and objectively.

Often, though, you won't—or can't—take that kind of time with an assignment. Our students have to accomplish four drafts of six or seven papers in fifteen weeks; this schedule doesn't leave a lot of time for sitting on a draft. Like many compositionists, we believe that the more writing students do, the better they will become, so our students write a ton. And many professional writers—feature writers, columnists, reviewers, journalists—can't take a lot of time with a given piece either;

like them, you need to learn to switch off your creative side and switch on your critical side quite quickly.

When you've received some feedback from other sources, revise into another draft that takes that feedback into account; then make up a list of questions for yourself similar to those we gave you for tutors and instructors. Read through your draft and attempt to answer those specific questions for that draft. Try to stay objective and detached rather than thinking of all the time you've spent on this assignment already; think only of honestly answering the questions, as if this were someone else's paper. Here are some possibilities:

1. The group said my paper was confusing, needed reorganizing. Have I done significant reorganizing from the last draft to this one?

2. The instructor told me I needed to improve my transitions. Have the beginnings and endings of my paragraphs changed significantly? Are there now transitions that help the logical flow of the paper?

3. My last draft(s) had quite a few comma splices. Working with what my instructor showed me, have I examined my commas to best ensure against comma splices in this draft?

We recommend that you actually write out a similar series of questions for each of your papers. Don't rely completely on memory. As we've mentioned before, you can also use any of the heuristics we or your instructor gave you on drafts of your own papers. The key to getting good feedback from yourself is similar to getting good feedback from anyone else: Have a lot of writing done, and have a plan for what sort of feedback you need or want to receive.

13

REVISING AFTER RECEIVING FEEDBACK

■ ■

You can go on endlessly gathering responses from your group, instructor, tutors, friends, your dog. At some point, though, you need to take this feedback and use it to revise.

This is a tricky part for us to write because you can receive so many different kinds of feedback. It's very difficult to find neat categories or labels for what sorts of revising you might need to do based on the feedback you've received. We've decided to borrow categories from a teacher and writer we both have a lot of respect for, Donald M. Murray, who identifies these five in his book *The Craft of Revision*. We're going to talk about revising for audience, for meaning, for order, for evidence, and for language. And finally, we'll throw in a few words about editing and proofreading.

REVISING FOR AUDIENCE

Most of you at one point or another in your lives have behaved very differently around your parents than you have around your friends. Even as adults, many of us still do. We are different around different audiences. So if you're going to present basically the same message to your closest friends one hour, then to your employer the next, you're going to deliver that message in far different ways, right?

The same, of course, holds true for your writing. Who your readers are and their relationship to you and to your message have everything to do with the way you present that message. So thinking about your readers should be primary when you think about revising.

Much of the global revising our students need to do centers on matters of audience; doing group allows them to discover firsthand how their readers react to their writing: what readers already know about their topic, what they don't know and need to know, what they really want to hear more about, that sort of thing. Working in groups, our students spend much of their time asking the writer questions, filling in information that isn't there yet, exchanging stories that each paper reminds each student of. Writers sometimes discover that they had the wrong audience in mind all along, that the paper they've written isn't really appropriate for their peer group and instructor audience, and that they need to better define just who their intended readers are.

We all need to learn how to do this, and that's really the purpose of this section of this chapter. We're going to give you a hodgepodge of concerns that relate directly to who your readers are and how you wish to affect them, and we're going to give you some advice about different ways of approaching revising for audience.

A Social Perspective

Much of the feedback you'll receive from other readers will concern what they know or don't know about your topic after reading your draft. Many of the questions they may ask you will revolve around parts of your paper where you haven't included information your readers need. Some of the comments they make will suggest to you that they already knew enough about such and such and that perhaps you've said a little too much about it. So primary among your responsibilities as a writer is to take a social perspective of the needs of your readers. Whether or not you've received some feedback, here are some questions (which appeared in part 3 as well) you need to ask yourself as you revise your work:

1. What do my readers already know about my topic? What have I told them that I may not need to repeat?

2. What don't my readers already know about my topic? Are there key concepts or terms that I haven't sufficiently explained? Are there key events I haven't touched on? Are there examples I've left out that I could use?

3. What does my audience already know about my topic that I need to repeat in order to make my point clearer? What needs to be repeated or stressed for me to make my point?

4. What are my audience's opinions and feelings about my topic? Taking those opinions and feelings into consideration, how can I more effectively present my topic to my audience?

We think you can see how the answers to these questions might affect how you revise your work. Not considering how much your audience already knows about your topic may have lead you to write too much that your audience already knew. You may have defined terms that you can safely assume your audience already understands; you may have done too much explaining about concepts or people that you find your audience is already familiar with. In most situations, for example, you'd hardly need to tell your readers that Elvis Presley was a famous rock and roll star. That would be a wasted line because you can safely assume that the great majority of your readers already know that. In a paper about railroads, you probably wouldn't need to define the term *locomotive* because most of your readers will already know what one is.

Considering what your readers *don't* know also often leads to a lot of revising. A student writing about rock climbing can safely assume that most of us don't know a piton from a crampon, so that student will need to define those terms. It's usually best to avoid specialized jargon for the most part, but when you need to use it you will have to define it.

REVISING FOR LANGUAGE

Word Choice, Logic, and Political Correctness

Some things we've overheard recently from student writers talking about their work and the work of others:

One white student asked another, "What kind of kids went to your school?"

"Mexicans."

"Oh, so it was a ghetto school."

From a student who went to a high school that represented a wide range of socioeconomic groups: "Rich kids are snobs."

From a female Chaldean student: "Chaldean guys like to date American girls because they're loose."

As you begin revising your work, especially as you revise your first draft into something you intend to share with an audience, we need to spend a little time talking with you about your language—the words you choose to express your thoughts, why you use the words you do, what effects those words have on others, and your responsibility for taking care over the words you use. Our message is simple: If you care about how your writing represents you and how well your writing will work, there are facts you'll have to accept about language.

Language: You Are What You Say

Think about how the word used to describe a thing can affect the way we perceive that thing. Let's say that you and a friend are visiting Washington, D.C., and in a subway station you come across an ill-dressed man who seems to have everything he owns in a old duffel bag that he's currently using as his pillow. You look at the man and think, Homeless, while your friend looks at the same man and thinks, Bum. What do you suppose that says about each of your attitudes about the person to whom you're attaching the label? Does your use of the more neutral term *homeless* indicate your own more open and perhaps compassionate attitude toward this man? Does your friend's use of the term *bum* convey her negative attitude toward the homeless? It's possible, right? The point is that language is not arbitrary. Though at times you may feel that what you say or write is "just words," this is very rarely the case.

Even on the off chance that your friend attaches no special negative connotation to the word *bum,* if she uses the word in a conversation with others, do you think those others will consider it a neutral term? In educated company, who do you suppose will come off as more compassionate with their listeners: you, using the word *homeless,* or your friend and her *bum?* If your purpose in communicating with these folks is to talk, not argue the issues of homelessness and vagrancy, you are better served by using a term that won't incite an argument.

Logic

At the moment, you're writing in a college course, and the discourse that goes on at this level requires of you certain standards of logic and presentation that may not apply as much to situations outside college. Here's another fact to accept: academic writing has to be a lot more logical and evenhanded than much of the writing done outside colleges and universities. You're being required to write at levels of objectivity and fairness that make word choice—like the difference between *homeless* and *bum*—important.

Much of what we're saying here should be fairly obvious. You're going to want to avoid words that can be considered offensive or stereotypical—racial, religious, or otherwise. You're going to want to respect people's wishes to be referred to as African Americans, Korean Americans, women, and so forth. People from these communities feel that the words we use to refer to them play a part in shaping the way we look at them and think about them. We think you can see the logic behind that. You can certainly tell the difference in attitude between someone who uses racial slurs and someone who uses more neutral, respectable, or nonoffensive labels.

So while we hope that you don't engage in racist or other negative modes of thought, you must see the absolute need to avoid stereotyping in your language while you're writing in college.

Avoiding Racial and Other Stereotypes and Insensitive Labels

We're sure that for the most part we can appeal to your common sense here. The reasons for avoiding racial, cultural, religious, and other stereotypes are at least in part fairly obvious. So be sensitive to that language. Don't engage in it yourself, and don't allow others around you to do so, at least not here, in your college classes. Try to be sensitive to what different racial, cultural, ethnic, and religious groups would actually prefer to be called. If you're uncertain, ask your instructor.

Also, try to eliminate references to a person's race or religion or culture where those references aren't necessary. For example, did you ever notice that race most often gets mentioned only when people are referring to nonwhites in our culture? Somehow, in attempts to describe people by height, weight, hairstyle, and so on, we tend to only hear about their race if they're "black" or "Mexican" or "Arabic"; rarely do we hear someone say, "Well, he's a white guy, about five-eleven. . . ." So when a person's race or culture or whatever really doesn't play a role, don't even mention it.

Who Your Readers Are Affects the Language You Use

You also know that a lot of language of the street is very controversial; language as presented in rap lyrics is a good example. Perhaps in your day-to-day exchanges with friends and family your language is peppered with slang or curses that are acceptable or usual in your particular culture. But in the college composition classroom, you're not writing only for your friends, only for others of your religion or race or sex;

you're writing for a mixed, academic audience, so you'll want to avoid the sort of language that might unnecessarily offend people in your audience. And we say *unnecessarily* because we recognize that writers may have a reason for offending their readers—as a way of stirring them out of complacency and into action, for example. But we warn you that only the most skilled writers pull this off without also losing their readers. Most likely, if we offend our readers, we've lost any chance of making our purposes and messages clear to them.

Another consideration: Slang and slurs often are the sign of writers who don't have the language to express themselves. These types of words signal an inability to communicate within the rules of the house. They shout, "Notice me; I want to offend you." If you can write well, with power and voice, you don't need to do a lot of shocking your readers. You want to keep your reader on focus with writing that uses language to convey meaning, not draw attention to itself.

Now this isn't to say that slang, vulgarity, and racial slurs may never appear in your writing. We academics may be politically correct, but we're not prudes. Generally (meaning, mostly, when it's okay with your instructor), it's all right to use these words if you're writing dialogue and that's the way this person you're writing about actually talks. That's part of characterization; you're recording the things that people say. So in a narrative piece, maybe about a time you were pressured by peers into doing something you knew was wrong, you might be using a lot of dialogue, and you might have had a friend or two with pretty colorful language; okay, do it, but just don't overdo it.

Nonsexist Language

An issue that has become important for writers in recent years is sexist language. Up until the later part of the twentieth century, our language use had been quite sexist. Browse through some older textbooks sometime, and you will see that "a lawyer" invariably becomes a "he" and a "him," while a kindergarten teacher will almost always be a "she." Our everyday language has been filled with gender-specific and therefore gender-biased terms: *policeman, fireman, chairman,* to name just a few.

It is just possible that the male-biasedness of the language continues to make the struggles of women for equality that much harder. It's possible that we continue to associate males with professions such as law enforcement and firefighting and with leadership positions such as chairing important committees at least partly because of the male-biasedness of our language and our thinking. And if even that possibility exists, perhaps you can understand the concerns of men and women everywhere and respect their desire to try to make our language less gender-biased.

So we ask you to follow the National Council of Teachers of English guidelines regarding nonsexist language. Basically, what we're asking is that you use nonsexist terms whenever possible.

Instead of:	Use:
Policeman	Police officer
Fireman	Firefighter
Chairman	Chair
Anchorman	Anchor
Repairman	Serviceperson

In addition to obviously gender-biased labels of professions and actions, pronoun use becomes a concern when we try to make our writing bias-free. This doesn't have to be the case, though. Whenever possible, use plural nouns. When you're writing about students, use the plural so that your pronouns will be *they* and *them* and *their,* rather than the *he* and *him* and *his* that were traditionally the choices for "a student," and rather than the more awkward *he or she* and *him or her* and *his or her.*

Don't: A good student takes a lot of notes, outlines the chapters in his textbook, and looks at the course syllabus every day.

Do: Good students take a lot of notes, outline the chapters in their textbooks, and look at the course syllabus every day.

Even where you have nouns that traditionally have been considered singular (everyone, no one) and therefore "correctly" are given a singular pronoun, you may use a plural pronoun to avoid sexist language use.

Don't: Dr. Helms asked everyone to open his text to chapter 15.

Do: Dr. Helms asked everyone to open their texts to chapter 15.

Or, better yet: Dr. Helms asked the class to open their texts to chapter 15.

One more thing: This may be self-evident by now, but it is amazing how deeply things have become ingrained in our subconsciouses. This one, we hope, can be replaced quite quickly. It is the use of *man* as a false generic, the use of the word *man* or *mankind,* when you really mean *people.*

Don't: Man has always struggled with his attempt to control his surroundings.

Do: People have always tried to control their surroundings.

We hope this section has been helpful, not only for you as you think about revising your language, but also for how you think about the way you classify your world. Academic writing demands that you pay attention to your language when you write, and we've advised that you do that as you revise, from rough to next draft and from that draft to subsequent draft to final draft.

Here are some questions to help you concentrate on revising for language:

1. Have I thought about how my word choice can reveal personal bias, opinion, and the like? (This isn't always a bad thing if we do this intelligently.)

2. Have I familiarized myself with guidelines on nonbiased language?

3. Have I taken the time to identify groups with the title I believe they prefer?

REVISING FOR MEANING

Our students say it all the time: "But that's not what I meant." Well, the group says, "That's what you said." Everyone experiences the frustration of knowing what they want to communicate but not having the words to say it. This problem is exacerbated in writing, since we want to be so clear, so concise. In speaking we can back up, make changes, resay something a half-dozen ways. In writing, we feel, one chance is all we get. So we want to make the most of it.

We hope we've made the point by now that this isn't really true. Revision gives us the opportunity to say something wrong many times until we finally find the way to say it so our readers understand. Drafting and getting feedback are the perfect opportunities to practice saying it right until all agree that we have communicated effectively.

But I Thought I Meant . . .

And it is not only that we sometimes need to write something several times and try things out on different people before we can communicate precisely but also that sometimes the very process of clarifying our words for a reader will help clarify our thoughts. Sometimes we write things, especially in prewriting and early drafts, that puzzle even ourselves. We just aren't sure what we mean. Revising for meaning means thinking very deeply, asking loads of questions of our audience and ourselves about what the words seem to suggest. Sometimes things will come out in our writing that we didn't even know we thought. This is part of the process of writing as discovery. Writing helps you understand things. Sometimes these are things that are very far removed from what you thought you believed.

As you can surely see, revising for meaning isn't simple or neat. It is taking something that may be a bit vague and wondering if it is vague because you just aren't sure what you mean by it. Students who are very clear about a feeling are rarely vague as they write about it. If your readers don't understand how you feel about something, ask yourself whether you really understand. Don't be afraid to think something you may not have thought before. This is a part of the process of discovery that comes with being skilled at revision. This is also evidence of the circular nature of writing. Learning that you want to say something that you hadn't said before returns you to the invention piece of the writing process.

From Mouth to Page

Another concern when you are thinking about revising for meaning is the frustration associated with transferring your words into writing. This may be one of the simplest things to take care of. Often in group someone will ask a writer, "What did you mean in this sentence?" And the writer will answer, "I meant that he was the best friend I ever had." And the group member will think for a moment and say, "Then why didn't you just say that?" Recall something we have talked about in previous chapters. Students want their writing to sound different from the way they sound, so they throw in abstract words, thesaurus words, and textbook words to say the simplest things. We all would write better if we trusted our speaking voices a little more and wrote more like the way we speak. Meaning is often hidden beneath layers of unfamiliar language.

Here are some questions to use to focus yourself on revising for meaning. Ask them of yourself, or lead others to focus their responses on these concerns:

1. Does this sound like me? Are there words or phrases that feel odd coming from my pen?

2. What about this paper is vague? Are those passages vague because I have discomfort committing to the ideas? Should these vague ideas be clarified?

3. Are there ideas that still may benefit from further examination of my thinking?

REVISING FOR ORDER

One of the most common complaints students have about their own writing process is that they just don't know how to organize their ideas into something that "flows." Often, it is not that their writing is disorganized at all; students are mistaking misordering for choppiness. A paper that has many short sentences and switches ideas very quickly is a paper that doesn't flow and feels choppy. A paper that is disorganized will most often be confusing when it is read or heard by another student. It will be confusing because the chain of events or thoughts does not occur in an order that makes sense to someone who is not privy to your thought process.

So, how do you revise for order? What do you do when someone tells you they aren't understanding the relationship between the chain of events you describe? Here are some strategies that will help you think about the order of your story, your argument, and your points.

Organizing Stories (Narration)

When you are narrating an event or telling a story, see if all the background information is given to the readers before they will need it. For example, if you really hate a certain place where your friends tend to gather, and a friend of yours says, "Let's go there," we won't understand why this is a cruel thing to say unless we know, in advance, that this friend already knows you are uncomfortable going to this place. This is just a matter of using some forethought and taking your reader into your story gently. At other times, you may want to withhold certain pieces of information in order to create a desired effect. Perhaps you are interested in shocking your reader with a particular detail. This is fine if it is done wisely, with consideration for why you are doing it.

When organizing events, think first about presenting them chronologically—that is, in the order they happened. This will allow your reader to come along with you in the feelings that accompanied the event. They learn what you learned in the order you learned it. But often when you read a paper of this sort to your group, they have a complaint such as "It sounds like a police report" or "It's so dry." This may be a time to think about how to reorganize the paper into a more interesting form. Remember, nothing has to be inherently wrong with the organization in order to think about revising it some. You just might want to spice it up, to make something into a really exciting piece of writing.

You may want to try telling the story as a flashback, meaning presenting the results of the incident first and then going back and describing how you came to be in that position. Maybe you want to start a paper by telling how it felt to sit in the principal's office at high school as you waited for the principal to enter and decree your punishment. Then, the rest of the paper could be your memories of the incidents leading up to this moment. Yes, the paper would probably work by just starting at the beginning, but look at the dramatic effect you get by starting close to the end. Rethinking the order that you present events is one of the simplest ways to make your writing style more sophisticated.

Organizing by Degree of Strength

How about organizing a paper that has several supporting points? If your group believes your arguments at the end are stronger than those at the beginning, ask them if they think it works best that way. There is no hard-and-fast formula for ordering your arguments by degree of strength. There are times when it is best to begin with one of your stronger arguments so that you hook your reader right away; there are many times when it may be wisest to have your most resonant punch at the end. This takes asking, experimenting, and practice. (Go back to the chapter on composing for a fuller discussion of organizing arguments.)

The most crucial thing to learn about ordering material as you revise is to ask questions of those who hear your work in early stages. (Of course, this is important in all types of revision activities.) Order is a tricky thing; it is nearly impossible to see other ways to tell a story or present an argument when you are very close to it—as a writer always is. Use the tools of those around you to help.

Transitions Help

Transitions are another concern when you're thinking about order. Now is a good time to look back at the transitions you have made from one idea to the next. A transition is simply a way to get from one idea to the next one without making your reader feel as if you have abruptly taken a turn. Transitions can be single words (*but, after, next*), phrases ("on the other hand," "after all that work," "while in the navy"), or sentences ("Then again, my sister never was a very good cook"; "My friend Frankie is one of those people"). Skilled writers use transitions in such a way that the paper feels put together and natural. There are innumerable transitions, but they are so subtle that they go unnoticed. If readers say your writing is choppy, look at how you get from idea to idea, point to point, event to event. Sometimes you will find that you have no transitions. Other times it may be that your transitions lack grace. More than a very few "on the other hands" or "First," "Second" will also feel choppy. Work hard on integrating transitions into your writing. This will give your work a flow.

Following are some focused questions to help you get and give feedback on organization and order:

1. Have I organized my ideas in the only way possible? In the best way possible? What other techniques might I try?

2. Have I used transitions to help get my reader from point to point? Where might my transitions need some strengthening? Where are they obvious to the point of distraction?

3. Can I see how the chain of events or sequence of ideas fits together? How might I do better?

REVISING FOR EVIDENCE

Don't immediately think of prosecutors and district attorneys when you think about evidence. Yes, they use evidence to defend or prosecute alleged offenders, but this physical, tangible evidence most often used in our court systems isn't the only kind.

Writers use evidence all the time. They prove arguments through a series of supporting details. How do I know that your best friend is an excellent chemistry student? You proved it by offering me evidence of his/her(?) accomplishments: science prizes, straight A's, commendations from teachers. How do I know that Animal Rights Activists wish to boycott a certain brand of Tuna Fish? You proved it by recalling a news story you viewed last night. The specific details that writers use are the evidence they offer their readers.

Very often, as you move from draft to draft, you will find that your readers will need you to provide more evidence and more examples or to refine your evidence more and more. Revising for evidence, then, can be a matter of giving us more information about your topic, or it can be challenging just how good the evidence you've given us really is. Remember that you are always struggling to prove the points that you make. Some beginning writers have trouble fully supporting the things they say. They have a terrible fear of giving too much information; perhaps they don't want to bore their readers, so they give only the sketchiest details, which simply is not enough. You will learn gradually that you can't assume your readers will buy what you have to say unless you present loads of evidence to back up your ideas.

Perhaps the most common advice that writers get from a group of peers looking at a draft is to give them more information about X, Y, or Z. Take this as a code for saying "You haven't given me enough evidence. Prove it."

Right Evidence, Wrong Argument

Sometimes it isn't that your evidence is merely insufficient; sometimes it just doesn't prove what you think it does. This is still a further opportunity to listen carefully to the feedback you get. Your argument and support may be abundantly logical to you; to others, it may sound completely contradictory.

Some of this may go back to the other revision concerns we discussed earlier in this chapter. Maybe your arguments are sound, but you aren't communicating them effectively. Maybe you have misread how much your audience knows or doesn't know. Maybe your language is in some way alienating the very people you want to invite. These are all concerns we have discussed before, all things to think about.

But there is also this possibility: Maybe you know something, you believe it absolutely, but you just can't prove it. This is a problem of evidence. Talking out your beliefs usually helps the most. Or go back to prewriting and list the possible reasons for believing as you do, no matter how wild you think they may be. Write some support that you know doesn't really answer your readers' questions; then take it to someone as a draft. No doubt they will be able to help you decide if you are getting close to proving your point.

More often than you think, if you recall the section on meaning, the evidence suggests something different than you had imagined you meant. Once again, it is fine to go with this.

What Is Academic Evidence?

Evidence can be in the form of numbers (if you use library research), survey results (if you are doing some primary research of your own), anecdotal information (things you've seen or heard), data culled from laboratory experiments, and interviews with a representative sampling of classmates, among the many possibilities. In a research course, your teacher will talk extensively about valid and invalid forms of evidence. Once you have learned how to view evidence skeptically, you will become even more adept at critically evaluating the evidence you hear in papers that your classmates present to you. The study of evidence in the social and natural sciences, the humanities, and technical and professional education is a discipline unto itself.

In writing, take evidence and consider it from all angles. Most important, let others view your evidence (as part of a peer review of your writing) through their lenses to see what they observe.

Here are some questions ideal for concentrating on evidentiary revision. Use them on your work and on your classmates' work. Ask others to concentrate on them when hearing a draft of your paper:

1. What is the evidence for the main point? Is it strong and convincing? Be sure you can articulate the exact evidence and how it supports the views presented.

2. Is there evidence you know of that may be even more convincing? What else is there to think about?

3. Has the evidence been gathered from credible sources? Is much of the evidence based on supposition and third-person accounts?

We think you've gotten it by now. There are many different concerns that writers have when they go to revise their work. Of all these, our most valuable pieces of advice come from the very beginnings of this section: Do revise. Do get feedback. If you do nothing else, these two activities will improve your writing. Once you begin them, you will never be satisfied with writing that doesn't include these two crucial steps.

14

EDITING

■ ■

Editing is like combing your hair before going to work. It doesn't change you substantially; it shows only that you took time to worry about your presentation.

Please notice that we've made editing the final concern of the writing process. We will stress once again that you should try not to let your concerns about spelling, punctuation, grammar, mechanics, sentence structure, and paragraph structure interfere with your production of text. Especially during invention, be free of these concerns as you use writing to think and as you try to determine where your writing might take you.

Even when we discussed composing, we really didn't direct you to think too much about editing concerns. We called a bit of your attention to paragraphing, but nowhere did we ask you to be concerned about the correctness of the draft you were composing.

Even as part of revising, we didn't concern you too much with matters of correctness. We want you to think of revising on a larger, more global level and to turn your attention to correctness separately. So we treat editing separately, as something you do when you're just about to give your writing to readers in some "finished" form.

This doesn't mean that editing isn't important or that correctness isn't important. Correctness is vitally important because it determines what your writing looks like to your readers. Most readers won't give you much credit and won't stay with your paper, reading it for what it says, if it's so filled with errors that it's difficult to read. English teachers may read through your errors to your content; most real-world readers won't. When most of us go to buy a car, we form our first impression of that car by looking at the outside and then at the condition of the interior. If the car is trashed, filled with rust spots and unrepaired dings and dents, and the upholstery dirty and the headliner torn, most of us won't hang around to experience the great engine lurking under the hood. Mechanics might—those men and women who are really into engines. Consider them the English teachers of the auto world. The rest of us—we're history.

So be concerned with how your paper looks when you present it to an audience. We ask our students to edit their papers before their first group, to do their best to make sure that each draft is the best and the most correct that they can possibly make it. But we also tell them that these first drafts will change dramatically as the result of global revisions that are needed, so we don't concern ourselves too much with editing at that point.

It is important that the paper be correct enough so that errors don't distract or detract. There is a time when you need to call something the best you can do for now. This is the time when correctness gets pushed into the forefront. We try to teach students certain strategies that can make their editing easier, which we'll present to you here in an order of the most difficult to the less difficult things to deal with.

TESTING YOUR PARAGRAPHS

For Development

It takes specifics to properly develop all ideas, so when we test for paragraph development, we're asking, "Is the idea this paragraph presents properly explored through specific examples?" To test your paragraphs for good development, try to determine what the main idea of your paragraph is. It will usually be some sort of abstract statement, such as "My first job was very difficult." Go on to see if you've offered enough specific examples of how that job was difficult so that you've really shown us just how difficult it was. Especially on early drafts, don't be afraid of overkill, of offering too many specifics. When revising, you will find it much simpler to delete unnecessary specifics than it is to provide new specifics.

For Unity

Paragraph unity means that each of your paragraphs develops only one main idea. As you read over a draft of your paper, try reading each paragraph as a separate entity. Try to forget, as much as possible, whatever context is provided by the previous paragraph and whatever the next paragraph goes on to do. Read each paragraph and ask yourself, Does this paragraph develop one main idea?

If your paragraph has a major shift of some sort—from one idea to another, from one day to another, from one location to another—you want to consider providing a paragraph break: new idea (or location or whatever), new paragraph. Then, of course, you need to make sure that each idea is properly developed, as we discussed before.

For Coherence

We use the term *coherence* to refer to how your paragraphs hang together and how they flow logically. Here you're reading your paragraphs to make sure there are no big jumps in logic, location, emphasis, or the like that aren't accounted for by transitional devices within the paragraph.

What's a transitional device? Simply words, phrases, or sentences that point out the relationship between ideas, both within and between paragraphs. Some single-word transitional devices are words such as *then, next, however,* and *although.* Sometimes a phrase is necessary: "after that," "before that," "the next thing that happened," or "on the other hand." Sometimes you'll use a whole sentence: "When I woke up the next morning, I was . . ."; "Once I found out just where we were heading, I . . . " Refer back to Chapter 13 for a further discussion of transitions.

Where there are leaps that don't appear accounted for by some transitional device, and where you can determine that what follows the leap belongs in the same paragraph, try to assure the coherence of your paragraph with some sort of transition.

Consider the following paragraph from Nicole's paper about going to the dentist. Notice that the paragraph is well developed, unified, and coherent.

```
I guess it's the whole dentist atmosphere; I adore noth-
ing like a place full of bad, outdated magazines, corny
elevator music, and annoying reminders on every wall in-
forming you to deprive yourself of all your favorite
snacks. These informing displays show happy teeth being
```

supplied with rabbit like or nature's food—YUM! If that's not bad enough, you can count on being kept a prisoner there for an extra half hour. I'm convinced this is just to get you in a worse frame of mind. Well, for me, I usually sit and think, I should've brushed my teeth one more time. Not to mention I just brushed the hell out of them and flossed for the first time this year. So now I'm already in pain before the overly-sadistic hygienist has gotten her sanitized hands on me.

Notice, too, that Nicole's paragraph provides a transition into the paragraph that will follow it. You're expecting that she will be moving into her visit with the hygienist, which is just what the next paragraph of her paper does.

TESTING YOUR SENTENCES

For Choppiness

While worrying a lot about correctness and attempting to avoid the infamous run-on sentence, a lot of inexperienced writers end up producing "choppy" writing. Choppiness, simply put, means you've strung together too many short sentences. Look for passages where each sentence is about the same length and is put together in about the same way. If you find this, you may have found choppiness.

One thing you can look for is a lot of sentences that begin with "I." We told you early on that there's nothing wrong with using "I" in your papers, but often you will find that you've got six or seven sentences in a row that begin with "I." And that often means that those sentences are about the same length and about the same structure, thus producing choppiness.

Give your paper a read out loud. If a section sounds singsongy, or if you're reading your paper like a shopping list or a police report, you might have choppy sentences.

And if you're using a computer, a simple way to test your writing for choppiness is to do the paper in a list fashion.

Go through your file, hitting a return at the end of each sentence, so that your paper now appears as a long list of individual sentences, just as we're doing here.

Are there longer ones?

Shorter ones?

Do they vary in length and structure, or are they all about the same?

If you find that they're all about the same, chances are your paper is choppy.

You see?

Our look at this list of sentences shows us that we've got a variety of sentence lengths and structures. When put together in proper paragraph form, those sentences won't add up to a choppy paragraph.

If you have problems with choppiness, you'll need to do some sentence combining and some rearranging in order to vary the lengths and structures and in order to eliminate the repetitive "I's." Be aware, though, that if you do have a problem with choppiness, once you start attempting more variation, you're probably going to start making some errors you didn't make much before: run-ons, comma splices, and the like. That's part of the learning process, and we hope that we and your instructors can teach you strategies for finding and correcting these errors. It can be frustrating, we know. Someone tells you that all your sentences are too short, so you lengthen them, and then they are all strung together. With experience, you will learn how to compromise somewhere between a whole lot of staccato sentences and a whole lot of lengthy ones.

For Other Sentence Problems

Fused-sentence run-ons and sentence fragments are serious sentence-level errors, serious because they interfere with the reader's ability to form meaning from your text. You'll find each of these errors discussed in the final section of this book. Here, we simply wish to say that you need to work with your instructor or a writing tutor to figure out what your particular pattern of error is. This holds true for all errors. These people can help you figure out how to find and correct your errors.

We've found that most of our students correct their own fragments and fused sentences when they read out loud. They provide the pauses that correct the run-ons, or they join their fragments to the preceding or following sentence, thus correcting the problem. So reading out loud is a great strategy for finding these sorts of errors. Sometimes you'll want someone reading along with you, someone who will stop you when you've paused where there's no period in your paper, or who will point out to you that you didn't pause at a period. You can then examine those differences to figure out if your pauses or lack of pauses in the paper is appropriate. Remember, you know a lot about language from listening to it. So when it comes to recognizing run-ons and fragments, you can probably trust your ears more than you can your eyes, at least for now.

TESTING FOR OTHER ERRORS IN GRAMMAR, MECHANICS, AND PUNCTUATION

As we mentioned before, errors happen in patterns; different writers have different patterns of error. Also, different sorts of errors occur as writers develop, which is why you might start making some run-on errors when you try to alleviate choppiness in your writing. So we can't really write much blanket advice that will apply to everyone.

Again, we reiterate that you need to establish a relationship with your instructor or a writing tutor. Ask these folks to help you figure out what your major errors are and the strategies for correcting them. Don't expect your tutor or instructor to be your proofreader; expect them to be coaches who will show you how to do it yourself.

Using Computer Programs

There are a number of computer programs that check grammar and punctuation. They are mostly descriptive; that is, they mostly tell you only what they find in your writing. Some will find possible fragments, which is good, but you can't immediately assume that your fragment is always inappropriate. Good writers use fragments quite often. Computerized grammar checkers are good at finding passive constructions, but that doesn't mean you never want to use a passive. Sometimes you do.

So generally we don't ask our writing students to use these devices. We prefer that they gain some experience with and control over the language that will make the information these computer programs provide really useful. Most grammar checkers, for example, will tell you not to begin a sentence with "And," which is advice we've chosen to ignore often in this book. We do have sentences that begin with "And"; we like them that way; they work.

TESTING FOR SPELLING

Use that spelling checker. It's pretty clear by now that we're sold on the idea that you should be using a computer throughout the writing process, so it's only obvious that we'd begin our spelling section by telling you to use the spelling checker on your computer. Spelling checkers are the neatest thing that's ever happened to bad spellers, and, believe us, most people—even a lot of good writers—are bad spellers.

How do computerized spelling checkers work? Understanding them will help you understand how to use them better. Spelling checkers are essentially on-line dictionaries. They check each word of your document, stopping at every word you typed that's not in the dictionary. Most good spelling checkers then suggest a couple of possibilities for the word you're looking for; when one of those possibilities is the correct word, you highlight it and replace the incorrect version in your text. That part's pretty simple.

There are limitations to understand, though. For one, not every word in the language will be in the dictionary—your last name, for example—so it's entirely possible that you've correctly typed a word that just happens not to be in the dictionary. That's when you tell the computer to skip or ignore that spelling.

Another limitation is that the computer can't tell the difference between correctly spelled words, so you have to know the difference between *then* and *than,* between *two, to,* and *too,* between *further* and *farther.* And sometimes you'll simply misspell a word so badly that the computer won't be able to offer any alternate spellings.

When that happens, most spelling checkers will let you try to respell the word right in the window where the word appears; you can then click a "check" or "look up" icon, which tells the program to look up the new spelling of the word. If the word is still wrong, perhaps you'll have gotten close enough for the spelling checker to figure out the correct alternative. One hint: When you find yourself in this position, try playing with the vowels first, replacing one vowel with another that can make the same sound in a word. We've found that most of our students' spelling-checker-stumping errors occur because they've used the wrong vowels. By changing the vowels and then telling the program to recheck that word, these students are usually able to figure out the correct spelling of the word.

There's a disadvantage to spelling checkers, as well. Because they're so easy to use and do so much of the work for you, you might be tempted not to pay much attention to the spelling errors you make. And so you might just continue making the same spelling errors over and over again. That's not such a hot idea when you consider that you won't always have that computer and that spelling checker keeping an eye on you. Don't get lazy.

Pay attention to your spelling checker at work. Pay attention not only to the words you commonly misspell but also to the kinds of words you often misspell—words that do or don't double a consonant when you add an ending, or words where the "I before E" rule applies. As you've no doubt been told before, it's a good idea to keep a list of commonly misspelled words near your work station, something that you will always see and that will remind you of what you need to be watching for.

Becoming a good speller is a matter of practice and patience. While we won't go into the "rules" about spelling here (see chapter 24, "Mixed Pairs"), learning a few of the rules from your instructor or other sources may be of help, depending upon what your particular spelling problem is. Once again, it's a good idea to work closely with your instructor or a writing tutor to figure out where your problems lie and what will work best for you.

TESTING FOR FORMAT

Perhaps you've had cause to wonder at some time why English teachers seem to be so persnickety about format—where your name goes, the date, the course name, the title, page numbers, and whatever.

Part of the reason gets back to rules—just about every profession has house rules concerning the format of the writing done in that field. It so happens that in English, as in much of the humanities, we follow a set of house rules laid out by the Modern Language Association (MLA) pretty closely. The *MLA Handbook* tells us where to put our titles and names, how to do our references pages, all that. And just believe us, it's important to have that sort of standardization in a field; it's good to have everyone playing by the same rules.

So chances are your instructor will be asking you to format according to the MLA guidelines or a similar set of guidelines. No matter the case, then, do it, and do it right.

After all, correct formatting is mostly a matter of carefully following directions, so if you haven't cared enough to follow simple directions, you're going to make a bad impression from the moment your paper hits your instructor's hands. In our field, sending something out for publication that doesn't carefully follow the publisher's guidelines might cause that publisher to reject it without even reading it.

So as you prepare your draft for readers, take a last look to make sure that you've followed whatever guidelines are in place: Have you centered your title? Did you remember the date? Are your page numbers where they were supposed to be?

As we said at the beginning, editing is a very individualized activity. There will be some errors that you will never have to concern yourself with simply because you do not make them. If that is the case, all the better. There will be some, no doubt, that occasionally cause problems for you and your reader. We've given more detailed explanations of the kinds of errors our students seem to make most in the following pages. Perhaps your instructor will refer you to these sections as a class or as an individual to get a little extra guidance on these conventions.

5

STUDENT WRITERS
AT WORK

15

SELECTIONS OF STUDENT WRITERS AT WORK

You can learn a lot by studying the writing processes of other writers. Most of the time, all we see is a writer's final product, which is probably why so many of us feel so intimidated by good writing. We get the sense that, geez, this is so good. I could never do that. But as we've told you much earlier in this book, good writing doesn't emerge fully blown as the good writing we ultimately end up reading. Writers revise. A lot.

For obvious reasons we can't show you the process a professional writer goes through on her novel. We don't have the space to show you Ernest Hemingway's 40 or so revisions of the ending of one of his novels. But we can show what some of our students have done with some of the writing assignments we presented to you earlier in this book. In this chapter we will show several versions of these students' papers, attempting to recreate for you what was discussed in groups and what sort of revising advice our students received from us one on one.

As you read these papers, notice that most of them grow from version to version. This is common for basic writers, as they discover during groups and when working with instructors that they haven't fully developed the ideas they began with. Pay attention to how these students clarify their ideas by adding details, description, dialogue, etc. Notice that they're all attempting to *show* more, and that much of the revising these students did was accomplished *before* they ever turned their papers in solely for their instructors, to read. Sometimes we were a part of their groups, but often their groups were facilitated by a peer tutor. In short, some of the good advice these students got for revising came from fellow students.

As you read through these students' papers, there are a few things you need to know. First, any work done on grammar, mechanics, and punctuation on the drafts was work between the student and the instructor. Discussion of error was never a part of the group work process. The comments you see written by the students themselves or by their instructors or tutors reflect what went on during groups, as do the explanations between versions of each paper. Be sure to read these narrative descriptions of what actually happened during group.

Second, there are two different typefaces to let you know who wrote what. The cursive handwriting indicates changes and/or comments the writers themselves noted on their drafts. The boldfaced printing is used for instructors' changes and comments.

STUDENT WRITER AT WORK—
HEATHER MASON

Heather was in R.J.'s class in fall of 1994. Her paper, "Only When I'm Sick," was written for the Double Experience, or Figure 8 assignment.

Heather Mason
Paper 3, Draft 1

ONLY WHEN I'M SICK

For as far back as I can remember my mom was always forcing me to drink Vernors when I was sick. Whether I was sick with the flu, sore throat, or a sprained ankle, my mom's cure was to drink Vernors. I used to think that this was my mom's home remedy and that it was some kind of medicine. As I got older I found out that both of these ideas were not true. Yet as a child I thought any illness could be treated with a glass of Vernors, hot or cold.

I can remember being in first grade and my throat started hurting during class and I started to get a fever. I asked my teacher if I could go down to the nurse. My teacher gave me permission and of I went to make a fool out of myself.

All I wanted was to get a glass of Vernors. It seemed like the longest walk of my life down that hall and I thought I would never get there. When I got down to the nurses office and she asked what was wrong I told her my throat hurt. She said she was going to call my mom to come and get me. I told her I didn't need to go home, that all I needed was a glass of Vernors and I would feel better. The nurse looked at me funny and tried not to laugh and called my mom any way.

When we got home I told my mom that the nurse at school wasn't a very good nurse because she didn't know that Vernors would make me feel better and that I didn't need to home. My mom just said that you aren't allowed to have pop in school and that's why she didn't give me any. My mom made me a nice big glass of Vernors and I thought I was cured. This actually only made me feel better for a while until I took a nap and then went to the doctor.

A few months ago when my mom was sick she had Vernors in the refrigerator and I thought I could handle drinking a glass. As I started drinking it, I almost made myself think that I was sick. I couldn't believe it. I thought that maybe I was just imaging things so I tried to finish the glass. But I wasn't imaging anything. My stomach started feeling upset and I had to put the glass down. It was then that I realized that my mother had scared me for life. I would never again be able to drink Vernors as a healthy person.

To this day I still drink Vernors when I'm sick. It still makes me feel better, and I guess it always will. I still cannot drink it if I'm healthy and I guess that is also something that will never change. This is not something that gets me upset in fact I think it's kind of funny. I know this is not something my mom did on purpose/ _RO_ she thought she was helping. I don't mind not being able to drink Vernors unless I'm sick because this way I have

*More dialogue
w/Mom, nurse
How does it feel
to be sick?
More description
of nurse*

something to make me feel better when I am sick that's not an every day drink.

The first thing we'd like you to notice is that in her first draft Heather has discovered the relationship between the two experiences, which is the essential requirement of the assignment. Through her freewriting and the composing of the first draft, Heather discovered her main idea and came up with something that clearly fits the assignment.

The next thing to notice is that Heather's draft is very short, which is not at all unusual for first drafts, as we've mentioned. So once the group got past confirming that Heather had a very good central idea, they worked with the first draft as a sort of sketch of what the paper might be. How to strengthen the paper? That was their central question.

Among the many things they discussed, Heather made particular notes to use dialogue, both with her mom and with the school nurse. That's a way of *showing* what happened as opposed to merely *telling* the readers about it. The group suggested that there were opportunities to describe more—perhaps the nurse, perhaps the feeling of being sick. And they toyed with the idea that Heather could reorganize her paper—start with the more recent experience, then flash back to her childhood experience as a way of explaining the more recent one.

Heather shared this in group on a Thursday, did some revising right after group, spent some time in the campus computer lab working on the paper, then returned to class the following Tuesday with this second draft:

Heather Mason
English 131
Paper 3, Draft 2

ONLY WHEN I'M SICK

It was late ~~at night~~ one night about two weeks ago when I started getting very thirsty *while* ~~from~~ studying. I walked down stairs to the kitchen to get something to drink. I opened up the refrigerator only to find a six pack of Vernors sitting there. It had been a long time since I had drank this and I thought it might be a nice change. As I cracked open the can and brought it towards my mouth I started getting a funny feeling in my stomach just from the smell. I kept on drinking it, and after drinking about half of the can, I knew I was definitely getting sick. I sat down at the kitchen table hoping to relax my stomach, and I started to remember some things from my past.

For as far back as I can remember my mom was always forcing me to drink Vernors when I was sick. Whether I was sick with the flu, *a* sore throat, or a sprained ankle, my mom's cure was to drink Vernors. I used to think that this was my mom's home remedy, and that it was some kind of medicine. As I got older I found out that both of these ideas were not true. Yet as a child I thought any illness could be treated with a glass of Vernors, hot or cold.

I can remember being in first grade, ~~and~~ my throat started hurting during class, and I started to get a fever. I asked my teacher if I could go down to the nurse. My teacher gave me permission and of I went to make a fool out of myself. All I wanted was to get a glass of Vernors. It seemed like the longest walk of my life down that hall, and I thought I would never get there. When I got down to the nurse's office, I knew I was doomed. I could see right through the fake smile on her face. It was like the only reason she was even there was for the money. She had gray hair rolled up in buns on each side of her head and she had no bangs. Her teeth were stained yellow and every time she opened up her mouth you got sprayed.

"Hi there, honey, what can I do for you today?"

"Well, uh, I have a sore throat and my head hurts, and I want a glass of Vernors so I feel better and can go back to class."

"I really don't think a glass of Vernors is going to make you feel good enough to go back to class. How about I just call your mom and she can come get you and you can go home and take a nap. Does that sound good?"

"I don't want to go home. I just want a glass of Vernors so I can go back to class, and if you don't give me one then I'll call my mom and tell her you are being mean to me."

"Go have a seat in the other room while I get you your glass of Vernors, Heather." Not realizing that she was just tricking me, I fell asleep waiting for the nurse to come back and woke up to my mom in my face. I was so upset I didn't say anything the whole way home.

"I hate the nurse at school, Mom. She is so mean. I told her that I wanted a glass of Vernors so I could go back to class, and she said she was going to get me one, but really she called you.

"She isn't mean, honey, and you don't hate her. She isn't allowed to give out pop in school and that's why she called me because she knew if you went home I could give you some. Now go watch T.V. and and I'll make you a nice tall glass of Vernors."

My mom made me a nice big glass of Vernors and I thought I was cured. This actually only made me feel better for a while until I took a nap and then went to the doctor.

Then I remembered another time maybe about a year ago, that I gad gotten sick off of Vernors that I had forgotten about. My mom had been sick and there was Vernors in the refrigerator. Thinking I could handle drinking it I poured a nice big glass. As I started drinking it, I started to feel sick to my stomach. I couldn't believe it. I thought that maybe I was just imaging things so I tried to finish the glass. But I wasn't imaging anything. My stomach started feeling upset and I had to put the glass down. It was then that I real-

ized that my mother had scared me for life. I would never
again be able to drink Vernors as a healthy person.

   To this day I still drink Vernors when I'm sick. It still
makes me feel better, and I guess it always will. I still
cannot drink it if I'm healthy, and I guess that is also
something that will never change. This is not something
that gets me upset, in fact I think it's kind of funny. I   comma splice
know this is not something my mom did on purpose she   run-on
thought she was helping. I don't mind not being able to
drink Vernors unless I'm sick because this way I have something to make me feel better when I am sick that's not an
every day drink.

Do spell check & clarify last sentence

   Clearly, Heather made a lot of use of the advice she got during the
first group. Her paper is reorganized, beginning with the more recent
experience and flashing back to childhood. The nurse's office experience is drawn out in far greater detail, and we even get to see the
nurse's hair rolled up in buns. Heather has used a lot of dialogue here,
and all of it works pretty well. She's *showing* in this draft. And because
of this, her paper has grown quite a lot.
   When Heather took this second version to group, the group had
much less to say about it than her first one had. They thought it was a
good paper, and about all they thought needed improving was some
clarifying and expanding of the conclusion. Heather worked with that
advice, and several days later turned in a third version to R.J.
   Because the changes between the second and third drafts were relatively minor, we won't reproduce the third draft here. R.J. read and
marked the third draft and commented that he thought she'd made
good progress on it. His main suggestion was that Heather should expand her conclusion and try to say, on a more philosophical level,
what she thinks she's learned from these experiences (which is what
the assignment asks for).
   As you look at Heather's final draft, you will see that she has successfully used the advice she received from groups and from her instructor. Notice that most of her revising was done before she had
turned her paper in to her instructor, and that her final product is a
pretty good paper.

Heather Mason
English 131
Dr. Willey
12/8/94
Paper 3, Draft 4

ONLY WHEN I'M SICK

It was late one night about two weeks ago when I started getting very thirsty while studying. I walked downstairs to the kitchen to get something to drink and I opened up the refrigerator only to find a six pack of Vernors sitting there. It had been a long time since I had drank this, and I thought it might be a nice change. As I cracked open the can and brought it towards my mouth, I started getting a funny feeling in my stomach just from the smell. I kept on drinking it, and after drinking about half of the can, I knew I was definitely getting sick. I sat down at the kitchen table, hoping to relax my stomach, and I started to remember some things from my past.

For as far back as I can remember my mom was always forcing me to drink Vernors when I was sick. Whether I was sick with the flu, a sore throat, or a sprained ankle, my mom's cure was to drink Vernors. I used to think that this was my mom's home remedy and that it was some kind of medicine. As I got older, I found out that both of these ideas were not true. Yet as a child I thought any illness could be treated with a glass of Vernors, hot or cold.

I can remember being in first grade and my throat started hurting during class. Then I started to get a fever and knew I couldn't take it anymore I asked my teacher if I could go down to the nurse. My teacher gave me permission, and off I went to make a fool out of myself. All I wanted was to get a glass of Vernors. It seemed like the longest walk of my life down that hall, and I thought I would never get there. When I got down to the nurse's office, I knew I was doomed. I could see right through the fake smile on her face. It was like the only reason she was even there was for the money. She had gray hair rolled up in buns on each side of her head, and she had no bangs. Her teeth were stained yellow, and every time she opened up her mouth you got sprayed.

"Hi there, honey, what can I do for you today?"

"Well, uh, I have a sore throat and my head hurts, and I want a glass of Vernors so I feel better and can go back to class."

"I really don't think a glass of Vernors is going to make you feel good enough to go back to class. How about I just call your mom and she can come get you and you can go home and take a nap. Does that sound good?"

"I don't want to go home. I just want a glass of Vernors so I can go back to class, and if you don't give me one then I'll call my mom and tell her you are being mean to me."

"Go have a seat in the other room while I get you your glass of Vernors, Heather." Not realizing that she was just tricking me, I fell asleep waiting for the nurse to come back and woke up to my mom in my face. I was so upset I didn't say anything until we got home.

"I hate the nurse at school, Mom. She is so mean. I told her that I wanted a glass of Vernors so I could go back to class, and she said she was going to get me one, but really she called you."

"She isn't mean, honey, and you don't hate her. She isn't allowed to give out pop in school, and that's why she called me because she knew if you went home I could give you some. Now go watch T.V. and and I'll make you a nice tall glass of Vernors."

My mom made me a nice big glass of Vernors, and I thought I was cured. This actually only made me feel better for a while until I took a nap and then went to the doctor.

Then I remembered another time maybe about a year ago that I had forgotten about. I had gotten sick from the Vernors this time also. My mom had been sick and there was Vernors in the refrigerator. Thinking I could handle drinking it, I poured a nice big glass. As I started drinking it,I started to feel sick to my stomach. I couldn't believe it. I thought that maybe I was just imagining things, so I tried to finish the glass. But I wasn't imagining anything. My stomach started feeling upset, and I had to put the glass down. It was then that I realized my mother had scared me for life. I would never again be able to drink Vernors as a healthy person.

To this day, I still drink Vernors when I'm sick. It makes me feel better and I guess it always will. I cannot drink it if I'm healthy, and I guess that is also something that will never change. This is not something that gets me upset, I think it's kind of funny. I never would have thought that you could condition someone so easily. You always hear about people getting brainwashed, but I never thought it could happen accidentally. I know this is not something my mom did on purpose. My mom thought she was helping and didn't think it was going to affect me mentally. I don't mind not being able to drink Vernors unless I'm sick because this way I have something to make me feel better when I am sick that's not an every day drink.

STUDENT WRITER AT WORK— ANGIE ALRAIHANI

Angie took R.J.'s class in the fall of 1994. Her paper, "My Old House," was in response to an assignment to write a paper about a place. She chose to revisit a place from her past.

Angie Alraihani
English 052
Dr. Willey
Date 10/8/94
Paper Three, Draft One

MY OLD HOUSE

It is a sunny Friday afternoon. I am sitting at the corner of Ventura and 13 mile rd, in Southfield City, right in
front of my old house. I had been living in this house for
about four years. For as long as I can remember, our house
has been the same color (beige). My father loves nature so
I remember him decorating the trees, bushes, flowers, and
his favorite, the garden. In the summertime he would always bring me, and my two younger brothers outside to appreciate the fruits and vegetables of his garden. He would
sometimes bring us out at night, if he got home from work
late, and look through the garden with a flashlight. My
younger brother, who at that time was five, would get the
advantage of picking the vegetables. I can remember how
good the fresh cucumbers and tomatoes tasted.

Not only do we have a garden, but a variety of flowers
all around the house. My father planted them for my mother,
because he knew how much she loved flowers. So my mother
would walk around the house with a empty vase in ~~his~~ her hand
and come inside after five minutes with the most beautiful
bouquet of flowers. The aroma was like none other . It was
sweeter and more pleasing than any other flowers. My mother
would set the vase on the kitchen table, and whoever would
walk in the house would be greeted by the fresh smell.

When I came home the first thing I would see . . .

It is the beginning of October and the grass around my
old house is covered with rust-colored leaves. It is about

six o'clock and the sun is still shining. The rays of light pass through the tree on the side of the house. The light creates a romantic scene, but there is no one here to share it with. When I look at the tree with the gleaming sun shining upon it, a feeling passes through my body. It is a feeling of warmth and love. The sight is so beautiful that I don't want to look away. As my eyes are fixated on the tree I remember When my grandfather used to trim the tree and I would always help him. He passed away the year we moved in and I always remember him by looking at a tree. As I turn my head away from the tree I look at my old house. The house looks a lot better, the new people fixed it up really nice, but in my memories i will always remember they way the house looked before.

Across the house there is aluminum siding. There is one particular part where a cylinder-shaped piece of metal was surged through it . Them metal was stuck in the siding, but fell off after a few days. However, it left a small hole in the siding of our house. My mother was going to get it fixed, but my father wouldn't allow it when he noticed that the birds had made a home of it. This was about four years ago. And as I look at the hole ~~their~~ **there** are birds who still live in it. I wonder if it's the same birds. I guess I will never ~~know~~ **find out**.

The sound of dogs barking, reminds me of the many animals we had over the past years . If I remember correctly, it was about two cats, two hamsters and a lot of fish. I can remember the smell of these animals, which is why we don't have any now and never will have. My favorite animal was Snoopy. A white cat who was adorable. In winter he would play in the snow, and sometimes we couldn't even see him because of his pure white color. Snoopy was always a cheerful and playful cat, which always got him into trouble with the other neighbors cats. He ran away, and I miss him a lot

The sun is setting and it is beginning to get chilly outside. I can feel a cool, sharp breeze which makes my hair fly back, and gives me goose bumps. The sound of the birds chirping, the dogs barking, and the children playing outside create the perfect mood. The sight of the sun setting, and the sweet memories of my past experiences in my old house leaves me with only one thought in my mind ...it feels wonderful to be alive.

Add more detail in the introduction.
Add a paragraph about "how I feel about the changes in the house."

After Angie read her paper in group the first time, she got a lot of positive feedback. Everyone thought she was starting to do a good description of the house and that somehow those descriptions were starting to evoke her feelings about it. They asked if she could describe things yet more concretely, add more details about the house inside and out.

As they talked about adding more details about the exterior of the house, they noticed that the first paragraph would be pretty big, loaded with detail, and not particularly unified. So they searched for a place to divide into two paragraphs, in that way discovering the real boundary between the intro and the body of the paper.

And finally, the group wondered if Angie couldn't make her feelings about the place even more a part of her paper. She was beginning to evoke her feelings, and they wanted those feelings to be more explicit.

When Angie returned to class the next session, she brought the following version of the paper to group:

Angie Alraihani
English 052
Dr. Willey
10/10/94
Paper Three, Draft Two

MY OLD HOUSE

It is a Friday afternoon. I am sitting at the corner of Ventura and 13 Mile Rd, in Southfield city, right in front of my old house. I had been living in this house for about four years, till we moved to my Grandmother's house because we were supposed to move to California. But that never worked out. So we are stuck here for the time being.

For as long as I can remember, our house has been the same color (beige). My father loves nature, so I remember him decorating the trees, bushes , flowers, and his favorite, the garden. In the summertime he would always bring me, and my two younger brothers outside to appreciate the fruits and vegetables of his garden. He would sometimes bring us out at night, if he got home from work late, and look through the garden with a flashlight. My younger brother, who at that time was five, would get the advantage of picking the vegetables. I can remember how good the fresh cucumbers and tomatoes tasted.

Not only did we have a garden, but a variety of flowers all around the house. My father planted them for my mother, because he knew how much she loved flowers. So my mother would walk around outside with an empty vase in her hand and she would come inside after five minutes with the most beautiful bouquet of flowers. The aroma was like none other. It was sweeter and more pleasing than any other flowers. My mother would set the vase on the kitchen table, and when ever I would walk in the house I would be greeted by the fresh smell.

That would be the first thing my eyes laid on when I walked in the house. And that'*s* all I needed to make my day.

It is the beginning of October and the grass around my old house is covered with rust-colored leaves. It is about six o'clock, and the sun is still shining. The rays of light pass through the tree on the side of the house. When I look at the tree with the gleaming sun shining upon it, a feeling passes through my body/ ~~It is a feeling~~ of warmth and love. The sight is so beautiful that I don't want to look away. As my eyes are fix*ed*~~ated~~ on the tree I remember When my grandfather used to trim the tree and I would always help him. He passed away the year we moved in, and I always remember him by looking at a tree. As I turn my head away from the tree I look at my old house. *a*nd I never missed it so much till now.

Across the house there is aluminum siding. There is one particular part where a cylinder-shaped piece of metal was surged through it. The~~m~~ metal was stuck in the siding, but fell off after a few days. However, it left a small hole in the siding of our house. My mother was going to get it fixed, but my father wouldn't allow it when he noticed that the birds had made a home of it. This was about four years ago. *a*nd as I *now* look at the hole there are birds who still live in it. I wonder if it's the same birds. I guess I will never know.

? I don't get it here.

The sound of dogs barking/ reminds me of the many animals we had over the past years . If I remember correctly. it was about two cats, two hamsters. and a lot of fish. I can remember the smell of these animals, which is why we don't have any now and will never have again. My favorite animal was Snoopy. *a* white cat who was adorable. In winter he would play in the snow, and sometimes we couldn't even see him because of his pure white color. Snoopy was always a cheerful and playful cat, which always got him into trouble with the other neighbors cats. He ran away, and I miss him a lot

As I look at my house I can see the many different changes throughout the house. I can see they painted the

CS _____ garage. It looks a lot better now. As I turned my head I

see

~~saw~~ all the flowers were gone. They threw all the flowers away and they grew grass instead. That

is

~~was~~ very disappointing. The house looks a lot bigger now. I think because now we live in a smaller house, ~~t~~hat my old house seems a lot bigger. Now I go inside and I see many different minor changes. They painted the house gray. they changed the tile. and they changed many other things. It didn't look like my house any more. But at least nice people took over the house. And that makes it better.

The sun is setting and now it is beginning to get chilly outside. I can feel a cool, sharp breeze. which makes my hair fly back, and gives me goose bumps. The sound of the birds chirping, the dogs barking, and the children playing outside create the perfect mood. The sight of the sun setting, and the sweet memories of my past experiences in my old house leaves me with only one thought in my mind . . . it feels wonderful to be alive.

Angie's paper has grown some, a practically inevitable outcome of revising, especially for basic writers. She thought hard about all the reactions she received in her first group and did her best to make use of them. She has added more description of the house inside and out, found the boundary between her intro and the body of her paper, and she has tried in several places to make her feelings more explicit.

The next group, which was joined by R.J., praised the content of the paper, the changes Angie had made. They then turned their attention to places in the paper where they had trouble reading or following, where they thought there may be something wrong, where they stumbled for whatever reason. During discussion, R.J. was able to translate their concerns: there are some fused sentences in the draft, some confusing changes in verb tense, and no one seemed to get the passage about the piece of metal "surged through" the aluminum siding.

Angie's third draft, which we won't reproduce here, attempted to address all these concerns and was pretty successful. She needed more help from R.J. on the verb tenses and some other line-editing sorts of concerns, and then produced the following final draft:

```
Angie Alraihani
English 052
Dr. Willey
10/10/94
Paper Three, Draft Four
```

MY OLD HOUSE

It is a Friday afternoon. I am sitting at the corner of Ventura and 13 Mile Rd, in Southfield, right in front of my old house. I lived in this house for about four years, till we moved to my Grandmother's house because we were supposed to move to California. But that never worked out. So we are stuck here for the time being.

For as long as I can remember, our house has been the same color (beige). My father loves nature, so I remember him decorating the trees, bushes , flowers, and his favorite, the garden. In the summertime he would always bring me and my two younger brothers outside to appreciate the fruits and vegetables of his garden. He would sometimes bring us out at night, if he got home from work late, and look through the garden with a flashlight. My younger brother, who at that time was five, would get the advantage of picking the vegetables. I can remember how good the fresh cucumbers and tomatoes tasted.

Not only did we have a garden but a variety of flowers all around the house. My father planted them for my mother because he knew how much she loved flowers. So my mother would walk around outside with an empty vase in her hand and she would come inside after five minutes with the most beautiful bouquet of flowers. The aroma was like none other; It was sweeter and more pleasing than any other flowers. My mother would set the vase on the kitchen table, and whenever I would walk in the house I would be greeted by the fresh smell. That would be the first thing my eyes laid on when I walked in the house. That's all I needed to make my day.

It is the beginning of October, and the grass around my old house is covered with rust-colored leaves. It is about six o'clock and the sun is still shining. The rays of light pass through the tree on the side of the house. When I look at the tree with the gleaming sun shining upon it, a feeling passes through my body of warmth and love. The sight is so beautiful that I don't want to look away. As my eyes are fixed on the tree, I remember when my grandfather used to trim the tree and I would help him. He passed away the year we moved in, and I always remember him by looking at a tree. As I turn my head away from the tree, I look at my old house, and I never missed it so much till now.

Across the house there is aluminum siding. There is one particular part where there was a big hole on the side of the house. My mother was going to get it fixed, but my father wouldn't allow it when he noticed that the birds had made a home of it. This was about four years ago, and as I look at the hole now there are birds who still live in it. I wonder if it's the same birds. I guess I will never know.

The sound of dogs barking reminds me of the many animals we had over the past years . If I remember correctly, it was about two cats, two hamsters, and a lot of fish. I can remember the smell of these animals, which is why we don't have any now and will never have again. My favorite animal was Snoopy, a white cat who was adorable. In winter he would play in the snow, and sometimes we couldn't even see him because of his pure white color. Snoopy was always a cheerful and playful cat, which always got him into trouble with the other neighborhood cats. He ran away, and I miss him a lot

As I look at my old house I can see the many changes. They painted the garage; It looks a lot better now. All the flowers are gone. They threw all the flowers away, and they grew grass instead. That is very disappointing. The house looks a lot bigger now, I think because now we live in a smaller house. I go up to the door and I knock; Tommy opens the door and he lets me in. I've known him for several years because are mothers are very good friends. Now I go inside and I see many different minor changes: They painted the house gray, they changed the tile, and many other little things.

I begin to climb the stairs, and I remember how my little brother used to slide down the stairs. All the rest of my memories in this house came back, and that makes me smile. My room looks very different because now it a boy's room. In my closet where my clothes hung now hangs boy's clothes. I remember where I had pictures of my friends, many different posters, and several little different knick nacks are hanging there. And now posters of cars and girls are hanging there. I can feel a tear going down my check, so I go downstairs, and tell Tommy I will talk to him later, and I leave.

Now, the sun is setting, and it is beginning to get chilly outside. I can feel a cool, sharp breeze, which makes my hair fly back and gives me goosebumps. The sound of the birds chirping, the dogs barking, and the children playing outside creates the perfect mood. The sight of the sun setting and the sweet memories of my past experiences in my old house leave me with only one thought in my mind...it feels wonderful to be alive.

STUDENT WRITER AT WORK—
STEPHANIE HINSHON

Stephanie was in R.J.'s class during the fall of 1994. Her paper, "Mel," was written in response to an assignment to write about a person who was influential in her life.

Stephanie Hinshon

Eng 131

3:00 t,r

2nd paper 1st draft

My most vivid memory of a person ~~that~~ who has made a tremendous impact of my life happened in the prime years of my tennis career. While investigating the camps throughout the state of Michigan, I came across a very competitive, yet econom- ical camp in detroit. The camp provided a lot of involve- ment along with comradery within the group. The instructures were young adults ~~who were~~ playing tennis at the college level, who had fought their way up the ladder and portrayed themselves to the children as role models for the future tennis players. The instructors would steer the younger generation toward the things the students would have to accomplish to reach the desired level of achievement.

Before actually entering the camp, I had a private les- son with a /Pro/ to determine in which group I belonged. The "pro" happened to be black, which was okay with me. It didn't ~~doesn't~~ make a difference one way or the other to me. Pre- ceding the lesson, I decided to join the camp, and the first day came almost too soon.

While walking on the tennis courts, I realized that I was the only white person in the ~~W~~whole camp, ~~W~~which was pretty odd considering my usual experience is that I am not amongst the minority in the crowd. I pretended that I didn't notice, but who was I kidding? Everybody else certainly noticed. I felt I was the center of attention with a big spotlight following me with every move, every flinch, every gesture I made.

The first couple of weeks, I felt isolated and wondered if people were going to accept me. Then I found someone with whom I could bond ~~with~~. **Mel** ~~He~~ is a young black man who grew up in an all white neighborhood. He understood what it was like to be different **from** ~~then~~ the rest of the group and to not live with his own people. He was not accustomed to being in an all black group and felt a little more comfortable after finding someone more familiar to him. As the weeks progressed, I began talking more and was able to let my guard down, relax, **and** learn to enjoy myself.

Of course~~, s~~ince I was the only white person, many of the African American people were curious about me, as I was curious about them. Our differences maybe even made us closer. They wanted to know if they could touch my hair, my skin, lookat my hands and facial features. Not only did our appearences differ, but our music and our jargon **were** ~~was~~ also (veyr) different. This brought on even more questions, which seemed to bring us even closer together, because it provided us with plenty to discuss. I made many new friends that summer.

Mel became
~~I also met this guy that was~~ very special to me, ~~Mel~~ but one big factor that was keeping us apart was that he is black and I am white. Deep down I didn't care, but~~, I~~ wondered if my friends and family could accept this relationship. I came to relize how sensitive this issue is.

which people?

(People) made many nasty comments. They called me a "nigger lover" and jeered that "Once you go black you never go back", I soon found out who my real friends were. Some people seemed to toatlly disregard me, as if I never existed. Others exhibited hatred and disapproval.

One thing that bothered me was that I got a reputation. I was known as the girl who had jungle fever. Not the funny, outgoing, happy-go-lucky person reputation I used to have. Many people learned to ignore or deal with my situation by not aknowledging it. But I also got to be very annoyed with the people who knew about my relationship, because people would say derogatory statements not necessarily to me but around me. For example people would say "nigger" not trying to affend me but would realize that I was around and they would apoligize to me but They weren't really sorry, they were just sorry they said it in front of the wrong person.

This lack of understanding and disapproval grew as our relationship grew stronger. And like a vicious circle, it seemed as if our relationship generated power in spite of and maybe even because of the ignorance of those others. They could not understand why I would lower myself to go out with an African American person, as if they are a (lessr) class of people. But what people fail to realize is that we all are equal.

Mel has taught me many things, such as respect, honesty, and trust. Through our relationship I learned to care and love someone on my own with out support from my friends and part of my family. I also feel that Mel has taught me to be more open minded toward people different *from* ~~that~~ myself.

This is a paper that starts out and stays pretty detailed, which initially threw the group for a bit of a loop. They had already become accustomed to very short papers where what was needed for improvement was more obvious. They were filled with positive things to say about Stephanie's experience, about Stephanie's and Mel's parents, and thus about Stephanie's paper. R.J. was a part of the group and encouraged the positive discussion, figuring Stephanie was learning a lot about how her paper affected her readers.

As the discussion went on, R.J. asked when the group really got interested in what Stephanie was writing about. They all agreed it was when she met Mel and that maybe it took a little too long for the paper to get there. Perhaps there was too much detail leading up to actually meeting Mel, too much for readers to read before they know why they're reading it. So the group discussed what options writers have in these situations, exploring the possibility that Stephanie could write an intro that comes out and says what her paper is going to be about, or the possibility that Stephanie could cut down on actually getting to the camp and get to Mel more quickly. They also discussed the fact that there are quite a few obvious errors in the first draft, enough to be distracting to the reader.

```
Stephanie Hinshon

Eng 131

3:00 t,r

2nd paper 2nd draft
```

"Mel"

```
                                    who
My most vivid memory of a person  t̶h̶a̶t̶ has made a tremen-
                   n
dous impact o̶f̶ my life happened in the prime years of my

tennis career. Being the daughter of a great devoted ten-    dangling modifying

nis player, he had some of the inside scoop of searching     clause

for a camp that he would get his money worth. He was look-

ing for a competitive, yet economical camp. We found a camp

that provided a lot of involvement along with camaraderie

within the group. The instructors were young adults who

were playing tennis at the college level, who fought their

way up the ladder and portrayed themselves to the children

as role models for the future tennis players. The in-

structors would steer the younger generation toward the

things the students would have to accomplish to reach the

desired level of achievement.


    The first day of camp came almost (to) soon() I was getting

a little timid and nervous about going to a place where I     SP

didn't know anybody.While walking on the tennis courts, I
```

realized that I was the only white person in the ~~W~~hole camp, Which was pretty odd considering my usual experience is that I am not amongst the minority in the crowd. I pretended that I didn't notice, but who was I kidding? Everybody else certainly noticed. I felt I was the center of attention with a big spotlight following me with every move, every flinch, every gesture I made.

The first couple of weeks, I felt isolated and wondered if people were going to accept me. Then I found someone ~~with~~ who~~m~~ I could bond with⊙ Mel⊙ a young black man who grew up in an all white neighborhood. He understood what it was like to be different from the rest of the group and not to live with his own people. He was not accustomed to being in an all black group and felt a little more comfortable after finding someone more familiar to him. As the weeks progressed, I began talking more and was able to let my guard down, relax, ~~and~~ learn, and enjoy myself.

As the time progressed so did our friendship; Mel And I hung out more and more⊙ We went out to the movies, the parks, played tennis and just did the friend thing. Our friendship eventually grew to a relationship⊙ we now would classify ourselves as a couple. But there are many differences from being a couple of the same race and being a couple of two different races. People tend to have to work harder for the relationship to work to in a^n interracial relationship.

Many people exhibited hatred and disapproval. We would get many different looks and comments from people we didn't know, along with those we knew. Many people would call me a nigger lover, and tell me consistently that⊙ "Once you go black you never go back⊙" Former friends of mine used to ask me why a cute little Jewish girl would want to go out with a "NIGGER" (their words) as if they were lesser people. His friends would call him a sell out because they said a minority who goes out with a white person not only ~~does it~~ minimizes the selection of people for that particular race it also lessens the race. Others seemed to totally disregard me, as if I never existed.

One thing that bothered me was that I got a reputation. I was known as the girl who was dating a black person. Not the funny, outgoing, happy-go-lucky person reputation I used to have. many people learned to ignore or deal with my situation by not acknowledging it. People would also forget I was in (there) presence and would say "nigger" not trying to offend me but wouldn't realize that I was around, until after it was said. They would apologize to me, but, they weren't really sorry they were just sorry they said it in front of the wrong person.

This lack of understanding and disapproval grew as our relationship grew stronger. And like a vicious circle, it seemed as if our relationship generated power in spite of and maybe even because of the ignorance of those others. They could not understand why I would lower myself to go out with an African American person, as if they are a lesser class of people. But what people fail to realize is that we all are equal.

The odd thing in my situation was that both of our families were very supportive. Both of us were hesitant to meet each others parents, because we ~~have~~ had already endured much hatred from others who we thought were our friends, but as the result they weren't . We were very relieved that our families wanted to play a part in our relationship. Mel was invited to many holiday functions, and was treated as the person he is, not as an intruder. I was also invited to his holidays get together. Since we celebrated different holidays, it was easy to attend each other's *s/b parties*

~~partys~~. Both of our family's were big tennis ~~family's~~ so it was easy to ~~strict~~ up many conversations that I feel was the initial bonding for us. We would play in many doubles tournaments together. My dad and Mel played in numerous tournaments together and he was not only considered my boyfriend ~~to my dad~~ he was also my dad's friend. My parents approval of my boyfriend means alot to me it's very comforting.

Mel has taught me many things about his culture. We had much information to exchange about our differences. I found Mel to be very intriguing and motivat~~ing~~ *he* *ed me* to be true to your self and never let others alter your way of thinking. I think many people are afraid of going with there true selves , out of fear of standing alone. But I have learned through much experiences ~~by~~ ~~me~~ *that* standing alone, I have become a much stronger and independent person. Mel has also taught me how to respect and trust myself and others. Through our relationship I also learned to care and love someone on my own with out support from my friends . Not only did we have a great relationship we had a very intense learning experience.

Stephanie chose to try to get to Mel more quickly in her second draft by cutting down a bit on the details of how she got to the camp. She has left in feeling as if she were in the spotlight, her feelings of discomfort about being the only white in the camp. And that's good because those are ideas central to the paper and to her experience with Mel.

Although she has done some cutting, her paper hasn't gotten any shorter because she's beginning to add more details about Mel and their relationship. The next group probed for more yet, pointed out again that the level of error in the paper was a problem for them as readers, and Stephanie revised this into a third draft that grew a bit more and began to more explicitly state how she feels about Mel and what she learned from him. You will see that her final draft is a pretty good paper and that Stephanie made use of everything she learned in groups and from R.J.:

Stephanie Hinshon
Eng 131 T,R 3:00
Dr.willey
Paper #2 Draft #4

"MEL"

A person who has made a tremendous impact on me was a part
of my life in the prime of my tennis career. My Dad is a
great, devoted tennis player, he had the inside scoop on
a tennis camp for me that he would get his money's worth.
He was looking for a competitive, yet economical camp. We
found a camp in Detroit, that provided a challenge and ca-
maraderie within the group. The instructors were young
adults playing tennis at the college level, who fought
their way up the ladder and were role models for the future tennis players. The instructors directed the younger
generation toward the things the students would have to
accomplish to reach the desired level of achievement.

The first day of camp came almost too soon : I was getting a little timid and nervous about going to a place
where I didn't know anybody.While walking on to the tennis courts, I realized that I was the only white person in
the whole camp, which was pretty odd considering my usual
experience is that I am not the minority in the crowd. I
pretended that I didn't notice, but who was I kidding?
Everybody else certainly noticed. I felt I was the center
of attention with a big spotlight following me with every
move, every flinch, every gesture I made.

The first couple of weeks, I felt isolated and wondered
if people were going to accept me. Then one day , I was
approached by a young guy named Mel. The first thing he said
to me was, "Is your phone number 937-8009?"

I was shocked. I proceeded to say," How did you get my number?" He said, "I had a dream and your number appeared in my dream". Then he told me the truth: " I saw it on the tennis roster." Ever since Mel made that first move, we had an automatic bond.Everyday after that I would wake up extra early and go to camp early hoping he might get there early so, we could talk and maybe practice together. Everyday after camp was over we would hang out and go to the park, or go out to eat, or hang out in his neighborhood and play tennis at his neighbors tennis court.

Mel was a young black man who grew up in an all white neighborhood. He understood what it was like to be different from the rest of the group and not to live with his own people. He was not accustomed to being in an all black group and felt a little more comfortable after finding someone more familiar to him. As the weeks progressed, I began talking more and was able to let my guard down, relax, learn, and enjoy myself.

As the time progressed so did our friendship: Mel and I hung out more and more. We went out to the movies, the mall, and just did the friend thing. Our friendship eventually grew to a relationship. We now classified ourselves as a couple. But there are many differences from being a couple of the same race and being a couple of two different races. People have to work harder for an interracial relationship to work.

Many people exhibited hatred and disapproval. We got different looks and comments from people we didn't know, and from those we did knew. Many people would call me a Nigger lover, and tell me consistently that, "Once you go black you never go back." Former friends of mine used to ask me why a cute little Jewish girl would want to go out with a "NIGER" (their words), as if black people were lesser people. His friends would call him a "sell-out" because they said a minority who goes out with a white person not only minimizes the selection of people for that particular race, it also lessens the race. Others seemed to totally disregard me, as if I never existed.

One thing that bothered me was that I got a reputation. I was now known as the girl who was dating a black person. I used to be known as the, funny, outgoing, happy-go-lucky-person. Many people learned to ignore or deal with my situation by not acknowledging it. People would also forget I was in their presence and would say "Nigger," not trying to offend me but they wouldn't realize that I was around, until after it was said. They would apologize to me, but they weren't really sorry. They were just sorry they said it in front of the wrong person and sorry I heard it.

This lack of understanding and disapproval grew as our relationship grew stronger. And like a vicious circle, it seemed as if our relationship generated power in spite of and maybe even because of the ignorance of those others. They could not understand why I would lower myself to go out with an African American person. But what people failed to realize was that I didn't see those differences.

The odd thing in my situation was that both of our families were very supportive. Both of us were hesitant to meet each other's parents because we had already endured much hatred from others who we thought were our friends, but as it turned out they weren't. We were very relieved that our families wanted to play a part in our relationship. Mel was invited to many holiday functions and was treated as the person he is, not as an intruder. I was also invited to his holiday get togethers. Since we celebrated different holidays it was easy to attend each other's parties. Both of our families were big tennis families so it was easy to up many conversations. That, I feel, was the initial bonding for us. We played in many doubles tournaments together. My dad and Mel played in numerous tournaments together, and he was not only considered my boyfriend, he was also my Dad's friend. My parents' approval of my boyfriend means a lot to me. It's very comforting.

At first I thought that Mel taught me about his culture. When trying to elaborate on what I had learned ,I realized that what made our relationship work was our similarities not our differences. We shared the same values, education, family, morals, integrity and honesty.

I found Mel to be very intriguing, and he motivated me to be true to myself and never let others alter my way of thinking. I think many people are afraid of going with their true selves, out of fear of standing alone. But I have learned through experience that by standing alone, I have become a stronger and more independent person. Mel has also taught me how to respect and trust myself and others. Through our relationship, I also learned to care and love someone on my own without support from my friends . Not only did we have a great relationship, we had a very intense learning experience.

Melvin and I talk to this day, but he attends Morehouse College in Atlanta, Georgia, and he lives in St. Louis. Even though our relationship isn't the same as it was a few years ago, we still have a strong, healthy, happy friendship.

STUDENT WRITER AT WORK— JENNIFER GONZALES

Jennifer was in R.J.'s class during the fall of 1994. Her paper, "College," was in response to the first writing assignment of the semester, to explore her reasons for being in college, and to explore the sorts of sacrifices she'd have to make and what she hopes to gain from attending.

Jennifer Gonzales
ENG 131
Dr. Willey
9-8-94
Paper 1, Draft 1

COLLEGE

~~The~~ Reason~~ing~~s for attending college differ for all people. Some go because their parents are making them go, or
maybe becuase they have nothing better to do. ~~While~~ Others
go to achieve a promotion in their current job or to get
the right training for the career they are hoping to
choose. My reasoning has a lot to do with the last reason
I listed. But there's more to it for me than that. I would
also like to achieve a higher education for my own personal benefit.

Stopping school after high school can seriously limit career choices. Plus, with the advancements in technology,
the upgrades will be taught to you as each occurs. With
the career I would like to go in to, photography, I feel
it is important to obtain a bachelor's degree in order to
succeed. I was told by Detroit's professional sports photographer, Mark Hicks, when a company is looking to buy a
picture or hire you to do a shoot~~ing~~, they'll look for a
college degree, hoping the higher education will make you
more dependable.

Photography has been a love of mine since I took my first
photography class, my sophomore year in high school. I had
always enjoyed taking pictures since I got my first camera
when I was about **seven** ~~7~~, but after I took the class I realized
that there was a lot more involved in photography than just
snapping shots of your friends and then taking the film to
Perry's to get developed. I still have a lot to learn about

the subject, and I'm hoping college will help me in furthering my knowledge as far as photography goes. Plus, the problem with taking the class at the high school I went to, is the equipment in the dark room is so old fashioned, that walking into a newer darkroom ~~like~~ such as the one here at OCC, I have no idea how to work any of the equipment. It's all foreign to me.

Besides, what would I be doing if I wasn't in college? Probably not much. I'd probably have a full-time job somewhere at a sports or music store, making just above minimum wage. Is this something to depend on for the rest of my life? No. Many people go through special training to become skilled laborers, and these people have respectable jobs that can support themselves and a family. But that is not what I would want to do for a living.

~~Although,~~ Many sacrifices are needed to succeed in college. For some, money would be a big issue. As for me, I'm lucky that my parents will pay my way through college, wherever I may choose to go. But the big sacrifice in my life will have to be part and only part of my social life. Not all, because I feel that socialization is a necessity in life because we are human beings. While some people are work work work, and no play, I don't find that way of living to be very healthy. In my opinion, a student who cuts out their social life completely, will eventually burn out, and then possibly rebel against their previous beliefs and morals.

Besides, college is a time to learn more to benefit your personal needs. For example, a college course can teach what is needed to know for a certain profession, but we have to go beyond that. To get the best out of life, we must learn as much as we can, and explore as many knew concepts as possible. What better way to do this than continuing an education after high school.

Why?

This is a short, sketchy first draft, not at all uncommon for the first draft of the first assignment of the semester. After she read her paper to group, the group agreed that she had a good start on her assignment, that she could treat this as something of a detailed outline of her paper. She's touched upon most of what the assignment asked her to, but she needs to expand on nearly everything. Paragraph by paragraph, the group asked Jennifer to expand on the ideas in her paper, which she did orally, to which the group commonly responded, "Put it in the paper."

As you can see from her second draft, Jennifer did indeed "Put it in the paper":

```
Jennifer Gonzales
ENG 131
Dr. Willey
9-8-94
Paper 1, Draft 2
```

COLLEGE

Reasons for attending college differ for all people. Some go because their parents are making them go, or maybe because they have nothing better to do. Others go to achieve a promotion in their current job or to get the right training for the career they are hoping to choose. My reasoning has a lot to do with the last reason I listed. But there's more to it for me than that. I would also like to achieve a higher education for my own personal benefit.

Stopping school after high school can seriously limit career choices. Plus, with the advancements in technology, the upgrades will be taught to you as each occurs. With the career I would like to go into, photography, I feel it is important to obtain a bachelor's degree in order to succeed. I was told by Detroit's professional sports photographer, Mark Hicks, that when a company is looking to buy a picture or hire you to do a shoot, they'll look for a college degree, hoping the higher education will make you more dependable. So after I finish what I have to here at OCC, I'm hoping to transfer to Wayne State University, where of course I am planning on majoring in Photography.

Photography has been a love of mine since I took my first photography class my sophomore year in high school. I had ~~always~~ enjoyed taking pictures since I got my first camera when I was about seven, but after I took the class I realized that there was a lot more involved in photography than just snapping shots of your friends and then taking the film to Perry's to get developed. Because with snapshots, you, the photographer have no control over what you want in the picture and what you would like to eliminate. With an enlarger (a dark room tool, used to expose the light sensitive paper to the light coming through the negative), you can take a small part of a picture and adjust the enlarger to make that the focus of the picture. Or, if the negative is too light or too dark, that can be controlled in the dark room all well. I still have a lot to learn about the subject, and I'm hoping college will help me in furthering my knowledge as far as photography goes. Plus, the problem with taking the class at the high school I went to, is the equipment in the dark room is so old fashioned that walking into a newer darkroom such as the one here at OCC, I have no idea how to work any of the equipment. It's all foreign to me.

There are many different types of photography, such as studio photography, portrait photography, photography for events in a newspaper or magazine-for example sports photography (photojournalism), and many other types that I just haven't learned about yet. Right now my choice is sports photography. ~~The reason for my choice is~~ All my life I have loved sports and played them as well. My favorite being hockey. There's not much I can do with sports professionally‚ so the next best thing is shooting pictures of the sports.

Besides, what would I be doing if I wasn't in college? Probably not much. I'd probably have a full-time job some-where at a sports or music store, making just above mini-mum wage. Is this something to depend on for the rest of my life? No. Many people go through special training to become skilled laborers, and these people have respectable jobs **and** ~~that~~ can support themselves and a family. But that is not what I would want to do for a living.

Many sacrifices are needed to succeed in college. For some, money would be a big issue. As for me, I'm lucky that my parents will pay my way through college, wherever I may choose to go. But the big sacrifice in my life will have to be part and only part of my social life. Not all, because I feel that socialization is a necessity in life because we are human beings. While some people are work work work, and no play, I don't find that way of living to be very healthy. In my opinion, a student who cuts out their so-cial life completely will eventually burn out and then pos-sibly rebel against their previous beliefs and morals.

Sacrifices have to be made for the career I am choosing to major in. Photography is an expensive subject to study. First of all, the cost of a camera can ~~range in prices~~ **vary**, but even a camera on the lower ~~cost~~ end is hundreds of dol-lars. Plus once I am more involved in photography, I plan on setting up my own dark room in my house. An enlarger will have to be purchased along with chemicals, negative carrier, safe light, filters, and other necessary dark room accessories. The cost of these is all high. Also film will **SP** be needed to purchase every time I run out along with light sensitive paper needed to develop the pictures themselves.

This is coming to-
gether nicely; you've
made some signifi-
cant changes
here—good ones.

also
~~Besides,~~ College is a time to learn more to benefit your personal needs. For example, a college course can teach what is needed to know for a certain profession, but we have to go beyond that. To get the best out of life, we must learn as much as we can and explore as many knew concepts as possible. What better way to do this than continuing an education after high school⑦

Jennifer's paper has become much more detailed throughout. She has better explained her love of photography and taken the time to tell us about what type of photography she hopes to do as a career and why. And she's added more about the sacrifices she expects to have to make to achieve her goal.

She'd done a good job on this revision, the group agreed. The group thought that now it might be nice to add a little something about her high school experience, agreeing that not doing so well in high school was a large part of the reason many of them were in this community college. And they suggested that she expand her conclusion, try to give the paper more of a sense of closure.

Jennifer addressed these concerns in her third version, which we needn't reproduce here. By the time she turned it in to R.J., they could then work together on a few minor line-editing concerns. Once again, most of the major revising Jennifer did on this paper, she did before she ever turned it in to her instructor.

Jennifer Gonzales
ENG 131
Dr. Willey
9-8-94
Paper 1, Draft 4

COLLEGE

Reasons for attending college differ for all people. Some go because their parents are making them go, or maybe because they have nothing better to do. Others go to achieve a promotion in their current job or to get the right training for the career they are hoping to choose. My reasoning has a lot to do with the last reason I listed. But there's more to it for me than that. I would also like to achieve a higher education for my own personal benefit.

My experience in high school was not that great. I wasn't the best student. Attending a catholic high school for my entire high school career got boring and I started to really hate the school. This was because the school, Marian High School, was extremely small and dumpy looking. Plus, it was an all girl school, so by the end of my senior year in high school, I really started to hate girls and the way they all talked about each other behind their friend's backs. Also, after having the Catholic religion stuffed in my face day after day made me resentful toward the church and everything it taught. In fact, I just barely graduated in time. But when I finally got through that school, I decided that I wouldn't put myself through that again. Deciding that I am going to do better in college is one thing, but now I have to prove to myself that I can do it.

Stopping school after high school can seriously limit career choices. Plus, with the advancements in technology, the upgrades will be taught to you as each occurs. With the career I would like to go into, photography, I feel it is important to obtain a bachelor's degree in order to succeed. I was told by Detroit's professional sports photographer, Mark Hicks, that when a company is looking to buy a picture or hire you to do a shoot, they'll look for a college degree, hoping the higher education will make you more dependable. So after I finish what I have to here at OCC, I'm hoping to transfer to Wayne State University, where of course I am planning on majoring in Photography.

Photography has been a love of mine since I took my first photography class my sophomore year in high school. I had

enjoyed taking pictures ever since I got my first camera
when I was about seven, but after I took the class I realized that there was a lot more involved in photography
than just snapping shots of your friends and then taking
the film to Perry's to get developed. With snapshots, you,
the photographer have limited control over what you want
in the picture and what you would like to eliminate. With
an enlarger (a dark room tool used to expose the light-
sensitive paper to the light coming through the negative),
you can take a small part of a picture and adjust the enlarger to make that the focus of the picture. Or, if the
negative is too light or too dark, that can be controlled
in the dark room as well. I still have a lot to learn about
the subject, and I'm hoping college will help me in furthering my knowledge as far as photography goes. Plus, the
problem with taking the class at the high school I went
to, was the equipment in the dark room was so old fashioned that walking into a newer darkroom such as the one
here at OCC, I have no idea how to work any of the equipment. It's all foreign to me.

There are many different types of photography, such as
studio photography, portrait photography, photography for
events in a newspaper or magazine-for example sports photography (photojournalism), and many other types that I
just haven't learned about yet. Right now my choice is
sports photography. All my life I have loved sports and
played them as well, my favorite being hockey. There's not
much I can do with sports professionally, so the next best
thing is shooting pictures of the sports.

Besides, what would I be doing if I wasn't in college?
Not much. I'd probably have a full-time job somewhere at
a sports or music store, making just above minimum wage.
Is this something to depend on for the rest of my life?

No. Many people go through special training to become skilled laborers, and these people have respectable jobs and can support themselves and a family. But that is not what I would want to do for a living.

Many sacrifices are needed to succeed in college. For some, money would be a big issue. As for me, I'm lucky that my parents will pay my way through college, wherever I may choose to go. But the big sacrifice in my life will have to be part and only part of my social life. Not all, because I feel that socialization is a necessity in life because we are human beings. While some people are work work work, and no play, I don't find that way of living to be very healthy. In my opinion, a student who cuts out their social life completely will eventually burn out and then possibly rebel against their previous beliefs and morals.

Sacrifices have to be made for the career I am choosing to major in. Photography is an expensive subject to study. First of all, the cost of a camera can vary, but even a camera on the lower end is hundreds of dollars. Plus, once I am more involved in photography, I plan on setting up my own dark room in my house. An enlarger will have to be purchased along with chemicals, negative carrier, safe light, filters, and other necessary dark room accessories. The cost of these is all high. Also, I will need to purchase film every time I run out along with light-sensitive paper needed to develop the pictures themselves.

College is also a time to learn more to benefit your personal needs. For example, a college course can teach what is needed to know for a certain profession, but we have to go beyond that. For example, if we decide on a profession and major in it, then change our mind later in life, we will have learned more than our major. Plus, our generation is supposed to have many career changes because of our forever advancing society. Continuing our knowledge is, in my opinion, one of the most important decisions in life we'll ever make. And the consequences of continuing are rewarding. To get the best out of life, we must learn as much as we can and explore as many knew concepts as possible. What better way to do this than continuing an education after high school?

STUDENT WRITER AT WORK—MIKE HUSAK

We begin with Mike's second draft here because he didn't make many changes from his first draft to his second. This sometimes happens—perhaps the group just didn't come up with much good advice, or perhaps Mike wasn't ready to make use of the advice. But that's why we always go to group more than once—his second group was very useful.

Mike's paper, "The Kid," was in response to an assignment to write about someone whom he didn't know or hadn't known well but who somehow had a great influence on his life.

Mike Husak
English 131
Dr. Willey
10-11-94
Paper 2, Draft 2

THE KID

When I first started going through the assignment for my second paper, it seemed fairly easy what was being asked until I came across the part where it said to stay away from parents, relatives, friends or coaches from the past. I tried to think about someone that walked in and out of my life, or who I also observed closely but never meet, yet I felt that I've known forever. Perhaps I could write about him because I've seen him on T.V. or read about him in a book or in a paper.

After thinking about it, the only person I really wanted to write about that meant a great deal to me is Ken Griffey, Jr. In case you don't know who he is he is probably one of the greatest baseball players of all time. I know you wanted this paper to stay away from boring "Oh, your my hero" type papers, but this player means a lot more to me than just statistics.

I guess you could say that Ken could be all those things, but perhaps some of his qualities are just a little different then the other normal people.

When he was a young man in high school, Ken had gone through several rough years. During those few years of high school, Ken had many major problems. One of those being his father. His dad was a professional baseball player for the Cincinnati Reds. He was really never around to do those father and son things. Never really around to help him with his homework, or with those teenage years of growing up. That's when he had gotten a little out of control. During his sophomore year, he started to hang out in a gang and began getting in trouble with stealing. The gang got him into drinking alcohol during school, that lead to his grades falling dramatically. Halfway through his sophomore year he was moments away from committing suicide because he thought his life was getting to be uncontrollable.

During his Christmas break, his father thought he was losing the communication level with his oldest son and really started helping him make future decisions about what he wanted to do in school and what kind of direction he wanted to take in life. After thinking about the talks and discussions he had with his father, he thought it might be time to start playing the sports he had been playing before high school to keep him out of trouble. His favorite sport out of the two he liked to play was football.

However, he was equally as good at baseball. After really working hard to get his grades picked up to where they used to be, it was baseball season. As soon as he set foot on the baseball field in Pennsylvania, it was like he had never missed a step. Throughout the season he had the best batting average, the most stolen bases, the most home runs and the greatest number of runs batted in the whole state. Toward the end of the season when everyone thought he had done it all he did more. At the age of eighteen, Ken Griffey, Jr. was signed by a professional baseball team, the Seattle Mariners. He was the number one player drafted into the Majors that year, not to mention the youngest player ever in baseball history. He really could have chosen football and played in college but he knew the money was in pro baseball.

With all the great odds against him and down times throughout his life, who would have thought he would be in the major leagues. From the very beginning of his life in the BIG'S he had started turning heads. Breaking team records in home runs, on-base averages, runs batted in, and the least errors in the outfield throughout the season. In 1991 the Seattle ball club picked up Ken Griffey, Sr. as a free-agent and signed him to a one-year contract. Now if playing a professional sport with your father on the same team isn't a dream come true, I'm not really sure what would be. They were the first ever father and son in professional baseball to hit back to back home runs on the same team.

When I thought I had seen everything Ken had done, he did it again. It was a cool Friday night at Tiger Stadium, and the Tigers were playing the Mariners in a four game set. I was lucky enough to have four tickets to three out of the four games. I had been shootin' the shit with him from the opening pitch in game one. I was really getting on his back to sign a baseball jersey. Finally in the third game, he said "If you come to the dugout after the game I'll sign your jersey." Just hearing him say that to me would have been enough to make my year. After the game was finished, I walked over to the dugout and he was there waiting to sign my jersey and finally shut me up. I was the only person out of a crowd of about two hundred people that got his signature. That day was my birthday and his signing my jersey made it that much better.

After that game, I followed him to Cleveland to see him play and tried to read every possible book or magazine ever written on this guy. That's why I really believe that Ken was the one person that walked in and out of my life and made the greatest impact. We all have really rough times in our lives where we think there could be no way things could possibly get better. But if you really believe in your self and put your mind to it you can really do just about anything. Like when Ken thought he had no were to go with his life he really turned it around for the best. Which is what I hope to do. I didn't have the greatest succces in school through out my high school career but with some hard work and determination, I think I may just be able to get somewhere around a 3.5 or greater through higschool. The only thing different from my paper is that I got to meet the person that made a difference in my life.

This is a pretty good, detailed second draft. The group agreed that Mike had told them a lot about Ken Griffey, Jr. and had managed to capture and keep their interest.

As they considered the assignment, they thought that Mike hadn't yet said enough about his own life, that he hadn't yet sufficiently shown how Griffey influenced him. They asked Mike to add a lot more detail about himself. And they suggested he rewrite his intro, make it something that anyone could understand, even people who weren't a part of their writing class.

You can see from Mike's third draft that he did some of what the group told him:

Mike Husak
English 131
Dr. Willey
10-18-94
Paper 2, Draft 3

INFLUENCE

When I first started going through the assignment for my second paper, I thought it seemed fairly easy until I came across the part where it said to stay away from parents, relatives, friends, or coaches from the past. I tried to think about someone "that walked in and out of my life, or who I observed closely but never (meet), yet I felt that I've known forever." Perhaps I could write about him because I've seen him on T.V., or read about him in a book or a paper.

s/b "met"

Now, try to write a new intro, one that better sets up the paper you've actually written.

After thinking about it, the only person I really wanted to write about that meant a great deal to me is Ken Griffey, Jr. In case you don't know who he is, he is probably one of the greatest baseball players of all time. I know you wanted this paper to stay away from boring, "Oh, (your) my hero" type papers, but this player means a lot more to me than just statistics.

SP

I guess you could say that Ken could be all those things, but perhaps some of his qualities are just a little different **from** ~~then~~ other people.

When he was a young man in high school, Ken went through several rough years. During those few years of high school, Ken had many major problems. One of those was his father.

His dad was a professional baseball player for the Cincinnati Reds. He was really never around to do those father and son things. He was never really around to help him with his homework, or with those teenage years of growing up. That's when he got a little out of control. During his sophomore year, he started to hang out in a gang and began getting in trouble with stealing. The gang got him into drinking alcohol during school, that lead to his grades *comma splice* falling dramatically. Halfway through his sophomore year he was moments away from committing suicide because he thought his life was getting to be uncontrollable.

During his Christmas break, his father thought he was losing the communication level with his oldest son and really started helping him make future decisions about what he wanted to do in school and what kind of direction he wanted to take in life. After thinking about the talks and discussions he had with his father, he thought it might be time to start playing the sports he had been playing before high school to keep him out of trouble. His favorite sport out of the two he liked to play was football, but he was equally as good at baseball. ¶After really working hard to get his grades picked up to where they used to be, it was baseball season. As soon as he set foot on the baseball field in Pennsylvania, it was like he had never missed a step. Throughout the season he had the best batting average, the most stolen bases, the most home runs, and the greatest number of runs batted in the whole state. Toward the end of the season when everyone thought he had done it all, he did more. At the age of 18 ~~eighteen~~, Ken Griffey, Jr. was signed by a professional baseball team, the Seattle Mariners. He was the number one player drafted into the Majors that year, not to mention the youngest player ever in baseball history. He really could have chosen football and played in college, but he knew the money was in pro baseball.

With all the great odds against him and down times throughout his life, who would have thought he would be in the major leagues? From the very beginning of his life in the BIG'S, he ~~had~~ started turning heads. Breaking team records in home runs, on-base averages, runs batted in, and the least errors in the outfield throughout the season. In 1991 the Seattle ball club picked up Ken Griffey, Sr. as a free-agent and signed him to a one-year contract. Now if playing a professional sport with your father on the same team isn't a dream come true, I'm not really sure what would be. They were the first ever father and son in professional baseball to hit back to back home runs on the same team.

When I thought I had seen everything Ken had done, he did it again. It was a cool Friday night at Tiger Stadium, and the Tigers were playing the Mariners in a four game set. I was lucky enough to have tickets to three out of the four games. My seats were located three rows behind the on-deck circle. I had been shooting the shit with him from the opening pitch in game one. I was really getting on his back to sign a baseball jersey. Finally in the third game, he said, "If you come to the dugout after the game I'll sign your jersey." Just hearing him say that to me would have been enough to make my year. After the game was finished, I walked over to the dugout, and he was there waiting to sign my jersey and finally shut me up. I was the only person out of a crowd of about ~~two hundred~~ 200 people that got his signature. That day was my birthday, and his signing my jersey made it that much better.

Find a different expression. <u>Show</u> us what sort of stuff went on.

After that game, I followed him to Cleveland to see him play and tried to read every possible book or magazine ever written on this guy. That's why I really believe that Ken was the one person that walked in and out of my life and made the greatest impact. We all have really rough times in our lives where we think there could be no way things could possibly get better. But if you really believe in yourself and put your mind to it, you can really do just about anything. Like when Ken thought he had no where to go with his life, he really turned it around for the best, ~~W~~hich is what I hope to do in school and in my life's career. I didn't have the greatest success in high school but with some hard work and determination I have already begun the healing process.

The reasons that I look up to Ken are because of all of the ways he succeeded in overcoming all of his obstacles. Some of my similar obstacles were my parents going through a divorce when I was twelve years old. The breakdown in the family structure, and the support foundation that was lost was very difficult and distracting. Because of those distractions, my grades had fallen like Ken's during high school. Like Ken and his father not having good communication, my mother and father also found it difficult to communicate, and that was difficult for me. Finally the hurt of the divorce went away and my parents were able to communicate with each other and with me and my brothers. My natural father, my natural mother, and my step-father all show~~ing~~ _ed_ their love and support _and_ helped me to get back on my feet. It was in my junior year of high school that I realized I needed to focus more on academics. Even though I didn't have the reward of getting drafted into the major leagues, I had the opportunity to see my grade point average double in a year and a half. I think I may just be able to get somewhere around a 3.5 or greater through college. The only thing different from my paper is that I got to meet the person that made a difference in my life.

You're able to say _so much_ about his life and really relatively little about your own. If he's been a great influence on you, you should be able to say more about your life.

You can see that Mike has added information about his own life to this draft, which strengthens the paper and brings it closer into line with what the assignment asked for. For some reason, though, Mike didn't change his intro, so it's no surprise that when he turned it in to

R.J., one of the first comments he wrote was for Mike to change his intro. He also asked Mike to try to provide more material about himself to better balance out the paper. You can judge how well Mike has managed from his final draft:

```
Mike Husak
English 131
Dr. Willey
12-4-94
Paper 2, FINAL
```

INFLUENCE

Out of all the famous people, relatives and friends, there has really only been one true influence in my life. Ken Griffey Jr. In case you don't know who he is, Ken is probably one of the greatest baseball players of all time. I know you wanted this paper to stay away from boring, "Oh, your my hero" type papers, but this player means a lot more to me than just statistics. I guess you could say that Ken could be all those things, but perhaps some of his qualities are just a little different from other people.

When he was a young man in high school, Ken went through several rough years. During those few years of high school, Ken had many major problems. One of those was his father. His dad was a professional baseball player for the Cincinnati Reds. He was really never around to do those father and son things. He was never really around to help him with his homework, or with those teenage years of growing up. That's when he got a little out of control. During his sophomore year, he started to hang out in a gang and began getting in trouble with stealing. The gang got him into drinking alcohol during school, that lead to his grades falling dramatically. Halfway through his sophomore year he was moments away from committing suicide because he thought his life was getting to be uncontrollable.

During his Christmas break, his father thought he was losing the communication level with his oldest son and really started helping him make future decisions about what he wanted to do in school and what kind of direction he wanted to take in life. After thinking about the talks and discussions he had with his father, he thought it might be time to start playing the sports he had been playing before high school to keep him out of trouble. His favorite sport out of the two he liked to play was football, but he was equally as good at baseball.

After really working hard to get his grades picked up where they used to be, it was baseball season. As soon as he set foot on the baseball field in Pennsylvania, it was like he had never missed a step. Throughout the season he had the best batting average, the most stolen bases, the most home runs, and the greatest number of runs-batted-in in the whole state. Toward the end of the season when everyone thought he had done it all, he did more. At the age of 18, Ken Griffey, Jr. was signed by a professional baseball team, the Seattle Mariners. He was the number one player drafted into the majors that year, not to mention the youngest player ever in baseball history. He really could have chosen football and played in college, but he knew the money was in pro baseball.

With all the great odds against him and down times throughout his life, who would have thought he would be in the major leagues? From the very beginning of his life in the BIGS, he started turning heads: breaking team records in home runs, on-base averages, runs batted in, and the least errors in the outfield throughout the season. In 1991 the Seattle ball club picked up Ken Griffey, Sr. as a free-agent and signed him to a one-year contract. Now if playing a professional sport with your father on the same team isn't a dream come true, I'm not really sure what would be. They were the first ever father and son in professional baseball to hit back to back home runs on the same team.

When I thought I had seen everything Ken had done, he did it again. It was a cool Friday night at Tiger Stadium, and the Tigers were playing the Mariners in a four game set. I was lucky enough to have four tickets to three out of the four games. My seats were located three rows behind the on-deck circle. From the very first pitch my friend and I were yelling and trying to get his attention. I was really getting on his back to sign a baseball jersey. Finally in the third game, he said "If you come to the dugout after the game I'll sign your jersey." Just hearing him say that to me would have been enough to make my year. After the game was finished, I walked over to the dugout and he was there waiting to sign my jersey and finally shut me up. I was the only person out of a crowd of about 200 people that got his signature. That day was my birthday and his signing my jersey made it that much better.

After that game, I followed him to Cleveland to see him play and tried to read every possible book or magazine ever written on this guy. That's why I really believe that Ken was the one person that walked in and out of my life and made the greatest impact. We all have really rough times in our lives where we think there could be no way things could possibly get better. But if you really believe in yourself and put your mind to it, you can really do just about anything. Like when Ken thougt he had no where to go with his life he really turned it around for the best, which is what I hope to do in school and in my life's career. I didn't have the greatest success in high school but with some hard work and determination I have already begun the healing process.

The reasons that I look up to Ken are because of all of the ways he succeeded in overcoming all of his obstacles. Some of my similar obstacles were my parents going through a divorce when I was twelve years old. The breakdown in the family structure, and the support foundation that was lost was very difficult and distracting. Because of those distractions, my grades fell like Ken's during high school. Like Ken and his father not having good communication, my mother and father also found it difficult to communicate, and that was difficult for me. Finally the hurt of the divorce went away and my parents were able to communicate with each other and with me and my brothers. My natural father, my natural mother and my step-father all showed their love and support and helped me to get back on my feet. It was in my junior year of high school that I realized I needed to focus more on academics. Even though I didn't have the reward of getting drafted into the major leagues, I had the opportunity to see my grade point average double in a year and a half. I think I may just be able to get somewhere around a 3.5 or greater through college. Even though I'm not as old as he is, I'm sure I'll be able to look back at his experiences the older I get, and still be able to compare them with mine. The only thing different from my paper is that I got to meet the person that made a difference in my life.

STUDENT WRITER AT WORK— COLLEEN LICKORAI

Colleen was in Jennifer's class in the fall of 1994 and in R.J.'s class in the winter of 1995. In Jennifer's class, Colleen decided to write her paper on a significant place about her grandparents' house in Boston.

Following is her first draft, done after much freewriting and thinking through why this house always elicits such strong emotions from her:

A PLACE FROM THE PAST - DRAFT 1

Every year my parents my brother and I packed up our blue station wagon, with coolers and suitcases, coloring books and crayons,, gum and juice. And whatever else that would keep two young kids occupied. My family and I would start off at around 5'o clock in the morning. Driving and driving what seemed like days to my brother and I. Well, it was about 26 hours before we reached our destination. My grandma and grandpa Lickorai's house, in Boston Mass. We'ld pull into the long driveway with the grass and shrubs and suddenly it was like we were in a differnt world. The houses were so close, and two families lived in each one. My great aunt and uncle lived on the top level of my grandparents house. The neeighbors all knew eachother , because they lived there for so many years. I walk up the steps to the screened in front porch. And the smell of something good was lingering in the air.There house was a double house.As I walked into there house there was always something good to eat on the table and pop in the refrigerator. A kids dream. The floors were shiny and spotless. And there were always fresh tomatoes laying on the window sill. This would just seem like an or-dinary house to anyone else, but not me. Hiding in this house was a basement like no other. It wasn't finished. But, it was spotless. This is where I loved to play. There were toys hiding in the boxesand a T.V. and a little bench to sit on. My aunt and uncles basement was also connected. If you walked through a door you were some place else. It was cool and relaxing. And nobody would come down there and bother you. I would rollar skate around on the cement floor for hours until I got bored. Then I end up in the backyard, which seemed so big to me. There was a garden surrounding it and underneath the porch you could be in a second. To play in the shade↓When my granddparents got on my nerves I'ld truck upstairs to fun. THis is where my aunt and uncle lived. They were always argueing. But they were great fun. My aunt would always be so happy to see me. S he woul let me roam around the house until I found something interesting to keep my-self occupied. She would give me lots of candy and pop. And we'ld watch T.V. for hours↓Well, as the years went by my family and I still kept packing up the station wagon and took our long trip to Boston. Now, when we got there the yard was still nice the grass and shrubs were still well taken care of, the smell of good food still caught your at-tention when you walked in the door. Yet something wasn't there. The basement was now even older and the only thing that I would go down there for would be a pop. The snacks on the table only looked fattening. And by the time we were supposed to go home I was already packed and ready. Almost begging to leave. I now missed my house and my friends. Not to mention my privacy I felt like everything I said or did was being analyzed. The only thing that was still hiding in that house were good memories. Instead of putting on a movie with cartoon characters we were putting on talk shows and news programs. The little kid in that house was gone. I didn't feel like exploring the house anymore. I felt like being back at my own. When I went there as a child things that appeared to be big are now so small. Things have dif-fernt meaning . But, one thing I know forsure is that house will always be special.

In Colleen's first draft, she has some good ideas. The problems, though, are so important that the group got a little confused trying to determine her main point. They wondered why things have "different meanings now." They asked why she had changed her feelings. Those were the main questions they asked her to work on for her next draft. Notice though, as they did, that in her first draft she really has something interesting to say about places that remain the same while people change. The group also recognized this strength and asked her to work on expanding it. Because they saw a strength, Colleen was excited to work on clarifying her ideas. She left the group anxious to get back to work.

Here is her second draft:

A PLACE FROM THE PAST - DRAFT 2

fragment ____ <u>Every year since I was born</u>. My parents, my brother and I packed up our blue station wagon, with coolers, suitcases, coloring books, and crayons, gum, and juice. <u>And whatever</u>
fragment ____ <u>else that would keep my brother and I as kids occupied</u>. My family and I would start off around 5 o'clock in the morning. Driving and driving for what seemed like days to my brother and I. Well, it was actually around 20 hours before we reached our destination. My grandma and grandpa Lickorai's house in Boston Mass.

We'd pull up the long driveway , with the grass and shrubs neatly manicured. And the houses so close you could touch them. And suddenly it was like we were in a different world. Each house was huge. They were all double houses. My great-aunt and great-uncle lived on the top level of my grandparent's house. The neighbors all knew each other, because they all lived there for so many years.

I walk up the steps to the old screened in porch. And the smell of something good was lingering in the air. And when I made it to the kitchen there was always something good to eat waiting on the table. And there was a whole refrigerator full of pop. A kids dream. The floor was shiny and spotless, and there were always tomatoes from my grandpa's garden laying on the window sill. This would just seem like an ordinary house to someone else but, not to me.

Hiding in this house was a basement like no other. It wasn't finished. But, it was spotless. This is where I loved to play. There were toys hiding in the boxes. And there was a T.V. with a little bench to sit and enjoy your favorite show. My aunt and uncles basement was also connected. If you walked through a door you were someplace else. It was cool and relaxing. And no one would come down there and bother us. I would roller skate around the cement floor for hours until I got bored. Then, I end up in the backyard which seemed so big to me. There was a garden surrounding it, and you could be underneath the porch in a second. Just to play in the shade.

When my grandparents got on my nerves I'd truck upstairs where my aunt and uncle lived. They were always arguing. But, it was great fun. My aunt would always be happy to see my brother and I. She let us roam around the house until we found something intersecting to keep ourselves occupied. She give us lots of candy and pop. And let us watch T.V. for hours.

Well, as the years went by my family and I still kept packing up our station wagon and took our long trip to Boston. Now, when we got there the yard was still nice, the grass and the shrubs were still well taken care of. And the smell of good food was still lingering in the air the minute you walked into the screened in porch. Yet, something wasn't there anymore. The basement was now even older and the only thing that I would go down there for would be a pop. The snacks on the table only looked fattening. And by the time we were supposed to go home I was already packed and ready. <u>Almost begging to leave</u>. <u>I now</u>   **fragment** missed my house and my friends. Not to mention my privacy. I felt that everything I did or said was being analyzed. The only thing that was still hiding in that house were good memories. Instead of putting on a movie with cartoon characters we were watching talk shows and news programs. The little kid in that house was gone. I didn't feel like exploring the house anymore. I felt like being back at my own. When I was a child things that appeared so big, like my grandparents backyard were now so small. Things that were so much fun to do just aren't anymore. All of the things that were special to you just aren't so special anymore. One thing that I know for sure that house will always be special to me.

Contradictory {

Notice especially the end of this draft. Colleen is really trying to figure out what it is about her that has changed in relation to the house. The group commented, though, that this end was still confusing. She says that everything that was special is special no longer, later telling us how special this house is. This is really a thinking struggle for her. She just isn't sure what she feels. This is a very common problem for a writer. As she writes, she realizes that she is feeling some contradictory emotions. Working them out in her next draft helps her see her experience more clearly.

Additionally, the group felt that the paper could be more fluid. They asked her to look at the sentences as part of one another, trying to combine and show relationships between ideas. After another two drafts where she still struggled with her end, Colleen came up with her final draft:

Colleen Lickorai

A PLACE FROM THE PAST #5

Every year since I was born, my parents, my brother and I packed up our blue station wagon with coolers, suitcases, coloring books, gum, and juice - everything that would keep my brother and I occupied. My family and I would start off around 5 o'clock in the morning on a drive that seemed like days to my brother and I. It was actually around 20 hours before we reached our destination: my grandma and grandpa Lickorai's house in Boston, Mass.

We'd pull up the long driveway with the grass and shrubs neatly manicured. The houses were so close you could touch them. Suddenly it was like we were in a different world. Each house was huge, because they were all double houses - two houses built on top of each other. To a young kid that is enormous. My great-aunt and great-uncle lived on the top level of my grandparent's house. The neighbors all knew each other because they lived there for so many years. This contributed to the good feelings around the neighborhood.

I walked up the steps to the old screened in porch. The smell of something good was lingering in the air. When I made it to the kitchen there was always something good to eat waiting on the table; not to mention a whole refrigerator full of pop. All that food was a child's dream come true.

The floor was shiny and spotless, and there were always tomatoes from my grandpa's garden laying on the window sill. This would just seem like an ordinary house to anybody else but not me. It seemed as though it was full of fun things to play with, and all the food that I wanted.

Hiding in this house was a basement like no other. It wasn't finished, but it was spotless. This is where I loved to play. There were toys hiding in the boxes, and a T.V. with a bench to sit and enjoy your favorite show. My aunt and uncle's basement was also connected to this one . If you walked through the door dividing the two you were in another world.It was cool and relaxing, and no one else would come down there and bother us. I would roller skate around the cement floor for hours until I got bored. Then,

I ended up in the back yard which seemed so big to me. There was a garden surrounding it, and you could be underneath the porch in a second to play in dirt.

When my grandparents got on my nerves with their nagging I'd truck upstairs where my aunt and uncle lived. They were always arguing , but, it was great fun to visit them upstairs. My aunt would always be happy to see my brother and I. She let us roam around the house until we found something interesting to keep ourselves occupied. She allowed us to sit in front of the T.V. for hours stuffing ourselves with candy and pop.

Well, as the years went by my family and I still kept packing up our blue station wagon and taking our long trip to Boston.Now, when we got there the yard was still nice, the grass and the shrubs were still taken care of. The smell of good food was still lingering in the air the minute you walked into the screened in porch. Yet, something wasn't there anymore. The basement was now even older, and the only thing I would go down there for would be a pop. The snacks on the table only looked fattening. By the time we were supposed to go home I was already packed - begging to leave.I missed my house and my friends not to mention my privacy.I felt that everything I did or said was being analyzed . The only thing hiding in that house was good memories. We were now watching talk shows and news programs instead of cartoons. The little kid in that (hose) was gone. I didn't even feel like exploring the house. I felt like being back at my own home. Everything in a person's life changes with time no matter how stagnant they may be.

It is important for you to notice that she may not have gotten every aspect of this complex idea into the paper. Remember, Colleen is a beginning writer. But look at the improvements she has made. She has unified her writing; she has come up with a reason for her attitude changes; she has better organized her text. All these things serve the paper well and will serve Colleen well as she goes on to future writing assignments.

When in R.J.'s class the following semester, Colleen was asked to do a more traditionally "academic" writing assignment. She read an article about stereotyping and wrote in response to the article (see the assignment, "Writing in Response to an Essay" in Chapter 5). This was the last writing assignment of the semester, and Colleen was only given a week in which to do two drafts—one for group, the second as the "final." Here is the first version of Colleen's paper:

Colleen Lickorai
Paper 6, Draft One

THE BLOND MISCONCEPTION

For years now blonds have gotten a bad rep. Any time a blond is mentioned there is a snide remark that comes with that. If you are blond many stereotypes come along with you. For instance being dizzy, or an airhead, bimbo, big breasted just to name a few.

I'm not sure who started these stereotypes but being a blond myself I tend to dislike them. Probably because these are the type of things that are expected of me. This is also the farthest thing from the truth. As a blond I am far from an airhead. I go to school and have very good grades. I can also hold my own with people and can communicate well. I am no where close to a bimbo. I haven't gone out with many guys and when I do nothing much ever happens. In the physical sense. Church is actually a big part of my life and I have my morals and values. I'm obviously not in the big breasted category either. I think that I really don't fit the mold of a stereotypical blond. Actually I really resent having to prove to others that because of my hair color I am any different from them.

Hair color doe not make someone's personality. It also doesn't make someone easy or dizzy. I agree that there are blonds who can fit that stereotype but, there are also brunettes and redhaired people that can do a fine job fitting in. A person is what they make of themselves. Each one of us is different and each one of us has things that people dislike about us. I think that the moral of the story is don't judge a book by its cover. Because you could be very misleaded or miss out on meeting something special.

When Colleen took this first draft to group, the group first reviewed the assignment; it was apparent right away that Colleen had not done one significant thing the assignment asked her to do: react to the essay she'd read by summarizing the essay's main point. The group reinforced to Colleen that her instructor expected her to say something about the article.

Another key element of the assignment was to cite some example(s) of stereotyping from the media. Again, they pointed out to Colleen, she hadn't yet done that in this draft. She uses personal experience, but for this assignment she's being asked to do more. So the group felt that Colleen should say something about the article first, then go on to explore some example from the media, and then go on to her own experience. The group valued her experience and felt strongly that it should stay in her paper.

Colleen knew she only had one shot at this particular revision before the portfolio was due, soon; here's what she came up with. We think you'll agree she did a decent job with the group's advice, especially given the limited amount of time she had to work with:

Colleen Lickorai
Paper 6, Draft 2 (Final)

THE BLOND MISCONCEPTION

In the article, "Don't Let Stereotypes Warp Your Judgments," Robert Heilbroner talks of stereotypes being a kind of "gossip." This gossip makes us "prejudge people before we lay eyes on them." It also makes us lump people

in a class just by looking at them. This type of catego-
rizing is bad because a person can miss out meeting a wonderful person; when they first looked at them, they didn't
"look like their type."

The media help with making these stereotypes more bold.
In the television show Married With Children, the blond is
portrayed as an easy, stupid, air headed girl. She sleeps
with everyone and doesn't think twice about it. This type
of stereotyping of blondes makes it difficult for someone
who is not like the stereotypical blond.

For years now, blondes have gotten a bad rep. Any time a
blond is mentioned, there is a snide remark that comes with
that. If you are blond, many stereotypes apply to you. For
instance, you are dizzy, or an airhead, a bimbo, or big
breasted, just to name a few.

I'm not sure who started these stereotypes, but being a
blond myself, I tend to dislike them. Probably because
these are the type of things expected of me. They are also
the farthest things from the truth. As a blond, I am far
from an airhead. I go to school and have very good grades.
I can also hold my own with anyone who wants to debate or
argue. I work with people and can communicate well. I am
nowhere close to being a bimbo. I haven't gone out with
many guys, and when I do nothing much ever happens in the
physical sense. Church is actually a big part of my life,
and I have morals and values. I'm obviously not in the big
breasted category either. I think that I really don't fit
the mold of the stereotypical blond. Actually, I resent
having to prove to others that I am not any different from
them.

Hair color doe not make someone's personality. It also
doesn't make someone easy or dizzy. I agree that there are

blondes who can fit that stereotype, but there are also brunettes and red-haired people that can do a fine job fitting in. A person is what they make of themselves. Each one of us is different and each one of us has things that people dislike about us. I think that the moral of the story is don't judge a book by its cover. Because you could be very mislead or miss out on meeting something special.

STUDENT WRITER AT WORK—RITA GREEN

Rita was in Jennifer's class during the fall of 1994; she chose to begin a paper on societal expectations of people by discussing how her sister abuses the welfare system. Here is that paper:

Rita Green
Assn.#6 Draft #1

PROVING YOURSELF

The people in this state who receive assistance, and really don't deserve it , is growing by large amounts every year. They should have to prove to the state, that they really need the help. I have a relative in my family who is milking the government out of thousands of dollars. My younger sister is a good example of a person who takes advantage of the welfare system. She is married and has two kids. Her husband only works half of the year, and under the table, so they can make just under the right amount to recieve assistance. There is nothing physically, or mentally wrong with her. She is perfectly able to work, but she is lazy and doesn't want to. Neither my sister or her husband graduated from high school, but she could get free schooling and day-care to improve herself. The state has many free training programs for people who didn't graduate. Does this make sense? If someone graduates from high school, you have to pay for college or training school,but if someone didn't, they get free training in a specialized field. It's like the government punishes you for graduating high school.

My sister is the youngest in our family, and my mother always comes up with excuses for her. She'll say "Pam doesn't need to work, she needs to be at home with her kids."

Her kids attend school all day, so that excuse no longer works with me anymore. I get so mad at these comments all the time. On the other hand, my mother thinks its perfectly fine for me to work full time, and attend school, even though I have a family. They see nothing wrong with me doing this, they sort of expect it of me. Since I'm the oldest of three children, they expect me to set a good example for my two sisters. They always expected me to do my best, even though I always didn't want to.I'm tired of people thinking I always want to do everything!

For example, both my sister and I were pregnant with our first child at the same time. We were both in our eighth month, and I was kind enough to give her a baby shower at my home. She said to me "Oh Rita," "I didn't know if I was going to come, because I'm so tired all the time."

I couldn't believe it! Here I was in the same condition as she was, working full time, and giving her a baby shower. She had a lot of nerve to say that to me. My mother just sat there playing games, while I kept walking up and down the basement stairs carrying food and presents. I yelled to her "Mom do you think you can come up here and help me?"

Did they think I could do everything by myself? It seems like I always have to prove myself to everyone. Why? Just because I'm the oldest. I would like to be lazy just for once.

My company whom I've worked for the past six-teen years, expects me to do a certain amount of work, that exceed the rest of my fellow workers. My friends will say to me "Why are you working so hard for?" "Your making us look bad." "Why should I do more?" "Then they will expect this of me all of the time." So they do less work, and no one says anything to them. If I were to do the same thing my boss would be on my back, wanting to know why I wasn't at my certain level of work for that day.

Proving yourself to your family or freinds, is just as hard to do as to prove yourself at school or at work. Once you have shown yourself and other that you are aworthy person, shouldn't mean that you have to stay at that same level, for the rest of your life. You should be allowed to make mistakes, and to enjoy life. You shouldn't have to be the person that always has to be in control all the time. I feel that sometimes the order in which you were born in your family, has an effect on what kind of person you'll end up being in life.

Stay on the subject of family.

The group was quick to point out that Rita was writing about many different things in the same paper. They asked her to begin by taking out the part about her company. Rita did take out that paragraph, but when she brought the next version to group it was clear that much more needed doing. They asked her to try to make this paper more specifically focused on her. Though they thought the part about welfare was interesting, they found it a bit general. Someone suggested that she compare societal expectations of herself with those of her sister. Rita thought about this and came up with a much changed third draft:

Rita Green
Assn.#6 Draft #3

PROVING YOURSELF

The people in this state who receive assistance, and really don't deserve it is growing by large amounts every year. They should have to prove to the state, that they really need the help. I have a relative in my family who is milking the government out of thousands of dollars. My younger sister is a good example of a person who takes advantage of the welfare system. She is married and has two kids. Her husband only works half of the year, and under the table, so they can make just under the right amount to recieve assistance. There is nothing physically, or mentally wrong with her. She is perfectly able to work, but she is lazy and doesn't want to. Neither my sister or her husband graduated from high school, but she could get free schooling and day-care to improve herself. The state has many free training programs for people who didn't graduate. Does this make sense? If someone graduates from high school, you have to pay for college or training school, but if someone didn't, they get free training in a specialized field. It's like the government punishes you for graduating high school.

My sister is the youngest in our family, and my mother always comes up with excuses for her. She'll say "Pam doesn't need to work, she needs to be at home with her kids."

Her kids attend school all day, so that excuse no longer works with me anymore. I get so mad at these comments all the time. On the other hand, my mother thinks its perfectly fine for me to work full time, and attend school, even though I have a family. They see nothing wrong with me

First explain that both you and Pam have married, but Pam doesn't work.

doing this, they sort of expect it of me. Since I'm the oldest of three children, they expect me to set a good example for my two sisters. They always expected me to do my best, even though I always didn't want to. I'm tired of people thinking I always want to do everything!

For example, both my sister and I were pregnant with our first child at the same time. We were both in our eighth month, and I was kind enough to give her a baby shower at my home. She said to me "Oh Rita," "I didn't know if I was going to come, because I'm so tired all the time."

I couldn't believe it! Here I was in the same condition as she was, working full time, and giving her a baby shower. She had a lot of nerve to say that to me. My mother just sat there playing games, while I kept walking up and down the basement stairs carrying food and presents. I yelled to her "Mom do you think you can come up here and help me?"

Did they think I could do everything by myself? It seems like I always have to prove myself to everyone. Why? Just because I'm the oldest. I would like to be lazy just for once!

Before, I would never refuse my parents when they asked me for help. I now try to stand up to my family when they ask me for a favor. I tell my parents to ask my sisters instead. Their just as capable as I am to do errands for them. My mother for some reason, still calls me first. I try not to be disrespectful, but sometimes I lose my patience, and don't want to deal with my family anymore. I'm not very close with my youngest sister, and I hardly ever talk to her, because she always has an excuse for everything.

I've learned to say no more often to people. Sometimes people rely on a person too much,just because in the past they have proven to be a worthy person. I feel that sometimes the order in which you were born in the family, has an effect on what kind of person you'll end up being in life. Your so used to people expecting so much out of you, that you tend to push youself more.

This seemed to work better, so Rita submitted this draft. In an individual conference, she and Jennifer discussed the end. Jennifer wondered how having all these expectations placed on her influenced her adult behavior. They discussed working with those ideas in the conclusion. Here is Rita's final version; how do you feel she's done with all the advice she received?

Rita Green
Assn.#6

PROVING YOURSELF - DRAFT 4

When I was growing up as a child, I was taller than most kids my own age. People assumed I was older than I really was. By the time I reached ten years of age, I was already 5'7" in height. I looked like I was around thirteen or fourteen, and my family gave me responsibilities more fitted for that age, instead of someone who was only ten years old.

My parents would leave me alone all day to watch my two sisters. My sister Debbie was eight, and Pam my youngest sister wasn't even walking yet , so I guess she was under a year old. My mother would come up to me and say "Rita", "We are leaving for a few hours." "Take good care of your sisters, if you have any problems call your grandmother."

I didn't want to let my parents down,but I was frightened doing this. They would think I wasn't responsible! My sister Debbie and I, fought over silly things, and Pam was totally relying on me for her care. I knew how to feed her, change her diapers, and play little games with her. But, I was worried about something major going wrong. It would be all my fault. What if a stranger came to the door, should I answer it? What if something bad happened to my baby sister? I felt my parents were wrong in leaving me in control of my two sisters, but I dare say not a word to them. To them it would seem like I was letting them down. Sometimes they would leave me with them for the whole day. I was only ten, not a teenager who had babysitting experience!

Now that my sister and I have grown and are married, my mother still expects me to be more responsible. My sister is the youngest in our family, and my mother always comes up with excuses for her. She'll say "Pam doesn't need to work, she needs to be at home with her kids."

Her kids attend school all day, so that excuse no longer works with me anymore. I get so mad at these comments all the time. On the other hand, my mother thinks its perfectly fine for me to work full time, and attend school, even though I have a family. They see nothing wrong with me doing this, they sort of expect it of me. Since I'm the oldest of three children, they expect me to set a good example for my two sisters. They always expected me to do my best, even though I always didn't want to.I'm tired of people thinking I always want to do everything!

For example, both my sister and I were pregnant with our first child at the same time. We were both in our eighth month, and I was kind enough to give her a baby shower at my home. She said to me "Oh Rita," "I didn't know if I was going to come , because I'm so tired all the time."

I couldn't believe it! Here I was in the same condition as she was, working full time, and giving her a baby shower. She had a lot of nerve to say that to me. My mother just sat in the basement, playing baby shower games, while I kept walking up and down the basement stairs carrying food and presents. I yelled to her "Mom do you think you can come up here and help me?

My mother was only fifty-four years old, and there was nothing physically wrong with her,she was capable of helping me. She should of been helping me get everything ready. When she came upstairs she said to me "Oh, I guess you do need some help!" I was upset over this ,because she gave her total attention to my sister,and forgot about me.

Did they think I could do everything by myself? It seems like I always have to prove myself to everyone. Why? Just because I'm the oldest. I would like to be lazy just for once!

Before, I would never refuse my parents when they asked me for help. I now try to stand up to my family when they ask me for a favor. I tell my parents to ask my sisters instead. Their just as capable as I am to do errands for them. My mother for some reason, still calls me first. I try not to be disrespectful, but sometimes I lose my patience, and don't want to deal with my family anymore. I'm not very close with my youngest sister, and I hardly ever talk to her , because she always has an excuse for everything.

I've learned to say no more often to people. For instance, on the days that I don't have school,I sometimes take my father to his radiation and chemotherapy treatments. He was diagnosed with cancer last January. He is unable to drive because the treatments make him sick. One week I drove him on a Wednesday and Friday morning. My sister had the gull to ask me if I could take him on the following Monday.

"No", I said. "Just because I don't have classes that day doesn't mean that I don't have anything else to do!" "You'll have to take him, I have homework to do", I yelled back at her.

Sometimes people rely on a person too much,just because in the past they have proven to be a worthy person. I've changed my habits,even though my relatives still have high expectations of me. I feel that sometimes the order in which you were born in the family, has an effect on what kind of person you'll end up being in life. Your so used to people expecting so much out of you, that you tend to push yourself more.Since being brought up this way, I feel sometimes I put to high of expectation on myself.

STUDENT WRITER AT WORK— BRENDA SCHOOLER

Brenda took Jennifer's class during the winter of 1995. When confronted with a paper that asked students to take a childhood experience and examine how it might impact their adulthood, Brenda wrote about the lack of communication in her childhood home. Notice the many wonderful pieces of detail that she uses in this early draft:

Writing Assignment #3
Eng 131 - Ginsberg
Rough Draft - October 10, 1994

CAN WE TALK?

My reason for being in college goes back to my childhood. We're talking forty-something years ago. As I think back to 1956-57, my memories are vague, but I remember that as children, myself and my brothers and sisters were never talked to by our parents. They never discussed current events with us, or if we were having problems in school.

Parent-teacher conferences were the only time we got a "talking to", and that was only to tell us they were pleased with our report cards. If they were not pleased then there was a special conference (in the form of a whipping), set-up for you when my father got home. Even though we did not have these little discussions with my parents, I didn't think this was unusual and neither did my brothers and sisters, as I have come to find out. "Children are to be seen, not heard", seemed to be the unspoken rule in our home. There were seven of us children and always a LOT of noise, but never any family discussions.

Our house was filled with noise from sun-up to sun-down beginning with my parents alarm clock. *The* Next sound was the radio, then the shower along with singing and whistling as my father prepared to go to work. My mother prepared breakfast while the rest of the family got up and took turns in the bathroom rushing around trying to get ready for school. We all would grab some toast or morsel of bacon as we scurried out the door to catch a ride to school with my father. I don't even remember anybody saying "good morning". We sorta resembled soldiers in boot camp, trained to do everything by the book and by the clock. Funny thing though, I don't remember who did the training. I assume it was my mother, she seems the most likely person, but I have no vivid memory of her talking to me about personal hygiene, how to comb my hair, or about the "birds and the bees".

Gradually, in my twenties I began to open up more. Even when I got married and my husband and I went to his family functions, I rarely said anything. I felt so awkward and uncomfortable. I knew nothing about ennunciation, forming and completing sentences to converse with another person. What really made me determined to improve my communication skills was the fact that I noticed practically the same thing

Because of this I was never able to . . . . .

happening to my children. I could not and would not allow
this cycle to continue with another generation. I made it a
point to talk to my kids just about everyday as I picked
them up from school. I think that talking to them helped me
alot by having to know the answers to their questions. My
husband helped me alot. If I didn't know the answers to their
questions, I'd tell them "Let's go ask your father".

When I think about my parents now, I don't think they
knew any better. Their parents and grandparents raised
their families by the rod, and in some cases there was very
little concern by the parents whether the children had
questions or not, due to the racial situation in the south
which is where my ancestors grew up, and even though times
have changed, sometimes people don't. I feel that I've
changed in alot of ways since my school days. I've learned
to ask questions, have opinions, express my feelings and
appreciate the value of open communication.

You should add a real story about you and your kids.

Much was admired about this first paper. Then a group member
asked a key question—does Brenda have children? Brenda laughed
when she said she had five but had never considered that they would
be an important part of this story. Of course, she finally admitted, they
were. Her later draft shows her attempt to explain how she is as a parent through what occurred in her house when she was a child.

Brenda Schooler
Writing Assignment #3

THE DOUBLE EXPERIENCE - DRAFT 4

My experience goes back to 1956/57. My memory is somewhat
vague but I do remember how lonely I always felt. I come
from a family of eight children, so you would think that
I had plenty of people around to talk to. I shared upper

living quarters with five of my sisters and yes, there was plenty of "talking" - and arguing. What I wanted though was to be able to talk to my parents. This never happened. I can recall only one time sitting down at the kitchen table talking to my parents. That was the day I left home. I cried that day, not because I was leaving home but because it was sad to see them trying to talk me out of leaving. It seemed as though they suddenly had so much to say.

When I think back to my childhood, there was never any talks between parent and child.

Our home was filled with sounds and lots of noise from sunup to sundown beginning with my parents alarm clock.

The day would unfold with my father in the shower, bathroom filled with steam from the hot water, he'd be singing and whistling to the music from the radio in the bathroom as we tried to catch a few extra minutes of sleep. Our alarm clock was the aroma of fresh coffee brewing and the sound and smell of sizzling bacon as my mother prepared breakfast. As my father finished, we'd all rush to get to the bathroom trying to beat each other, in our haste to get ready for school. We resembled soldiers in boot camp, trained to do everything by the book and by the clock. Funny thing though, I don't remember who did the training. I assume it was my mother, she seem the most likely person, but I have no vivid memory of her talking to me about personal hygiene or about the "birds and the bees".

Because of this, I was never able to express myself verbally, or communicate on an adult level. Our (the children) opinion about family matters was never sought, hence family discussions was something I knew nothing about. I think this prevented my volcabulary from expanding to adult level and directly affected my self esteem.

I have not allowed this to happen to my children. I want my children to be able to talk to me and my husband whenever there is a need. I knew that if I wanted things to be different, I would have to make some changes. I first started by improving my volcabulary and communication. I spend a lot of time reading going to the library and using the dictionary and thesaurus whenever I need to know the correct spelling, pronounciation, definition and use of a word. I spend time with my children, listening to them when they talk to my husband and myself as well as when they talk to their friends. I don't just listen, I try to understand how they feel. I also encourage them to talk openly to us about problems or questions they might have and help them find solutions and answers to those problems. Also, including them in family decisions helps them develop a sense of importance and builds self-esteem.

Family communication is very important to me and my family. It isn't perfect yet, but we know it's something that gets better with time and practice.

I can see the benefits of good family communication in my children, my husband and myself. We've learned to talk to each other, express our thoughts and opinions and work out our problems together.

The group thought this was much better. However, they felt she had given up some of the good visual details that they had liked so much in draft #1. They asked her to try to give small stories that might illustrate her ideas more clearly. They thought comparing something that her father did to her in response to a specific incident, to something she did to her children, would be useful. Here is the final draft in response to those suggestions.

Writing Assignment #3
Eng. 131/Ginsberg
December 5, 1994

THE DOUBLE EXPERIENCE - DRAFT 6

My experience goes back to 1960. I was 10 years old and commonly referred to by my family and relatives as a loner. I spent the majority of my time alone. After school, I would go to my room and do my homework. When my homework was done, I would read until dinner time. Occasionally, I would fall asleep, skipping dinner. I come from a family of 8 children. The only place I could study in peace was my bedroom, which I shared with one of my five sisters. My sister loved NOT doing her homework, so I basically had the room to myself until bedtime.

From time to time, I would just sit by my window, watching the birds and squirrels playing on the lawns and in the trees. It was so peaceful.

My house was busy with activity and noise from sun-up to sun-down. Some of this activity was pleasant, and some was not so pleasant. There was always plenty of talking and arguing. Maybe this is what contributed to me wanting to be alone so much. I didn't want to be involved in any type of disagreement whatsoever.

I recall one occasion (and I don't remember what the circumstances were), being reprimanded by my father. This big looming figure stood before me yelling as loud as I could.

The tone of his voice frightened me and the resonance resembled that of a ferocious wild animal.

I was petrified!

Even though I knew this was my father, it didn't seem like him. I was afraid to move, let alone say anything to defend myself, or try to explain whatever it was I had done wrong.

I remember we were standing in the kitchen, and I knew I was going to get a spanking (or whipping, as it was called in my family), so I blanked out everything my father was saying and plotted my escape route.

My plan was to run under the kitchen table, weave around the table legs, brake for the back door and keep running. I figured I could out-run him and he would never catch me.

I had listened to the sounds of my siblings being punished by my father and I knew what I was in for. I didn't think I could survive if I hung around and let him whip me.

Too late!

He must have caught me off-guard. I got a whipping I will never forget.

One minute he was yelling - the next minute - WHAM!!

I felt totally helpless. I felt there was nothing any- body could do to save me.

That was enough to make me withdraw into a shell.

I never did anything to upset my father again. I got good grades in school and stayed out of trouble at home.

I spoke to my father only when I had to. My response to his questions were "Yes", "No", or "I don't know".

Because of this, I never expressed myself verbally, and my communication and vocabulary skills never fully developed to an adult level. This directly affected my self-esteem. I was always afraid of saying the wrong thing to people.

Turning the pages in the book of my life, here I am married, the mother of 5 children. The year is 1986. My 17 year old daughter is in her senior year in high school, when I receive a telephone call at work one day.

"Mrs. Schooler, this is Gail Mineci, Ronda's counselor at Ferndale". My heart stopped. I thought my daughter had been hurt and taken to the hospital.

"Yes, I said, is Ronda alright"?

"Well, not really. Ronda was involved in a physical confrontation with another student and must be expelled from school for a week, after which you or your husband will have to meet with the principal before she can return to school".

I was furious with my daughter!

My daughter - an honor student since 1st. grade through high school, a member of the National Honor Society, ranking 5th in her graduating class, with scholarships waiting for her after graduation - "involved in a physical confrontation"!

No way!

I was stunned. I couldn't wait to get home to Ronda to let her know how disappointed I was in her. This was going to get her grounded for at least 2 weeks!

I left work immediately.

On my way home, as I was going over everything I planned to say to my daughter, I flashed back to that day in the kitchen with my father. It occurred to me I hadn't even thought about asking my daughter what had happened. It was then that I realized that we had no family communication when I was growing up. I didn't communicate with my family either. It never dawned on me until that day that I was guilty of the same thing I accused my father of - not discussing anything with us, not wanting to hear our side of the story before taking a course of action. We were always "guilty as charged".

I thought of all the times in the past that I had spanked my kids without giving them a chance to explain.

I decided I had to change.

I called my husband and informed him of the situation with our daughter. He suggested we wait until he got home from work before we took any action.

That evening, after talking to Ronda, and the next day after meeting with the principal, witnesses confirmed my daughter's version of what happened. The confrontation was provoked by the other student involved. My daughter's suspension was recinded and she was allowed to return to school the next day.

After talking to my husband about my feelings and telling him how concerned I was about the importance of family communication, we decided to make an extra effort to listen to our children. We started by having "family talks", including our kids in family decisions and encouraging them to express their opinions with us as much as possible.

I've noticed the change in myself, my relationship with my husband and my children. My relationship with my parents and specifically with my father has improved immensely.

Learning to communicate has made a big difference in the way we talk to each other and the way we live.

Notice that we have omitted some of Brenda's drafts in this study of her work. In addition to getting the suggestions of the group and her instructor, she also worked with a tutor on refining her ideas. Because she had input from so many different sources, she was able to really move forward with her drafts. The end product is something she took great pride in.

STUDENT WRITER AT WORK—
DENNIS YOUNKIN

Dennis took Jennifer's class in the fall of 1994. When given free reign to write about whatever he wanted, Dennis chose to discuss the importance of a letter that his father had written to him. Here is the untitled first draft:

Dennis Younkin

UNTITLED - DRAFT 1

When I was young I never felt special. I always felt ~~a lit- tle~~ slow. like I didn't have what it takes to make it in school. At the end of my fifth grade year my parents told me I was going to take a reading class that would help me read faster. I was reading at a second grade level. I re- member feeling bad about myself because I wasn't like all the other kids in my class, and they would make fun of me. For the next two years I worked very hard at my reading skills and within two years was reading at my normal level.¶After I went to high school I lost interest and took classes that I needed just to get by. The grades I made were just average, ~~and plus I was never any good at sports either~~.

   As I got older I wanted to know how my parents did as they were growing up. Maybe deep down in side I wanted to find some anwsers as why I have so many problems with school. Both of them did fairly well, and my father made As' and Bs'. I think at that time there was alittle jeal- ousy against my parents because it seemed school came easy for the most part for them.

   Ever since my sixth grade year I wanted to join the Marines. Maybe part of it was watching all those war movies on tv. The Marines are toughest miliatry the United States has, and it was a chance for me to be on my own. College was not on my list for things to do because the last thing I wanted to do was go through sixth grade, and knowing that I would have to start school all over again.

Two months had passed and we had been in the field for three days. mail was the most important thing you could get in boot camp. It seems the only thing that links you to the outside world. I remember smiling every time I heard my name called during mail call. I would red the return address first to know where it came from. The guys in my squad would share there letters with others who didn't get mail. It was a way to help everyone cope with being away from home.

The letter I received that day was from my dad. I was surprised because he had never written before. In this letter he told me " I'm proud of you". At that moment my body was overwhelmed with pride unlike being a Marine. I remembered all that hard work I put into reading and trying to be like the other kids in my class. Now I felt was one up on then.

Ten years later the letter was on my mine. Why after all these years would those four words effected me so much. The letter is torn and faded from many reading. I pull it out every now and then to make sure its still around. I let my wife read the letter after six months of marriage. She smiled and told me "it was nice". She didn't understand but neither do I still. I thought I know the answer it was so easy. Because of feeling down about myself and feeling alittle jealous toward my parents. I thought the answer was I just wasn't proud of myself. I'm back to where I started, and not knowing why the letter is still around.

The group wanted Dennis to tell more about why this letter was so special to him. They felt there was something about the relationship that they did not yet understand that might help them see why this letter was so meaningful. They also wanted more of a feel for how hard this experience in boot camp was. Dennis incorporated many of those suggestions into his next version, called "The Letter."

Dennis Younkin

THE LETTER — DRAFT 2

When I was young I was never special, at the end of my fifth grade year. I remember my parents sitting down with me and telling me that next year I would be going to some special reading classes. They told me that I just don't learn as fast as other kids. I remember working very hard because I wanted to be like the other kids in my class.Within two years I was reading up to speed. but then when I when to high school I lost interest and I took classes that I needed just to get by. the grades I made in high school were just average plus I was never any good at sports either I played one year of football and two years of city baseball.

As I got older I wanted to know how my parents did as they were growing up. I was told that they both did pretty good, my father made A's and B's and played tennis, was quarterback of the football team and was almost Allstate in baseball. After graduation he went into the marines and after 4½ years he got out, went to work for Chrysler Corp. He is now head of the national help desk for chrysler.

Going into my junior year I made the choose to go into the United States Marines more for myself than anything because I knew if I stayed home and didn't go I would be working at McDonalds and having no life. Even though my parents told me they would pay for college, at the time college life wasn't for me. So on my seventeenth birthday I signed the papers to leave in 358 days. People tried to talk me out of going but my mind was made up nobody was going to change my mind. Time flue by and the time came for me to leave, I said my goodbyes and was off with 18 other kids to San Diego Cal where we were going to train.

Hell started when we landed at the airport in San Diego they made us sit on the airplane until everyone else on the plane got off , then the drill Instructor came into the plane and started screaming at the top of him lungs "get off the plane". At that moment total fear consumed my body and all I could think about was why in the hell did I do this I'm going to dye. They ran us to the other side of the airport to get on a bus to go to the base. When we stopped on the base we ran off the bus and recieved our issue and get a haircut. The first few days were long nineteen hours long we had all this testing,shots , classes,more issue,more testing and more shots. In the time of four or five days we were on the receiving end of about nine different shots.

After the first week things I started to get in the swing of things the training is more mind over matter "if you don't mind it don't matter". The day lasted from 4:30am to 9:30pm six days a week and on sunday the first four hours were for going to church,cleaning our rifles, polishing our boots and writing letters. The drill instructors called it constructed time I had been away from home for about two months and home was just a place you could only remember in your dreams. A place you never wanted to forget at least until you leave this place.

We had been out in the field for about 3 days and the mail from home was the most important thing you can get in boot camp, It seemed the only thing that linked you to the outside world. I remember every letter I received well I was gone and the first thing i would do would be read the return address so I knew were it came from. The guys in my squad would share there letters with every one so none felt left out. I can remember some of those days where I didn't receive any mail and you feel left out and forgotten. reading someones mail is fine but its just not from home.

The only thing was,this letter was from my dad. I was surprised because I had never recieved a letter from him before. I started to read the letter and I couldn't believe what I was reading My dad was proud of me,I never thought I would hear that from him. A wave of pride came over my body unlike the pride of being a marine. I'm sure everybody wants there parents to be proud of them for what they have become. Now after ten years of having the letter and carrying it all over the world with me the first four years . The letter is a white piece of lined paper and is torn and faded, from the many times it has been read. its the only letter i ever kept from those days. I pull it out every now and then just to make sure it still around.

As sometimes happens, Dennis took the suggestions of the group, and they didn't quite do what the group had wanted. They felt the added marines parts distracted from his main point. Also, they still weren't clear why this was such a troubled relationship for Dennis. Dennis himself wondered if he ought to do more to explain why he felt he failed his father for so long. This paragraph, then, about finding his father's childhood report card, became an important part of his next version. He also took a suggestion that a group member had about figuring out why he still thought so much about the letter and began to incorporate it into the end.

Dennis Younkin
Paper #1

NEVER FEELING SPECIAL - DRAFT 4

When I was young I never felt special. I always felt slow, like I didn't have what it takes to do good in school. At the end of my fifth grade year, my parents told me I was going to take a reading class. At that time I was reading at a second grade level. I remember feeling bad about myself because I wasn't like all the other kids in my class. I thought if they knew about my problem they would all laugh and make fun of me. For the next two years I worked very hard at my reading skills. By time I went to high school I was reading at my grade level. Throughout my high school years I lost interest and only took classes that I needed.

One day during my summer vacation of my freshman year, me and my grandmother were going through drawers of junk. She wanted to know what was in them. Seeing how see hadn't opened them in years. I pulled a stack of papers out and there was sitting in the drawer was a envelope with my dad's name on it. I asked her, "what was inside." She said "your dad's report cards." "Oh yea can I see them" wanting to know how he did in school. "Sure," she said and like a kid on Christmas morning I opened the envelope. He received As' and Bs' through all of school. At that moment a little jealousy against my dad leaked into my brain. It wasn't the answer of why I had so many problems with school.

Ever since my sixth grade year I wanted to join the Marines. Not having to go through more school and thinking by joining the Marines I would be getting out of school. College was not on my list. The last thing was I didn't want to do was go thru sixth grade again. Little did I know at the time I would spent almost a year in school for aircraft in the Marines. By the end of my junior year, I was leaving for boot camp right after high school.

Two months had passed and we had been in the field for three days. Mail was the most important thing you could get in the boot camp. It seems the only thing that links you to the outside world. I remember smiling every time I heard my name called during mail call. I would read the return address first to know where it came from. The guys in my squad would share there letters with the others who didn't get mail.

The letter I received that day was from my dad. I was surprised because he had never written before. In the letter it said, "I'm proud of you." At that moment my body was overwhelmed with pride unlike being a Marine. My dad being someone I looked up to,saying those words made me feel better than any A or B could ever in school.

Ten years later, I still have the letter. Every now and then I pull it out to make sure it is still around. The letter is torn and faded from many readings. I let my wife read the letter six months after we got married. She told me it was nice. She didn't understand but neither do I. Speculation is all I have for the letter. Not being able to figure out one clear reason for still having it. It really doesn't matter anymore. I can honestly say I can let the memory rest from now on. Most of all, I'm happy with this outcome.

You may find this final discussion still lacking some meaning. If you were in Dennis's next group, what might you tell him about it? What things might you praise him for that he has done up to this point? Dennis's paper is interesting to examine as a case study because he tried several things that failed. Ultimately though, those failures helped him to clarify what he did want to say.

STUDENT WRITER AT WORK—
REGINA BERARDI

Gina was a student in R.J.'s class during the fall of 1995. Her paper on AIDS stereotypes was written in response to the "Responding to an Essay" assignment you find in Chapter 5. Here we're beginning with her second draft; it differs little from the first, which is a common situation when a writer is struggling with her topic, with what she wants to say. This was a very difficult paper for Gina to write, and it took her some time to even come up with a first draft. So even after her first group, she still felt she had too many unanswered questions and not enough solid ideas of how to revise. Thus, her second draft has few changes from the first. We think you can see, though, that as a first or second draft, Gina has a lot to work with here:

Regina Berardi
English 131
Dr. Willey
10/13/95
Paper #2, Draft #2

In America today we not only view stereotyping and prejudice as a reality, but we also accept them as a constant factor in our lives. We see and hear it everyday on either television talk shows, in magazines ads, through gossip at the office, from the "clicks" at school, and even from family and friends. Robert Heilbroner clearly illustrates in his article how easy it is to stereotype and how often we do it. He also tells us how our preconceived notions or "standardized pictures" play a very large part in our perception of other people and of the world around us. For example, he tells us about a stereotypical situation, gives us possible reasons why this person or persons are stereotyping, then he takes you through the process and describes possible ways that we can modify this type of behavior. Heilbroner takes a very unique approach in explaining how and why we stereotype. He does an in depth analysis on the "traditional" approach that stereotype and prejudice are an inherited trait, took that information he found and specifically elaborates on all the different aspects of stereotypical behaviors.

Stereotyping comes in many different forms and affects us all in different ways as Heilbroner shows us in his article. One thing that he didn't discuss in the article was how stereotypes are taken so far sometimes that they can affect our own personal health and well being. Take AIDS for instance. When the public first became aware of the AIDS virus in 1981, it was already taking the lives of many people predominately in the gay community. Immediately, the stereotype that AIDS was only a "homosexual" disease was born. A short time after that we discovered that intravenous drug users were also contracting this disease through the sharing of needles, and from that another stereotype was born. In the minds of many Americans this was the truth. "You can't get AIDS unless you are gay or you use drugs." These were only the first of many stereotypes to come over the years as the AIDS epidemic grew larger.

By the late 80's and early 90's, AIDS had begun taking the lives of people in the heterosexual community. The media began to stress how important it was to protect ourselves in every possible way from this incurable disease. From this we started a whole new set of stereotypes. People thought that you could get AIDS from casual contact like, hugging, kissing and holding hands. We started to develop a prejudice against people with this virus. We no longer wanted them to have any part in society. We banned children that had AIDS from going to school and intentionally fired anyone we knew or even suspected had the AIDS virus. The Oscar winning movie Philadelphia is a perfect example of how unfairly a person with AIDS was treated in the workplace. The strong influence of stereotypes had not only taken over the minds of many Americans but was also taking away the constitutional rights of people with AIDS.

Today in 1995 the stereotypes of the past have been proved wrong by the medical field, and through education many of us have have learned to overcome these stereotypes of the past, though we still continue to stereotype people with this disease. They are still looked down upon as if they have committed some kind of crime. We view them as "dirty and "immoral." When we hear about someone with AIDS we automatically assume that their sexual promiscuity is the reason they contracted the AIDS virus. Stereotypes about AIDS are inevitable, for the simple fact that we use them to protect us from the reality of this deadly disease.

The teenagers and young adults of the world today are in the high risk area for contracting the AIDS virus. They are also very gullible to the stereotypes about AIDS that they hear from their peers. Some of the most common stereotypes that we hear in this age group about AIDS are that "you can't get the virus the first time you have sex", or that "you can't catch the virus if you are young and healthy." For some reason teenagers seem to think that they are not prone to this disease. They say "It won't happen to me, I use protection." That is just another misconception that makes them so vulnerable to this disease because it is a fact that condoms do not always work nor are they always applied and removed properly. ~~This is the reason that the media, parents and school administrators should be preaching "abstinence" and not "condoms."~~

Stereotypes are an unnecessary evil that somehow we can not seem to shake from our minds. In most cases their negativity is harmful to our own individuality and even more damaging to the person who is being stereotyped. Like AIDS, there is no cure for stereotyping. It is a disease that we all have inside of us. This is something we all have done at some time or another. If you haven't yet stereotyped,

it can almost be guaranteed that you will sometime find
yourself going into a situation with preconceived notions
or prejudgments.

The group was enthusiastic about Gina's draft. They all agreed that
she was indeed doing what the assignment asked her to do: she has
directly reacted to the assigned essay by summarizing what she feels
are the author's main points, and she has gone on to develop her own
examples of stereotyping in her world, focusing specifically on AIDS
stereotypes.

About the only thing the group took exception with in this draft is
the sentence you see lined out right before her last paragraph. The
group agreed that this statement about abstinence, while perhaps flowing logically enough from the ideas in the essay, took the essay off in
the wrong direction. The essay is about stereotyping, they said, not
about preaching or arguing abstinence. That statement may be a good
one in an argumentative essay, but it was out of place in Gina's stereotyping paper. Gina agreed, lining the sentence out as she sat in group.

This group spent most of its time helping Gina figure out how to be
more specific. Not everyone had seen *Philadelphia,* for example, so
Gina obviously couldn't assume everyone in her audience would be familiar with it. Tell us more about the movie, they asked. *Show* us how
it dealt with AIDS stereotypes.

The conversation came around to Ryan White, whose life became a
very public and celebrated case fairly early on during the AIDS epidemic. As they talked, the group recalled some details about Ryan
White, and Gina would go on to read a little more to aid her own recall. All agreed that Ryan would be an excellent example of how
stereotyping AIDS sufferers can lead to discrimination.

By the time Gina turned her third draft in to R.J., she had a good,
strong essay. We won't reproduce the third draft here, either, because
the only area that needed more work was her conclusion. The third
draft ended on a pretty down note, sounding almost as if there was simply nothing to be done about stereotyping, that it was an inescapable
fact of life. Talking with Gina, R.J. realized that this really wasn't the
way she wanted to end her essay; she really wanted us to take note and
try to change the way we think, especially the way we think about
AIDS. So in her final draft, Gina tries to do just that and has better success than with the ending of her third draft.

Here is Gina's final draft; we think you can see what good use she
made of the advice she received from her group and her instructor:

Regina Berardi
English 131
Dr. Willey
11/27/95
Paper #3, Draft #4

AIDS, A FACT OF LIFE

In America today we not only view stereotyping and prejudice as a reality, but we also accept them as a constant
factor in our lives. We see and hear it everyday on either
television talk shows, in magazines ads, through gossip at
the office, from the "clicks" at school, and even from family and friends. Robert Heilbroner clearly illustrates in
his article, "Dont let stereotypes warp your judgments,"
how easy it is to stereotype and how often we do it. He
also tells us how our preconceived notions or "standardized pictures" play a very large part in our perception of
other people and of the world around us. For example, he
tells us about a stereotypical situation, gives us possible reasons why this person or persons are stereotyping ,
then takes us through the process and describes possible
ways that we can modify this type of behavior. Heilbroner
takes a very unique approach in explaining how and why we
stereotype. He does an in depth analysis on the "traditional" approach that stereotyping and prejudice are an
inherited trait, takes that information he found, and
specifically elaborates on all the different aspects of
stereotypical behaviors.

Stereotyping comes in many different forms and affects
us all in different ways, as Heilbroner shows us in his
article. One thing that he didn't discuss in the article
is how stereotypes are taken so far sometimes that they
can affect our own personal health and well being. Take

AIDS for instance. When the public first became aware of the AIDS virus in 1981, it was already taking the lives of many people, predominately in the gay community. Immediately, the stereotype that AIDS was only a "homosexual" disease was born. A short time after that we discovered that intravenous drug users were also contracting this disease through the sharing of needles, and from that another stereotype was born. In the minds of many Americans this was the truth: "You can't get AIDS unless you are gay or you use drugs." These were only the first of many stereotypes to come over the years as the AIDS epidemic grew larger.

By the late 80's and early 90's, AIDS had begun taking the lives of people in the heterosexual community. The media began to stress how important it was to protect ourselves in every possible way from this incurable disease. From this we started a whole new set of stereotypes. People thought that you could get AIDS from casual contact such as, hugging, kissing, and holding hands. We started to develop a prejudice against people with this virus. We no longer wanted them to have any part in society. We banned children who had AIDS from going to school and intentionally fired anyone we knew or even suspected had the AIDS virus.

The Oscar winning movie *Philadelphia* is a perfect example of how unfairly a person with AIDS was treated in the workplace. The movie is based on the true story of Andrew Beckett, a young prominent attorney with a major law firm in Philadelphia. Beckett had just received a major promotion and was on his way to becoming a senior partner with the firm. Unfortunatly, before he got the chance to advance any further, a co-worker discovered he had the AIDS virus and that he was gay. The nightmare for Beckett began. He was no longer the portrait of perfection and excellence he once was. It seemed that overnight he became the butt of cruel locker room jokes about homosexuals by his co-workers. Almost immediately he was set up by the firm to look incompetent then fired supposedly for that reason only. The actual truth that Andrew Beckett was fired because he had AIDS.

Beckett was determined to fight this unlawful accusation by the firm. Through the long process of finding an attorney to defend an AIDS victim and the long process in court, Beckett was successful in proving that his termination was not due to incompetance but was the result of discrimination and ignorance. Thus, this is an example of how the strong influance of stereotypes had not only taken over the minds of many Americans but was also comprimising the constitutional rights of people with AIDS.

Ryan White was another victim of ignorance, stereotyping, and AIDS. Ryan was born with hemophilia, a disease in which the blood does not clot in the normal amount of time that it should. Living in the small town of Kokomo, Indiana, he led a normal life. Ryan was an honor student about to start junior high at Western Middle School, which was in Russiaville a few miles outside of Kokomo. In order for Ryan to remain healthy he had to use a blood product called Factor VIII, which was distributed to him by his mother almost daily. During the time he was receiving this product doctors were just begining to find out more about the contraction of AIDS and were not yet screening blood or blood products for AIDS. It wasn't until 1984 that there was any warning about AIDS and blood transfusions. By that time it was to late. Ryan was starting to get very sick. First he was diagnosed with hepatitis, then with pnemonia, and finally with AIDS.

The news spread like wildfire through this small town. Just like Andrew Beckett, Ryan was immediatly labled an outcast,and the media circus began. Longtime friends of Ryan and his family were seen on television saying that they saw him spitting on vegtables in the grocery store. Others said that Ryan was always a cronic biter in school. These accusations could not have been further from the truth, and Ryan was determined not to let this get in the way of him returning to school, but school was not ready for him. Some parents refused to send their children to school, and others warned their children to avoid any con- tact with Ryan. This hysteria led to the school banning Ryan. People thought they could get AIDS from Ryan if he sneezed or coughed on them. The sterotypes were so blown out of proportion that Ryan and his family could not go any place outside of their home without causing complete panic to the community. Therefore, Ryan and his family were forced to leave town, and start all over again not know- ing if they were going to face the same impossible obsta- cles as they did in Kokomo.

Fortunatly for Ryan he was able to go to school in his new town, and the people there were very compasionate and understanding about his disease. In the years to come Ryan turned from a victim of AIDS into a fighter and advocate for the prevention of this disease. In the hope to end the stereotyping and prejudice, he began educating children and adults all over the world about AIDS.

Today in 1995 the stereotypes of the past have been proven wrong by the medical field, and through education many of us have learned to overcome these stereotypes of the past, though we still continue to stereotype people with this disease. They are still looked down upon as if they have committed some kind of crime. We view them as "dirty" and "immoral." When we hear about someone with AIDS, we automatically assume that their sexual promiscuity is the reason they contracted the AIDS virus. Stereotypes about AIDS are inevitable, for the simple fact that we use them to protect us from the reality of this deadly disease.

The teenagers and young adults of the world today are in the high risk area for contracting the AIDS virus. They are also very gullible to the stereotypes about AIDS that they hear from their peers. Some of the most common stereotypes that we hear in this age group are that "you can't get the virus the first time you have sex," or that "you can't catch the virus if you are young and healthy." For some reason teenagers seem to think that they are not prone to this disease. They say, "It won't happen to me; I use protection." That is just another misconception that makes them so vulnerable to this disease because it is a fact that condoms do not always work nor are they always applied and removed properly.

Stereotypes are an unnecessary evil that somehow we can not seem to shake from our minds. In most cases their negativity is harmful to our individuality and even more damaging to the person who is being stereotyped. Ryan White and Andrew Beckett are both victims of a cruel society in which the truth is based on bias that we hear through the media or rumors that we pass on amongst each other. The fact of the matter is that as with AIDS, there is no cure for stereotyping at this time. Stereotypes about AIDS are inevitable for the simple fact that we use them to protect us from the reality of this disease, but we can change this unacceptable way of thinking. We can use the teachings and examples given to us by people like Andrew Beckett and Ryan White, to expand our knowledge of this disease, and pass it on to

others. Stereotyping is something we all have done at some
time or another. If you haven't yet stereotyped, it can almost be guaranteed that you will sometime find yourself going into a situation with preconceived notions or prejudgments, but we can put those feelingˢto an end by looking at
both sides of the situation before we make a judgment.

It is always interesting to see real work evolve. The papers represented here are varied in their skill level, their attention to detail, their
final polish. What they all have in common is a commitment to change
and improvement through revision. No writer can make the kinds of
true revisions needed to satisfy a reader merely by anticipating their
readers' responses. That is why individual and group feedback is the
cornerstone of a writing workshop.

STUDENT WRITER AT WORK—
MARY ANN KIRMA

Mary Ann thought a lot about how she wanted to approach her argument paper. She knew that because her family had been on welfare, she
had a unique perspective to present to her audience. She struggled a lot
in her prewriting stage with how she could frame her point of view.
Here is the first draft that she brought to group:

Mary Ann Kirma

Eng 131

Paper 6 Draft 1

~~Some people say that~~ our welfare system ~~is being~~ abused by
lazy people who take advantage of it. They say that people
who are on welfare don't try hard enough to find a job. There
are many myths about welfare. They say a typical recipient
is on welfare forever. Or that they make a fortune on welfare. Although a small percentage of recipients abuse the
system it also helps many people who are unfortunate.

There was a time in my life when my family was on welfare. My father who supported our family had been working

as a janitor at Chrysler Corp. for fifteen years. We were happy and satisfied with what we had, until one day my father who was the only person with an income, got laid off. This scared him very much. How was he going to support a wife and three kids without a job? It was difficult for him to find another job due to his lack of education and experience outside of janitorial work. My fathers search for a job began. He needed to find a job that paid him enough to support our family. He also wanted a job that provided some kind of health insurance like his job at Chrysler. After a year, my father ran out of the money he had saved. He had no choice but to apply to the welfare system. He needed help until he was able to get back on his feet. The system provided us with food stamps, which was what we used to buy food. We also received Medicare, which was health insurance. A check was also issued to us of $450 a month. This was the only way he could take care of us.

Give some ideas of how to change it. Talk about the struggle on welfare. Was it embarrassing? Was $450 a month worth the embarrassment? Did your life style change? Why was it so hard?

A year later, my father was called back to work at Chrysler. As soon as he returned we were able to stop relying on welfare. I don't know what would have happened to my family if there was no social welfare. It helped us during a rough time. I'm proud to say that we have a good welfare system. It has helped many people like my family through financial obstacles. The government wants to take welfare away even though it does not cost them very much when you think of the benefits. It provides medical care for the poor and elderly that have no one to take care of them. Most of all, welfare helps children who have no control over their lives. Try to image if there was no welfare. There would be so many people struggling. Welfare is for those who need the help. Unfortunately, people do abuse welfare, but we must remember the family's that depend on it to turn their lives around when they become the victims of unfortunate circumstances. They deserve that chance.

Her group was very interested in this draft, particularly because many of the members had always been critical of social programs like welfare. They felt that her strongest angle was the personal one. They wanted to hear more of her feelings, her family's experiences. Fresh from that first group, she wrote this list on the bottom of her paper:

Talk more about the struggle on welfare.

Was it embarrasing?

Did your life style change?

Why it was so hard?

Talk about how I would change it.

Certainly you can see how many valuable ideas Mary Ann got from her group. Instead of being faced with the need to revise but little idea how, she is ready to face a new draft with lots of areas to work on. It was now up to Mary Ann to incorporate the ideas given to her into future drafts.

Her next draft was problematic, for she seemed to feel overwhelmed by all her choices. She tinkered here, tinkered there, then brought an only marginally changed copy back to the next group. It was then clear that she needed even more specific guidance. The group went through the second half of her text with her and pointed to specific passages they thought could use expansion. Once she got a better idea where these things might go, she was able to go back to her original list and really work with it. Here is Mary Ann's much improved third draft:

Mary Ann Kirma
Eng 131
Paper 6 Draft 2

Some people say that our welfare system is being abused by lazy people who take advantage of it. Critics of social program say that people who are on welfare don't try hard enough to find a job. There are many myths about welfare. Critics say a typical recipient is on welfare forever. Or that they make a fortune on welfare. Although a small percentage of recipients abuse the system it also helps many people who are unfortunate.

There was a time in my life when my family was on welfare. My father who supported our family had been working as a janitor at Chrysler Corp. for fifteen years. We were happy and satisfied with what we had, until one day my father who was the only person with an income, got laid off. This scared him very much. How was he going to support a wife and three kids without a job? ~~My father's search for a job began.~~ It was difficult for him to find another job due to his lack of education and experience outside of janitorial work. My father was born in another country so he had a language difficulty. He needed to find a job that paid him enough to support our family. He also wanted a job that provided some kind of health insurance like his job at Chrysler. After a year, my father ran out of the money he had saved. He had no choice but to apply to the welfare system. He needed help until he was able to get back on his feet. Being on welfare our life style changed. My parents used to take us out every week to see a movie and have dinner. We were no longer able to afford this. I remember that year when I started high school. I wanted to go shopping to buy back to school clothing. My parents told me that I had to wear what ever I had.

The system also provided us with food stamps, which was what we used to buy food. I recall going to the super market with my mother. We were standing in line when a friend of my mother stood behind us. After a few minutes my mother pretended that she had forgotten an item. She was to embarrassed to let her friend know we were on welfare. We also received Medicare, which was health insurance. A check was also issued to us of $450 a month. This was not enough money. By the time my father paid his bills, we were left with nothing to spend.

An unexpected tragedy happened while we were on Welfare. My sixteen year old brother became paralyzed from the chest down due to an Arterio Vascular Malformation on the spinal cord. He spent three months in the hospital. If we were not on welfare, we probably would still be in debt.

A year later, my father was called back to work at Chrysler. As soon as he returned we were able to stop relying on welfare. I don't know what would have happened to my family if there was no social welfare. It helped us during a rough time. My parents learned from this experience. My mother got a part time job. She wanted the security so that this wouldn't happen again. Since I was in high school, I was old enough to get a job. From this experience I've learned how money can drastically change your life.

I'm proud to say that we have a good welfare system. It has helped many people like my family through financial obstacles. The government wants to take welfare away even though it does not cost very much when you think of the benefits. I agree that there could be some changes made because of those who abuse the system. For example if a recipient is not disabled, they should be able to find a job after a year. If they don't try to find a job the government should reduce their pay. If on welfare have limits on how many children a family can have. The government should have regular check ups on families on welfare. This will help the system to cut back on fraud.

Welfare provides medical care for the poor and elderly that have no one to take care of them. Most of all, welfare helps children. Image if there was no welfare. There would be so many people struggling. Unfortunately, people do abuse welfare, but we must remember the families that depend on it to turn their lives around when they become the victims of unfortunate circumstances. They deserve that chance.

Start with images - what if there was no welfare?
More feeling

The process of this paper teaches us much about the value of multiple stages of revision. Mary Ann got very solid help in her first group, however, she needed time and space to understand how best to use that advice. She just wasn't able to do what she wanted with her second draft. It took a more specific second group to get her on track. Different groups serve different purposes at different times in the process of writing and revising. Students who are just learning to work in groups are often frustrated because they feel they get conflicting advice from groups made up of different people. Some of this may feel frustrating, but it is all quite productive. First, people just need to get different kinds of help at different times. There is no use in explaining certain things when other things take precedence at this time. If a paper needs much help in organization, we may not spend a lot of time discussing expansion of a small idea. Yet once those organizational concerns are addressed, we may notice how much more needs adding to a given section. Second, even advice that is not taken is part of the process of learning to revise. We ask our students to carefully consider the ideas of everyone in a group. And we know full well that not all ideas will be helpful. Thinking through the process, though, is part of thinking through as a writer.

SOME COMMON GRAMMAR, MECHANICS, AND USAGE ERRORS

16

SENTENCE FRAGMENTS

■ ■

Sentence fragments are one of the really serious sentence-level errors in English. They're serious because fragments can interfere with the readers' ability to make meaning from your text. So it's important that, if you're having some sentence fragment problems, you learn to proofread specifically for that problem, and you learn what strategies you can employ to correct these errors.

A fragment, simply put, is an incomplete sentence, an incomplete thought that cannot stand alone as a sentence. Usually, part of the thought that would make the fragment complete is in the sentence before or after it. That's the most common form of fragment error: The writer tries to make a sentence out of a phrase or clause that should be part of the sentence before or after it. If you were raised on traditional grammar and want to know the technical terms, what we're saying is that most fragments lack either a subject or a verb, which is usually in the sentence before or after the fragment.

A lot of fragments begin with words such as *when, if, whether, which,* or *that,* and the sentence fails to address the questions raised by those words. These are called *dependent word fragments,* and usually you can find the answer to the "when" or the "if" or the "whether" in the next or previous sentence. Once again, those two sentences should probably be put together.

One of the best strategies for finding and correcting these errors is reading your own writing out loud, alone or with a partner or group, and reading only exactly what you've got on the page before you. Time and again, we hear students read their papers and correct their own errors as they read—joining fragments to the proper sentence before or after them. So if you read aloud and give a hard pause at each of your periods, you'll begin to hear the incompleteness of those fragments. Stop, look at the fragment again, then look at what comes before and after it, and see which of those sentences your fragment is dependent on for meaning, for completeness. When you've found it, join the two together, using the advice we've given you about when to use commas and when to use semicolons (see Chapters 17 and 18 on comma splices and run-ons).

If you're able to determine that your fragment problems usually occur when you begin a sentence with a dependent word such as *when,* then you'll always proofread your papers with a special eye out for those words. Target them; then make sure that the "when" gets answered within that sentence.

Here are some sentences we've culled from our students' writing. See if you can find the fragments and figure out how to fix them.

1. My only experience that I can recall is in the eleventh grade when I had to write a report on venereal diseases. Something that caught my attention in high school.

2. I was the kid in class who always acted like he was paying attention, but really I was thinking about other things. What I was going to do Friday night, my girlfriend, or making fun of the teacher in my mind.

3. When I started junior high. My English class was like going to a circus—the teacher never cared if you were present.

4. I have never been fond of writing because I am too afraid to hear what I have written. Afraid of being a little embarrassed, or that someone will not enjoy what took me hours and days to write.

5. If I had to rate this movie. I would give it a four, not on the story but on the graphics that they have in it.

6. From the stories I heard from an LRC teacher, I got the impression that college was supposed to be a lot of book reports and oral reports. Spending every waking moment in the library, researching material for these huge reading assignments. Then giving a 15-20 minute report to the class. Followed by an even bigger project that has to be done along with other classmates.

7. I wrote about what kind of cars we were going to have in the future. What I would be doing in the future. If I would be married, and where I thought I would live in the future.

8. I feel as if she is the only person I can share my true feelings with. Maybe it's because she's in my peer group. Easy to talk to, polite, and only uses good manners when she's in front of an adult.

9. They bother important people by calling them at 7:00 o'clock in the morning. Wake them, and put them on the spot about something they happen to be in the news about.

RUN-ONS

■ ■

Run-on is a term often misused. Most students are led to believe that a run-on is any sentence that's just too long and awkward for some reason. We've often had students tell us they have problems with run-ons, only to read their writing and discover that they don't.

The term *run-on* is used for a couple of different errors. A true run-on is a fused sentence. That's where you run together two complete sentences, complete thoughts, either of which could be written alone as a sentence, without any punctuation at all. They don't have to be long complete thoughts, either; they can be very brief. So run-ons don't necessarily have anything to do with the length of the sentence.

The fused sentence run-on is what this chapter deals with. The other type of run-on, the comma splice, we'll deal with in the next chapter.

Most of our students who have run-on problems self-correct the errors as they read out loud. They insert hard pauses where no such punctuation exists on the page before them. So, as with the fragments, a good strategy for proofreading for run-on errors is to read out loud, alone or to a friend or group, noting the differences between what you have on the page and what you say. As you practice this on the sentences in this chapter, you'll be looking for where you pause. Most of the time you'll be pausing between the two complete thoughts, at the point where some sort of punctuation is necessary to mark the boundaries between the complete thoughts.

What sort of punctuation will you use to correct these and your own run-on errors? Don't insert a comma alone; that would create a comma splice, another sort of run-on error. One choice is to insert a period, making the one sentence into two separate sentences. The nature of most basic writers' run-ons makes this a very common choice. If this is your only remedy, though, chances are you'll end up with another problem—choppiness. All your sentences will be short and of similar structure. You don't want to eliminate one problem like fused sentences in favor of another one. (See chapter 14, "Editing," for a fuller discussion of choppiness.) There are many strategies for eliminating fused sentences. Experiment and use all of them to learn when they are most effective.

If the ideas are closely related, so much so you feel they should be in the same sentence, you have two choices. One is to insert a semicolon between the complete thoughts. That's what semicolons were made for. The other choice is to use a comma with a joining word: *and, but, for, or, no, so, yet.* When you use a comma with a joining word between complete thoughts, you avoid a comma splice.

So see if you can identify the run-ons in these selections from our students' writing, and in each case see if you can figure out what you think would be the best way to correct them.

1. The report was great I did a lot of research on it I even brought in pictures to show the class, which brought a lot of amazement to the students.

2. I don't remember my English experience at that time that much all I remember is that all they would teach us is manners and how to behave ourselves.

3. When I got on the subject of sex it was all over I got really nervous and could not finish.

4. In English the situation was different I had to start all over from scratch.

5. I think if I were ever to write a book, I wouldn't even think about it I would sit down and just write.

6. A sudden rush of fear overwhelmed me I wanted to jump off the bus, yell at the lady to tell her to stop.

7. At the time I didn't feel guilt or remorse for what I had done instead I just pitied myself and sank into depression.

8. Lori hated being pregnant she complained constantly.

Some Common Grammar, Mechanics, and Usage Errors

9. My father and I still have a great relationship in fact I consider him one of my best friends.

10. As I exited the bathroom I ran into a friend from my old neighborhood we went over to the table where I had been sitting and I introduced him to Adam and Jeff.

18

COMMA SPLICES

■ ■

The comma splice is a common sort of run-on error. While it is not the sort of meaning-crippling monster that so many English teachers used to treat it as, it is a hangnail in otherwise good sentences.

Most simply put, a comma splice occurs when you use a comma between two complete thoughts—two parts of a sentence, either of which could stand alone as a sentence. To fix a comma splice, you can do one of several things. You can decide whether one of the joining words *(and, but, for, or, nor, so, yet)* works between the two or more parts of your sentence. If one does, then you can put it before the comma, making this a complete sentence rather than a comma splice; if one does not, then you can exercise other options: a semicolon, a colon, or a period that turns the one sentence into two. It is important to note that one strategy will not work for all comma splices. Turning each comma splice into two separate sentences may cause severe choppiness; using too many semicolons can create too many overly long sentences where the ideas don't really relate closely enough together. Vary your sentence structure to strive for the most natural writing. Once you begin to experiment, you will see how this works.

About the best way we've determined to help students who have comma splice problems is to tell you to do a proofreading specifically for this error. As you read through a draft, stop at every comma you've included. Read what comes before the comma; if it could stand alone as a sentence, you know you need to now read what comes after the comma. If it, too, could stand alone as a sentence, and you have no joining word with the comma, you'll know you have a comma splice.

Once you've identified the comma splice, you can make your decision as to which of the options we've told you about best fixes it. We've discovered that most students' comma splices occur when they're writing ideas that really are closely enough related that they belong in the same sentence, so a very common solution is to turn the comma into a semicolon. As we mentioned in the chapter about run-ons, that's really what semicolons are for—joining together two complete thoughts without a joining word.

Here are some sentences that may or may not contain comma splices; each is taken from our students' writing. See if you can determine which sentences contain comma splices and if you can choose the best option for correcting each.

1. I began writing a letter to my friend several months ago, that letter still sits unfinished in my dresser today.

2. This lady was unbelievable, she would make us write conclusions to every story we read.

3. I remember when I was in high school, the teacher would tell us, "If the grammar and the spelling isn't right, you will have to do the paper over again."

4. I thought this was so unfair, she could've given me a chance on my essays.

5. I went to my teacher at the beginning of the semester for help, I didn't get it.

6. I found out I wasn't the only student suffering, more than half of the class was suffering.

7. We had to define all the words, it was like hell, deep, dark, and red.

8. We had a house on Glen Lake near Traverse City, I had been spending summers there since I was two, and it was very important to me.

9. I looked around the room, it looked like a typical Friday night.

10. Now you're probably wondering where all of this leads, well it all ties in.

19

PRONOUN CASE

■ ■

We know. We know. Our mothers were the same way that many of yours were.

"Can you get Peter and me a snack?" R. J. would ask his mom.

"Peter and *I*," she'd correct him.

"Can you get Peter and *I* a snack?" he'd say.

The trouble is that our moms were wrong, and often.

In the first sentence above, *me* is the correct pronoun to use. And we'll try to teach you a really simple trick you can perform in most sentences that'll help you find the right pronoun most of the time.

The confusion usually arises when there are some other names along with the *I* or the *me*, such as in the sentence above: Peter and me. When you're faced with that situation, just leave the other name or names out of the sentence for a moment, and ask yourself what you'd say without it or them. In the case of our sentence, of course, you would say, "Can you get me a snack?" not "Can you get I a snack?" So, *me* is the right choice.

When Jennifer said to her mom, "Debbie and me are going to the park," and then her mom corrected her to say, "Debbie and *I*," she was right because you'd say, "I am going to the park," not "Me am going to the park." The trick works once again, and you'll find that it will much of the time.

The trick also works on sentences and in situations where you're trying to decide between *he* and *him* or between *she* and *her*. When R. J. said something like "Him and Jimmy went to the store" and his mom corrected him to say, "*He* and Jimmy went to the store," his mom was right. You can tell because you wouldn't say, "Him went to the store." But when Jennifer said, "I gave valentines to both Martha and her," and her mom tried to correct her to say, "I gave valentines to both Martha and *she*," her mom was wrong that time. You can tell because there's no way you'd say, "I gave she a valentine."

You see? (For those of you trying to recall your traditional grammar, what we're talking about here is the difference between objective and subjective pronoun cases. Objective cases are the *me, him, her, them*; subjective cases are the *I, he, she, they*.)

As for the *himself, herself, themselves, myself* (which traditionally are called the *reflexive* pronouns), just be aware that you use those when you're talking about things people do to or for themselves. So you can speak for yourself or watch what some people do to themselves, but if someone asks you who's going to the game Saturday, you're not going to say, "Uh . . . John, myself, Louise, and Amir." That's the case where you need the *I*.

Here are some sentences we've taken from our students' writing. See if you can figure out the correct pronoun.

1. Me and a few of my teammates ended up hanging out with each other a lot and became pretty good friends.

2. I yelled to Frankie to wait up for me. Frankie and me were talking about school and wondering if Timmy would be there.

3. As Joe, Greg, and Josh walked closer, I hung back, easing my way up to the gate. Greg then pulled out his camera and asked Joe and I to pose for this Kodak moment.

4. The guy looked all over town for us, asking around school, the local hangouts, even our church. I mean to tell you, this guy was really gunning for my brother and I.

5. We didn't really expect anything in return. But the lady gave Flo, Eddie, Mark, and I twenty bucks apiece as a reward for finding her poodle.

6. It didn't take long before Amy, Jennifer, and her figured out where they'd gone wrong.

7. Mark, Tony, Mohammed, and myself were the best soccer players that semester.

8. I thought hard about their lives, about how their parents and them had come to America with nothing and made themselves successful.

9. It was a secret only her and I would share.

10. It wasn't until much later that Emily and him decided they'd been wrong.

Chapter

APOSTROPHES

■ ■

They look an awful lot like commas that floated up to the top. Unfortunately, they also cause nearly as many problems as do commas. Apostrophes have very specific uses, but students often have trouble narrowing down those uses and finding the right places for the apostrophe. Remember, an apostrophe has only three primary uses.

First, an apostrophe is used to signal a contraction. Recall that a contraction is two words joined together. The apostrophe allows you to drop one or more of the letters, condensing the word. The apostrophe stands in as a substitute for those deleted letters. As well as being a time and space saver, it helps our writing sound more like our speaking. Listen in on any conversation. Notice how contractions abound.

Example: I do not want to go over my piano scales right now.

becomes

I don't want to go over my piano scales right now.

Other common contractions include *isn't, she'd, haven't, and it's* (for more discussion on this troublesome contraction, see chapter 24, "Mixed Pairs"). Students often have troubles with these kinds of contractions because they misplace the apostrophe. Be certain that it is located in the position that would have been occupied by the letter you are replacing.

Second, apostrophes indicate possession. When we want to indicate that someone (or something) has something else, we use an apostrophe. This is relatively simple when that thing is a tangible object: Courtney's golf clubs, Jess's new television. However, sometimes we want to indicate possession of a thought, idea, or other abstraction. The best way to think about this is to remember that an apostrophe used to indicate possession is really replacing the word *of.* To test for appropriate apostrophe use, remove the apostrophe and replace with the word *of.* If the sentence still makes sense, you've punctuated correctly. For instance, "Mark's idea" really means "an idea of Mark." That does make sense, so you know you've used this apostrophe correctly.

The exception to this rule is the word *its,* which is possessive without the apostrophe. *It's* means "it is," so we form the possessive of this word without the apostrophe.

Third, apostrophes are used to form the plural of letters (A's and B's) and numbers (6's and 8's).

And a final word about apostrophes is necessary—how to use one to indicate plural possession. For example, let's say you have more than one brother, and each has his own room. When referring to their rooms, then, you have a plural noun that needs a possessive apostrophe. In such cases, the apostrophe comes *after* the *s* that ends the plural noun. So in the case of your brothers, you'd write, "My brothers' rooms are larger than mine."

Following are some sentences that students have written. See if you can figure out where the apostrophe errors are and how to correct them:

1. As the semesters flew by, I started to work so hard that I could'nt even see my girlfriend anymore.

2. My customers attitudes are so often so rude. Theyre always treating me like a slave.

3. I got a lot of Cs and Ds in high school; now I am more serious.

4. My husbands obsession with drugs and alcohol made our married life impossible.

5. I borrowed Tonys sweatshirt and never took it off.

Chapter

DANGLING MODIFIERS

In elementary school, R. J. had a teacher, Mrs. H. Mrs. H. was a different sort of teacher when it came to language arts. You see, this was the era where writing instruction dealt mostly with drill in grammar and mechanics, "parsing" (diagramming) sentences, and phonetics, quite unlike the whole language approach that is much more common today. Mrs. H., however, made him write, a lot—book reports, "What I did on my summer vacation," "If I were president of the United States," that sort of thing. One thing above all else could drive Mrs. H. crazy and make her write in red ink all over her students' papers: dangling modifiers, most of which she referred to at the time as "dangling participles." As many of you may have discovered, there are still quite a few Mrs. H.'s around, teachers who will make dangling modifiers seem to be something you should be arrested for.

To put them in perspective—sure, properly placing modifying clauses within sentences is an important skill, and dangling modifiers can occasionally destroy the effectiveness of a given sentence. So you should learn what they are and how to correct them, since we all occasionally dangle a modifier or two and need to eliminate them during proofreading.

You will notice, however, that most sentences with dangling modifiers make sense anyway and that dangling modifiers don't always interfere with the readers' ability to understand the sentence. And this is the very thing that makes them hard to find and correct—they don't stand out the way sentence fragments or fused sentences most often do.

So let's get our terms straight first. A *modifier,* simply put, is a word or a series of words in a sentence that refers to and thus modifies a noun or noun phrase in another clause in the sentence. When you dangle a modifier, we're saying that you haven't provided the noun that it modifies or that you've placed it next to the wrong noun or phrase.

Notice that dangling modifiers most often occur at the beginning of sentences and that very often an *-ing* word, a participle, is part of a dangling modifier. Take this sentence:

Lost in thought, the ringing of the telephone startles me.

First of all, most of us understand the sentence. The person is lost in thought and startled by the ringing of the telephone. The thing you need to understand is that that's not *literally* what the sentence says. According to the rules of English grammar and syntax, the modifying clause "Lost in thought" *must* be followed by the noun that it modifies. The noun would be "I," not "the ringing," because the ringing is not lost in thought. Literally, then, the sentence says that the ringing is lost in thought.

So once you've dangled the modifier, how do you fix it? As a writer, you have choices. Somehow you've got to make the correct noun follow the modifying clause, or you've got to get the correct noun within the clause itself. For our sentence here, you could do this:

Lost in thought, I am startled by the ringing of the telephone.

Here, you've inserted the correct noun after the modifying clause. You could also do this:

Because I am lost in thought, the ringing of the telephone startles me.

Here, you've inserted the noun into the modifying clause (which technically means it's no longer a modifying clause). The choice is yours. Given this sentence, the first option looks better to us.

Now go on to take a look at some other sentences we've found in our students' writing, and see if you can figure out the various alternative ways to "correct" the dangling modifiers in each sentence.

1. When dealing with animals, they can be unpredictable.

Some Common Grammar, Mechanics, and Usage Errors

2. Not knowing that my teacher was going to make us read aloud, she called my name first.

3. After fumbling for my shoes and hunting for my keys, it was already 6:55.

4. After entering, small, neatly lettered signs led me through a maze of hallways and into a large room filled with people.

5. Once inside the bar it was filled with young teeny boppers dancing, drinking, and having a good time.

6. While reaching in her jacket for a smoke, a lighter fell to the ground.

7. While driving down Telegraph, the snow had just begun to fall.

8. Going through Allen Park, traffic was flowing along nicely, but once I entered Dearborn, something strange happened, or to use a more exact word, horrifying.

9. Down one to zero, the looks of chagrin appeared on the faces of all the Falcons.

GENERAL PUNCTUATION

■ ■

Though commas and periods get the most attention, there are many other marks of punctuation that, once mastered, can add depth to your writing. Let's start with the simple ones, the ones that most beginning writers are familiar with and accustomed to using.

The exclamation point (!) This is the punctuation mark that we learn in grade school and really like. If you have access to writing done by grade school-aged children, you will notice that they often rely on this punctuation mark to the exclusion of all others. A child might write, "He is so big!" to emphasize the size of someone. If you think about why, the shortfalls of the exclamation mark in more sophisticated kinds of writing become clear. Children use it because they don't have enough verbal and writing skills to emphasize their points in the ways they wish. They aren't yet able to use metaphors (to compare sizes) or sophisticated sentence structures that modify. Fortunately, you are. This is why exclamation marks should be used very sparingly in college-level writing. They really are just an easy way out, and thus very general. Instead, make your writing exclaim with vivid imagery, similes and metaphors, modifying words and phrases.

This isn't to say that exclamation points should never be used. It is only to ask you to think about what you are substituting them for, and why you aren't using words to express yourself. Any mark of punctuation is a technical tool. It has no real meaning, so don't use it to try to add meaning to your writing.

The question mark (?) Use it to cue a question. It is an interesting quirk of our language that we place the question mark after the sentence, since by then the reader is well aware that you have asked a question. (Other languages such as Spanish place question marks at the beginning and end of sentences that question.) However, this is how it is done. You'll notice that most inquiry sentences begin with indefinite pronouns that question, such as *who, how, which,* and *where.*

The colon (:) Colons are most often used in paper writing to introduce lists. Usually, the list is written as a continuation of the thought, such as "Three of the best foods in the world can be found at Chinese restaurants: egg rolls, wonton soup, fried rice." It can also be used to redefine a statement or to add an example to an explanation. This is the case in the following sentence: "My father brought home the best possible gift: a new dog." In this sentence, "a new dog" is a modifier used to add more information to the object of the sentence, "best possible gift." One final use of the colon is to join two independent clauses when the second one illustrates something about the first. "The best part of golf is its beauty: every course has its own unique look and feel."

The semicolon (;) When you think about the physical characteristics of a semicolon, you can almost guess its correct use. A semicolon is a period on top of a comma; you use it as a mark of punctuation when a period is too strong and a comma is not strong enough. Most often, a semicolon is used to join two independent clauses. Sometimes that sentence will have in it a transitional word like *thus, however,* or *furthermore;* sometimes it will not. In either case, a semicolon will join those two independent clauses into one sentence.

Next are some sentences that students have written, each containing an error in punctuation. Try to locate the error and offer at least one suggestion to fix it appropriately.

1. I have two uncles in my family who have different views on being a successful person, one uncle is a salaried worker for a large corporation.

2. All my life; I was told that high school was a breeze.

3. I never thought to ask, what about me.

4. Moving to a new town at the end of 5th grade was a wonderful opportunity to make new friends Tiffany, Justin, Corie.

5. I went to that class everyday, thus I should have gotten a much better grade.

6. It was a great party!

7. I want to better myself and get more knowledge in Business Administration, then I will follow my father's footsteps into the greatest of all companies Ford Motor.

Chapter

SUBJECT-VERB AGREEMENT

■ ■

For many of us, fortunately, our ears can tell us what verbs go with what subjects. If your native language is English, you will most likely know by instinct that there is something wrong with the sentence: "The dog are eating the bone." Because of the way we have experienced language, we hear the awkwardness of putting a plural verb (are) with a singular subject (the dog). Even if we don't know why it is wrong, we know that it sounds wrong, so it doesn't cause a problem in much of our writing.

There are times, though, when we can't rely completely on our ears to discern correct verbs for the subject. Subjects will either be singular (one thing) or plural (two or more) and corresponding verbs will be either in singular or plural case.

There are certain instances that cause people trouble in trying to maintain subject-verb agreement. In the examples, the subjects have been underlined and the verbs placed in bold.

Two singular subjects joined by *and* take a plural verb:

My <u>friend</u> and my <u>sister</u> **know** how to identify many birds.

Indefinite pronouns take the verb that best represents their meaning:

<u>Each</u> of us in the class **learns** all the software. (Each is singular, so it takes the singular form: learns.)

<u>All</u> students in the class **learn** the software. (*All* is plural, so it takes the plural form: learn.)

Collective nouns are words that stand for a group or unit. When these words stand for the group as a whole, they take the singular verb. When the sentence clearly discerns different members, we use the plural:

The baseball <u>team</u> **has** a losing streak that is a mile long.
The <u>senate</u> **disagrees** on how to handle cutting health-care costs.

These are the three most common classes of words that cause subject-verb errors for beginning writers. Perhaps you will make other errors that you can begin to identify through careful proofreading. If your teacher, another student, or a tutor tells you that you are having agreement problems, try to make it as simple on yourself as possible by recalling that singular subjects take singular verbs, plural subjects take plural verbs.

Following are some sentences that students have written. Some of them are correct, and some have mistakes in subject-verb agreement. See if you can locate the errors and recognize those sentences that are correct.

1. She and I believes that there should be a law that limits the television watching of children.

2. The old foot that presses on the gas of the car doesn't use as much force.

3. A few months ago the class drive to a local nursing home to see the seniors.

4. All people in the room takes several cookies and then left.

5. Physics are my favorite subject.

6. Jodi and Deanne run faster than I do; this caused many problems.

7. Each penny take on a life of its own once out of my hands.

8. Jennifer, Stan, Doris and I takes a bow at the end of the show.

9. The president's cabinet have endorsed the plan.

10. Everyone think he is a good painter; everyone, that is, but him.

MIXED PAIRS

■ ■

Spell checkers are wonderful things. Unfortunately, as we discussed in our section on spelling, they have limitations. One of the limitations is that they aren't as smart as we are. For instance, they can't distinguish usage. Think about the differences in the meaning of the words *no* and *know* in the following sentences: "I can't get no satisfaction" and "I don't know much about history." The difference in these two words may be fairly obvious to many of us; to the computer spell checker, they are both just viable, correctly spelled words. If you mix them up, the computer will never catch your error. You must be able to distinguish between words that sound the same but have different spellings and meanings.

Our students have trouble with the sets of words in the list that follows. After each set, we will give you a brief explanation of how you may best be able to keep them separate in your mind as you go about doing the final editing and proofreading of your paper.

No and *Know: No* is the negative ("The answer is still no"); *know* means "understand" or "recognize" ("I know you better than you know yourself").

There and *Their: There* indicates location ("I want to go there") or is used to introduce an inverted sentence ("There are many great songs"); *their* is the plural possessive ("I went to their soccer game").

To, Too, and *Two: To* forms the infinitive of a verb ("To be or not to be, that is the question") or is used as a preposition to signal where a person or thing is going ("Why not go straight to the moon"); *too* means "also" ("I am going too") or is used as an adverb meaning "excessively" ("It is too hot in here"); *two* is a number less than three, more than one.

Than and *Then: Than* is a comparative word ("I am bigger than you"); *then* shows a relationship between the timing of events ("I went to the show and then on to the mall").

Its and *It's: Its* is a singular possessive ("The table lost its shine"); *it's* is a contraction meaning "it is" ("It's a beautiful day in the neighborhood").

Are and *Our: Are* is the plural form of the verb "to be" ("We are going soon"); *our* is a plural possessive ("This is our favorite meal").

Further and *Farther: Farther* is used to indicate actual measurable distance ("Now that he's moved, he lives much farther away from me"); *further* is used to refer to matters of degree that can't actually be measured ("They fell further and further in love").

Less and *Fewer: Fewer* is used to indicate something than can actually be counted ("There were fewer people at the concert than we expected"); *less* is used when you can't actually count what is being referred to ("I feel less energetic today").

This certainly does not exhaust the list of mixed pairs that give students difficulties, but it does identify some of the most common problems. Before leaving this section, make a list of the words that you have problems with and try to give yourself a concrete example of their correct usage. Perhaps another student, a dictionary, or your instructor can help you with this. Here are some sentences written by students with the problematic word taken out. See if you can determine the correct one.

1. _____ were toys hiding in the boxes and a T.V. on a bench next to it. (*There* or *Their*)

2. We _____ all a little nervous about how she will react to the change. (*are* or *our*)

3. Her soup was so good I wanted seconds _____. (*two, too,* or *to*)

4. After all _____ fighting, it was good to see them kiss and make up. (*there* or *their*)

Some Common Grammar, Mechanics, and Usage Errors

5. My first glove smelled just like a _____ car, so I _____ I would like it. (*knew* or *new*)

6. If you don't _____ where you are going, you might get lost. *(know or no)*

7. It was better _____ a kick in the pants. (*then* or *than*)

8. My writing experiences were little _____ none. (*to, too,* or *two*)

COMMON COMMA USAGE PROBLEMS

Commas are the most difficult form of punctuation to master. Most people never do completely. Part of the problem is that we punctuate our speech much differently from what is called for in standard, written English. The best example is probably: "But, . . ." Many native speakers of English stick that comma after the *but* because that's the way so many of us actually speak. According to the rules of English grammar, though, when a comma is necessary along with the "but," it's going to come *before* it rather than after it.

Another problem is that commas are stylistically loaded. Writers often use them to affect the rhythms of speech or the syntax of sentences, despite hard-core rules saying that a comma might not belong in such and such a spot. Comma rules, maybe more than any of the other rules of grammar, can be broken often when breaking the rules works for the writing. However, breaking the rules is never wise until you have control of how those rules work. You shouldn't try an unorthodox golf swing until you have mastered the correct one. It's the same for punctuation.

So realize going in that what we'll be giving you is advice that should get you by in most instances. Since much expository writing should follow most of the rules of standard, edited English, what follows are pretty good guidelines for you to go by.

We'll approach this by covering the most often broken comma rules and defining where the rules say that commas *should* go; then we'll give you some examples of sentences that need to have commas added according to those rules. We'll try to finish by discussing how the commas actually affect the sentences.

First, you use a comma to separate complete thoughts that are linked together with a joining word—*and, but, for, or, nor, so, yet.* (If you were raised with the more traditional grammar terms, "complete thoughts" are "independent clauses," and "joining words" are "coordinating conjunctions.") Whenever you have a complete thought—something that can stand alone as a sentence by itself—on each side of a joining word, you use a comma *before* the joining word. In the parenthetical sentence above, there's a comma between *clauses* and *and* because each of the clauses is a complete thought. What's a complete thought? Simply, it is a set of words that has a subject (a noun plus its modifiers), has a predicate (a verb plus its modifiers), and expresses a complete idea. If you walked into a room and heard someone say only these few words, you should have a good idea of what they were talking about, for these few words would actually say something.

Second, commas go between *each* item in a series. This is an often-broken rule, partly because the practice in journalism, in most newspapers and magazines, is different. In those fields, what started as a typesetter's convenient shortcut has become practice. So in a newspaper you might read, "The candidate came prepared with notes, a copy of his opponent's book and throat lozenges," but the rules of standard, edited English dictate that you must put a comma before that final *and:* "The candidate came prepared with notes, a copy of his opponent's book, and throat lozenges." If you omit a final comma in a series, you are in effect telling the reader to treat the final two items as parts of a whole, as you would peanut butter and jelly.

Third, commas go after introductory phrases in sentences if the next clause is a complete thought. This is another frequent mistake. You'll notice that our own *first, second,* and *third* are followed by commas and that the clauses that follow the commas are complete thoughts—independent clauses that could stand alone if written as sentences. There are many one-word clauses that are common in English, such as *next, however,* and *furthermore.*

Aside from the one-word variety, introductory clauses can also be several words long. "Aside from the one-word variety" is an introductory clause followed by a complete thought and so preceded by a comma. Think of an introductory clause as a kind of a drumroll. Something, the main part of the sentence, is coming. This clause prepares you for it.

Fourth, commas are used around *interrupters* in a sentence, around words or phrases that add information not absolutely essential to the meaning of the sentence. Earlier we wrote, "This is an often-broken rule, partly because the practice in journalism, *in most newspapers and magazines,* is different." The italicized phrase is added, clarifying information. If you take it out, the sentence will still make perfect sense. This very sentence, another example, makes perfect sense without the added clause, and so we've used commas around it.

Fifth, you use commas between adjectives that modify the same noun. "At home R. J. has a small, white, constantly shedding dog named Calypso." In that sentence, *small* and *white* are adjectives that equally modify *Calypso,* so we put commas between them, and *constantly* and *shedding* work together to form a single modifier, so we didn't put a comma between them.

Sixth, you use commas with dialogue and to separate a person's name during direct address. "So in this sentence," he said, "commas follows *sentence* and *said.* And when we address you directly, Student, a comma also follows your name." This holds true in many cases: "Listen, Sweetheart"; "Hi, Tom,"; "Get a life, Dweeb."

There *are* other commas rules, such as those that pertain to such things as addresses; we've covered the main ones only, and we'll rely on you or your instructor to deal with the rest.

So here are some sample sentences taken from students' work. See if you can determine where commas are necessary.

1. When I first knew that I was going to move to Michigan I was really excited but now I don't know if I have made the wrong choice or not.

2. About one week later I received about a dozen more calls from various organizations some of which I had never heard of asking for donations or orders to buy things that were offered through their companies.

3. I remember getting up in the middle of the night to hide in the bomb shelter and that would sometimes last for a couple of days. It is really hard to stay in a bomb shelter which is a big, empty,

dusty room, where you do not have enough food, you cannot take a shower, you cannot sleep well.

4. She would try to explain that if you were on an escalator and it broke down then all you would have to do is walk, and if you were in an elevator under the same circumstances there's really nothing you could do except wait.

5. You could smell football in the air, and everything although cliché was very nostalgic.

6. First of all I don't get enough hours, which makes me so angry.

7. I remember having meetings and hearing "Dude I was so wasted" and "Oh my God you would not believe what that bitch said."

8. It was old, dark and cold.

9. My expectation was to find a small quaint cabin.

10. This was a traditional place to go if you were a middle class underaged teenager in California.

INDEX